James Coverley's
COMPENDIUM
of ROMAN HISTORY

until a chance period of the 3rd Century,
including the deaths of the Emperors

ISBN: 9798344440309
First Edition

James Coverley's
COMPENDIUM
of ROMAN HISTORY

until a chance period of the 3rd Century,
including the deaths of the Emperors

For Megan
without who, this would
not have happened.

CONTENTS

Preface

The idea of a preface is largely so the author can congratulate themselves on writing a book, which you're not in the least bit interested in, let's be honest. I can congratulate myself on my own time, not yours - this is your book, after all, not mine. So, instead, let me tell you a little about what this book actually is.

In writing this book, I have tried to avoid jumping through the increasingly precise hoops required of an academic work. The academic approach is essentially another form of self-congratulation, only this time you're openly boasting to other academics that you've done all your homework properly so that they too may do their homework properly by pointing out, in other academic tomes to other academics that you did your homework properly. In that respect, I have actively decided to avoid overuse of footnotes, references and notes. Don't get me wrong - a meticulously cited and referenced piece of work is a thing to admire, but by doing so, a 370-page book ends up with 250 pages of content and 120 pages of stuff nobody ever reads. So although this book does, where necessary, contain some references and citations, mostly I've contented myself will telling you who said it and where they said it and leaving it at that. Rest assured that I have done all the homework, but you didn't buy this book so I can show you how good at homework I am.

Unless you're an obsessive sort of person about the subject, most history is not very interesting and so, as you can probably tell from the title of this book, I've tried to include history that I think has the potential to be of some interest to everyone. When I was a child, history in school was simply an exercise in repeating information about the past back to children in the hope they could remember enough of it to get them through a series of end-of-year tests designed to see precisely how much information us kids could recall. Unfortunately, the majority of this information was about Corn laws and Jethro Tull - and I don't mean the standing-on-one-leg, prog rock, flute playing, cool Jethro Tull, either. I mean the bloke who invented the seed drill, whatever in hell that was. The information we were all dying to be told about was Vikings decapitating people, earthquakes destroying cities and witches being tossed into volcanoes, that sort of thing. All this fun stuff was dangled like a carrot before us as long as we got through the stuff about seed drills first. We never seemed to get that carrot. Carrots that had to be planted, don't forget, with the aid of a seed drill.

Finding the nuggets of treasure in a book about history is partly about your own voyage of discovery, like regular little Lewis and Clarks on your own adventure, and this book is partly about that. But sometimes it's also fun to let someone take you on an open-topped bus ride through the winding cobbles of the past, yabbering away about what you can see to your left and if you turn your head to the right, you can see so-and-so ... So I've also tried, in other chapters to give you a more detailed and narrative driven guide to Roman history as well. It has swearing in it because we're not children.

There is, of course, an awful lot of Roman history out there and almost all books on the matter attempt to narrow their focus down to certain timescales. I'm no different in that respect and knowing where to begin, or perhaps more importantly where to end, is vital in a short book. We begin, therefore, roughly at the time of the death of Julius Caesar (with the odd lurch back further for particularly juicy carrots) and end somewhere around the end of Roman Britain because it seemed like a good place to stop. In no way is the book meant to be a comprehensive guide to the intervening period. A compendium, by it's nature, offers a concise summary of it's subject matter. The information therein is therefore presented with that concise nature in mind. Where there are competing opinions, I have attempted to summarise them but nothing in this book should be taken as a definitive statement of veracity where competing narratives exist. Sometimes one narrative is relayed to the reader above another simply because it presents a more entertaining read. Other subject matter may be omitted not for narrative or editorial reasons, but simply because it's a bit boring.

Where I have provided extracts from source texts, they are presented as verbatim, with the normal use of square brackets - [and]- to indicate additional information added by the author. The passages are also presented with the grammatical oddities of the past and, as such, are subject to the often excitable translation practices of those who copied them. Don't blame me if it's weird, blame the monks!

As we now live in the Information Age, the TL;DR for everything I just said is:

It's a book with some facts in that you can flick through like you're watching cat videos on Tik-Tok and then there are other bits where someone who knows the subject explains shit to you.

I hope you enjoy it.

James Coverley
2 October 2024

Chapter One

ON THE
DEATHS OF THE
EMPERORS AND OTHERS

Julius Caesar

Let's be honest, someone was always bound to stab Julius Caesar in the back at some point and, so when it happened, on March 15, 44 BC, it didn't come as much of a shock. This was still a time when being a Senator meant something; before they became nothing but shuffling yes-men who were given a big shiny ring and a special toga to wear in order to fool them into thinking they mattered. In 44 BC, they still mattered, and they were determined to do something about Caesar.

A group of over thirty conspirators, including Gaius Cassius Longinus, Marcus Junius Brutus, Lucius Tillius Cimber and Decimus Junius Brutus Albinus, decided to act. Caesar was late to the Senate House. He had heard rumours of the plot but refused a bodyguard and that morning his wife, Calpurnia, after a terrible dream in which she saw his dead body, had begged him not to attend. Caesar initially sent Mark Antony to dismiss the Senate, but Decimus came to Caesar's home and persuaded him to come.

As he and Mark Antony entered the building, one of the conspirators stopped Mark Antony in his tracks, leaving Caesar to take his seat alone.

The common myth says that Caesar's last words were "Et tu, Brute?" (you too, Brutus?) This is a little bit of poetic licence from Shakespeare. Instead, Suetonius tells us his version of what happened next:

> As he took his seat, the conspirators gathered about him as if to pay their respects, and straight away Tillius Cimber, who had assumed the lead, came nearer as though to ask something; and when Caesar with a gesture put him off to another time, Cimber caught his toga by both shoulders; then as Caesar cried, "Why, this is violence!" One of the Cascas stabbed him from one side just below the throat. Caesar caught Cascas' arm and ran it through with his stylus, but as he tried to leap to his feet, he was stopped by another wound. When he saw that he was beset on every side by drawn daggers, he muffled his head in his robe, and at the same time drew down its lap to his feet with his left hand, in order to fall more decently, with the lower part of his body also covered. And in this wise he was stabbed with three and twenty wounds, uttering not a word, but merely a groan at the first stroke, though some have written that when Marcus Brutus rushed at him, he said in Greek, "You too, my child?" All the conspirators made off, and he lay there lifeless for some time, and finally three common slaves put him on a litter and carried him home, with one arm hanging down. And of so many wounds none turned out to be mortal, in the opinion of the physician Antistius, except the second one in the breast.

> The conspirators had intended after slaying him to drag his body to the Tiber, confiscate his property, and revoke his decrees; but they forebore through fear of

Marcus Antonius the consul, and Lepidus, the master of horse.

Antistius' examination of the corpse of Julius Caesar is widely considered to be the first known example of an autopsy.

Brutus.

As for Brutus, he was defeated in the civil wars that followed Caesar's death, at the Second Battle of Philippi by Octavian and Mark Antony.

Fleeing into the hills with what was left of his legions, he fell on his own sword rather than face capture. Brutus reportedly uttered a well-known verse from Euripides' *Medea*: "O Zeus, do not forget who has caused all these woes!"

Yeah, you did, Brutus. You did.

He was referring, of course, to either Octavian or Antony. What happened to his body depends on which account you believe, with one saying that Antony found it, wrapped it in the prestigious and sanctified purple cloak and cremated it, sending the ashes to his mother.

If you believe the story that Octavian found it, then he chopped the head off and planned to lay it at the feet of a statue of Caesar, but 'lost' it overboard during a storm at sea on the way home. Quite what he was doing with it when it slipped out of his grasp and into the foamy depths isn't explained.

Augustus.

The ancient Roman way of deciding what ailed an aging Roman Emperor was to metaphorically poke him with a stick, suck through your teeth and then say "Oooh. Looks bad. That'll be the plague, mate. Rub boiled donkey callouses in your eyes." Everything was 'the plague'. Broken leg? That's the plague. Eyes full of pus? That's the plague? Actually got the plague? Also the plague.

The standard treatment for all these plagues was to get something horrendous and rub it all over yourself, presumably because the doctor now had your money and just wanted you to go away again and if you went away with otter urine all over your face, or something equally unsanitary, your chances of coming back again to demand the return of your money were significantly reduced.

So what the health conditions Augustus suffered from at the end of his reign, and indeed most of the health conditions suffered by anyone in the ancient world actually *were* is speculative at best. They simply had no idea what was wrong with people. It was guesswork.

By 14AD, Augustus was seventy-five years old and had been sick for some time. Seventy-five wasn't especially ancient, but it was a good age for Roman times. Although the average life expectancy for a Roman was significantly lower than it is for modern humans, the major reason for this was child mortality which was alarmingly high. If you survived through puberty, you could expect to live as long as we do today unless someone decided to strangle you and throw the pieces in the Tiber.

He died on the 14th of August at Nola, near Naples, where his father, Gaius Octavius, had also died. He probably went there knowing that he was so sick that he would also die there, either from natural causes or 'urged on' in some way.

In the months before he died, he made significant preparations for the transfer of power, which was a new concept in the Roman world. Constitutionally, there was no need for an Emperor and there was no legal framework in place for a succession either. Augustus was only Emperor because the alternative, if you were a reluctant Senator, involved being smacked over the head with something heavy and ending up in the Tiber.

Lots of people ended up in the Tiber.

Having prepared to pass on power and having gone to Nola with the aim of dying somewhere nice, it was then rumoured that his wife Livia fed him poisoned figs. She was famous for her figs. Whether this is true or not isn't certain and he likely died of natural causes, but it's intriguing to speculate that the poisoned figs were just a form of assisted suicide.

Augustus' last words were, "Acta est fabula, plaudite" - "Have I played the part well? Then applaud as I exit" - which was a joke about the enthusiastic play-acting he had engaged in when he had invented the role of Emperor out of thin air. He had been making the whole thing up as he went along because there was no precedent. He was playing the role of Emperor and in doing so, he typecast the role for generations of Emperors that followed. Apart from the lunatic ones, of course.

Clodius.

Publius Clodius Pulcher was a politician and power-mad demagogue, which Rome had a few of. His main enemy was a fellow called Titus Annius Milo and they really, *really* hated each other.

Things came to a head between the two of them at around 1:30 pm on the 18th of January 52BC in a rather spectacular and somewhat ridiculous style. Clodius and Milo encountered each other about 13 miles outside Rome on the Via Appia near Clodius' villa in Bovillae. Milo's entourage was much bigger than his rivals, some 300 men compared to 26, but neither knew the other was also on the road and coming across each other was a surprise.

They passed each other slowly, bitter enemies eyeing each other with great suspicion, in total silence, glaring at each other like children in the playground.

It was all going fine until, with the last few men passing by, someone said something, or looked at someone the wrong way and it all kicked off. Everyone piled into the fight, like a wild-west saloon brawl. Clodius was wounded and carried to roadside inn to be treated. When Milo heard that Clodius had been wounded, he ordered his lieutenant, Marcus Saufeius, to kill him. Clodius was dragged out of the inn and stabbed to death. Then everyone ran away.

Clodius' body was found lying in the middle of the road by a Senator, Sextus Teidius, who came wandering up the road a few minutes later. He had it sent to Rome and presented to his, presumably rather surprised, widow, Fulvia.

Tiberius.

By March of 37AD, the 78 year old Tiberius was on his last legs. He had taken to his bed in the villa of one Lucius Licinius Lucullus at Misenum and was fading fast. Tacitus tells the tale of his final day.

However, Charicles [Tiberius' doctor] assured Marco [prefect of the Praetorian Guard] that Tiberius was sinking and would not last more than two days. There were conferences and dispatches to imperial governors and generals, hurriedly making all arrangements. On March 16th the Emperor ceased to breathe and was believed to be dead. Gaius [the incoming Emperor, Caligula], surrounded by a congratulatory crowd, issued forth to begin his reign. But then it was suddenly reported that Tiberius had recovered his speech and sight and was asking for food to strengthen him after his fainting-fit. There was a general panic-stricken dispersal. Every face was composed to show grief - or unawareness. Only Gaius stood in stupefied silence, his soaring hopes dashed, expecting the worst.

Marco, unperturbed, ordered the old man to be smothered with a heap of bed clothes and left alone.

Caligula

Caligula was boorish, puerile, mean and rude. None of which should come as a surprise, nor did it disqualify him from serving as an Emperor. He made a particular sport out of humiliating a certain Praetorian tribune named Cassius Chaerea, mocking the way he spoke and his supposed effeminate manner. Caligula would change the watchwords for Chaerea's duty to 'Venus', an incredibly feminine word, or 'Priapus', the name of a minor phallic god with a huge dick. When Chaerea bowed to kiss the Emperor's ring, Caligula would "hold out his hand to kiss, forming and moving it in an obscene fashion".

Chaerea could take no more. Although there were probably dozens of plots ready to go at any second, he struck first. Caligula was, shockingly, mingling with actors - male actors at that - in a narrow corridor below the palace when Chaerea drew a blade and stabbed him in the throat. The tight passageway, thronged with people, left no room for escape. Chaerea and his fellow plotters hacked wildly at the falling Emperor, stabbing those around him, too. Innocent Senators and bystanders fell under the whirling blades. Caligula's Batavian guards scrambled to stop them, but couldn't get near the dying Emperor.

In the ensuing bloodbath, dozens died. The assassins had worked themselves into such a determined fury to slaughter Caligula that they could barely stop. Not only were dozens caught in the crossfire of the feverish stabbing, but people were dying in the confusion and panic that ensued. They were stabbing everyone. It took the Praetorians to stop the slaughter.

In the end, Chaerea didn't have enough influence to dictate what happened next and in the chaos, the plotters hunted down Caligula's wife, Caesonia, and their young daughter, Julia Drusilla, cutting them to pieces. They ransacked the palace, looking for Claudius to chop him up, too, but the Praetorians found him first and swept him, somewhat reluctantly, to power. In all the mayhem, the Senate had toyed with the idea of simply doing away with the role of Emperor entirely as Caligula had left no heir, but before they could act, the Praetorians had declared Caligula Emperor and faced with either confirming that appointment or taking a dip in the Tiber, the Senate wisely chose the former.

Chaerea was arrested, one of the few who were. Nobody had the desire to hunt down everyone and there was nobody really looking for revenge, either. Nobody was really going to miss Caligula, after all. But Chaerea was sentenced to death and, being a soldier, he took the news rather matter-of-factly, only asking that if it were to be done, that it be done with his own sword. A request that was granted.

Sejanus

BY the end of 31AD, former Praetorian prefect, Lucius Aelius Sejanus, had managed to wriggle his way to the very top of the affections of Tiberius. Despite his relative lack of rank, he had been elected consul and with Tiberius out of Rome and unwell, Sejanus wielded significant power at the pointy end of Roman politics.

Tiberius' son Drusus, who was his father's heir, was jealous of the power Sejanus apparently wielded, at one point their enmity boiled over into a physical fight. Drusus died in mysterious circumstances in 23BC, likely at the hand of Sejanus.

What happened in October of 31 isn't clear, but Sejanus was arrested, seemingly on direct orders from 'outside Rome' and a trial was assembled for him within minutes at the Temple of Concord. He had been found guilty by the Senate before he even arrived, at which point he was instantly strangled to death and his body cast down the Gemonian Stairs for everyone to see.

The Gemonian Stairs linked the top of the Capitoline Hill and the Forum. There was nothing particularly special about the stairs, but they were right outside the Mamertine Prison, which is still there, so they were convenient for throwing traitors down. The traitor would be tortured, strangled, mutilated and then the body tossed down the stairs where it would be left to rot and be eaten by stray dogs before, you guessed it, being thrown in the Tiber. Sejanus' body lay there for three days.

Rome went absolutely bananas. Rioters took to the streets, smashing his statues and hunting anyone linked to him. The Praetorians were sent out to restore order and went bananas themselves, joining in the looting and mayhem.

His eldest son, Strabo, was captured and strangled. His wife, Apicata, killed herself. His slaves were tortured and executed. Eventually, all his children were rounded up just to add some more drama to the whole occasion. There was really no need for so much slaughter, but Tiberius was determined to make sure that whatever it was Sejanus did (again, it's not particularly clear what he was supposed to have done), that nobody else was going to do it again. For that, everyone had to go.

His lover, Livilla, Caligula's sister, was starved to death. Eventually, his remaining son, Capito Aelianus and Junilla, his daughter, were strangled and their bodies also cast down the Gemonian Stairs.

As the executioner tightened the rope around Junilla's neck, he pointed out that there was a constitutional problem. Junilla was a virgin and the execution of virgins was forbidden. So he solved that problem himself as he murdered her.

Messalina

When Valeria Messalina married Senator Gaius Silius in 48AD at a lavishly appointed wedding ceremony, it should have been a wonderfully happy occasion. People should have rejoiced, songs should have been sung and as they were two high-ranking people among Rome's social elite, perhaps even the Emperor himself should have given them his blessing.

The problem was, not only was Messalina still married and Silius her lover, but the chances of her new marriage being blessed by the Emperor, Claudius, were somewhat hampered by the Emperor being the person she was already married to.

Perhaps he wouldn't have noticed as Claudius was out of town overseeing the construction of his new super-port at Ostia. However, you'd think it might not have been a secret for long when he got back and found his wife married to another bloke. Either way, Claudius' freedman, Narcissus, who was one of the most spectacularly wealthy individuals in the Empire's history and Claudius' right-hand man, was right there in Rome when the wedding happened and immediately informed the boss.

Quite what Messalina and Silius were thinking is hard to pin down. Silius had divorced his own wife, Julia Silana, presumably with the intention of marrying Messalina and with Claudius at Ostia, it's hard to see the move as anything other than a rather brazen and ham-fisted attempt at a coup. However, it's also possible that the marriage was just for show, as part of a Bacchic ritual, as they were in the middle of celebrating Vinalia, a festival of the grape harvest. Who knows?

A sham marriage or not, Claudius was pissed, obviously, and sped back to Rome. Messalina rushed to meet him to try and calm him down before he went a bit crazy, and they came together on the road. She even brought along the leading Vestal Virgin, Vibidia, to try to keep Claudius from simply lopping off everyone's head, but when an angry Claudius barged into Silius' house, he found it stuffed full of Claudian family heirlooms that Messalina had simply given away.

To be fair to Claudius, he managed to resist simply having everyone eaten by lions on the spot and stomped off to sulk. Messalina begged to see her husband - Claudius, not the other one - but Narcissus, who revelled in the role of the Emperor's gatekeeper, refused to let her in to see him.

With Claudius' feelings softening, he asked to see her the next morning. Sensing his moment and acting before Claudius did something dumb, Narcissus forged an order to have Messalina executed. When the Praetorians arrived at the gardens of Lucullus, where she was hiding with her mother, she was offered the chance to take the honourable way out but she couldn't do it. Instead, one of the guards ran her through with his sword.

When Claudius was informed of her death, he didn't react and just ordered another glass of wine. Gaius Silius was executed, too. His former wife, Julia Silana, was a childhood friend of Claudius' niece and fourth wife (yes, they did that sort of thing back then), Agrippina the Younger, mother of Nero. At some point, the two of them fell out, and Julia spent her last years in exile in the miserable backwater of Tarrentum, dying there in 58. Tarrentum is the modern-day Taranto, after which tarantulas are named. There's an interesting fact for you. I told you there would be some.

Claudius

That the Emperor Claudius is still commonly viewed as something of a bumbling, stammering, physically weak fool can perhaps be blamed on writers like Robert Graves, whose masterpiece *I, Claudius* set the image of the Emperor in stone for modern generations. In turn, Graves got his view of Claudius' legacy from people who were writing about him in less than glowing terms, some of whom might have had something of a hand in his death. It was the fate of many of the Emperors that their memories were set in stone by people who were either deliberately charged with, or had a personal involvement in, ruining their reputation.

In reality, Claudius was a competent and adept ruler who might not have appeared to have the physical traits required of a conquering demi-god, but then not many of the Emperors did. His ability to command a room full of men by the sheer dominance of his presence alone might have been somewhat lacking, but otherwise, he was pretty good at his job. Which is partly why some people hated him so much.

He died on the morning of the 15th of October, 54AD, after a bout of violent and explosive (at both ends) food poisoning. It's likely that he was poisoned by his last wife, Agrippina the Younger, Nero's mother, in order to hasten the transition of power to her son and because, frankly, they fucking hated each other. Mushrooms were a favourite vehicle in ancient times for the budding poisoner, primarily because if the victim started retching and shitting themselves after eating poisoned mushrooms, you could just blame the mushrooms. A plate of mushrooms was Claudius' last meal.

The writer Seneca, Nero's tutor, had been exiled from Rome by Claudius for all sorts of reasons, including the rumour that he was having an affair with Agrippina. Either way, he had it in for him and was probably involved in the plot to kill him. After the Emperor's death, Seneca wrote a withering and mocking account of the deification of the Emperor called *Apocolocyntosis*. I say 'Seneca wrote it', but in reality the author was anonymous. Writing comedy books about the death of an Emperor, even if you hated him, wasn't the sort of thing it was a smart idea to own up to. But who else would write such a thing, in the style of Seneca than Seneca?

"Apocolocyntosis" is a word play on "apotheosis", the process by which dead Roman Emperors were recognized as gods. Where "apotheosis" can be translated as "deification", "Apocolocyntosis" can be translated as "pumpkinification".

In the *Pumpkinification of the Divine Claudius,* Seneca gives Claudius' last words as being:

"Oh dear, I think I've just shat myself."
That's not me being rude. That's precisely what he wrote.

Drusus

Tiberius Claudius Drusus, the eldest son of the Emperor Claudius, died 'just before coming to manhood', so anywhere between 12 and 18 years old, when he apparently threw a pear in the air, caught it in his mouth, and choked to death on it. Although 'caught it in his mouth and choked on it' can be translated as 'it was covered in poison and he ate it'.

Nero

Nero awoke on the 9th of June, 68AD, to find that all of his bodyguards had fled without him, which, for someone on the verge of losing power and already a little paranoid, must have been quite a sobering moment. Going to bed thinking that everyone is out to get you and then waking up to find your own bodyguard sprinting away down the forum doesn't do wonders for one's ambitions for a long and peaceful life.

Even at this point, had Nero not been a big, blubbering baby who had convinced himself that the fates had conspired against him, had started strangling a motherfucker or two and then getting some selected people flung into the Tiber where they belonged, he might have been able to save his reign. Instead he seemed not only willing to accept the hand that fate had dealt him, but convinced that there was absolutely nothing he could do about it. It's hard not to think that, in some way, he was rather enjoying the idea of having himself what he considered a romantic death

Gathering the few servants who had remained loyal, including a gladiator called Sporus who Nero had castrated and married, they fled on foot to the villa of his freedman Phaon, a few miles outside Rome. Nero spent the next few hours pacing around, gibbering. His servants urged him to take the sensible option of ending it and not leave his fate to the hands of the Senate. Nero ordered a grave dug and wandered about, whining. "Qualis artifex pereo!" ("What an artist the world is losing!") he moaned.

A letter arrived informing him that the Senate had declared him a public enemy and was sending men to capture him. He knew what that meant - public execution - and he wasn't about to be flogged to death on the streets and then fed to stray dogs.

He snatched up two daggers, tried them, and then lost his bottle. He begged Sporus to mourn him. He begged another servant to go first so he would know what to do. He started to argue with himself as his mind unravelled. "How ugly and vulgar my life has become," he whined "Come on, pull yourself together!"

Suddenly there was the sound of hooves on the cobbles outside as the soldiers came for him. He snatched up the dagger again and made everyone promise to bury him. And then, gripping the hilt tightly ... he couldn't do it. In the end, with the knife at his throat and his hand shaking, unable to make the final push, his secretary Epaphroditus put his own hand on the dagger and, with a little shove, drove it into Nero's throat. Suetonius takes up the story:

He was all but dead when a centurion rushed in, and as he placed a cloak to the wound, pretending that he had come to aid him, Nero merely gasped: "Too late!" and "This is fidelity!" With these words he was gone, with eyes so set and starting from their sockets that all who saw him shuddered with horror.

He was buried at a cost of two hundred thousand sesterces and laid out in white robes embroidered with gold, which he had worn on the Kalends of January. His ashes were deposited by his nurses, Egloge and Alexandria, accompanied by his mistress Acte, in the family tomb of the Domitii on the summit of the Hill of Gardens,which is visible from the Campus Martius.

In that monument his sarcophagus of porphyry, with an altar of Luna marble standing above it, is enclosed by a balustrade of Thassian stone.

Seneca

A conspiracy against Nero organised by Gaius Calpurnius Piso in 65AD resulted in the forced suicide of, obviously, Piso, but also the poet Lucan and the writer, philosopher, former tutor of Nero, pumpkin story inventor and asshole, Seneca the Younger, among many others.

Seneca took the traditional route of opening several veins in order to bleed to death quickly, but as he was a wheezy and portly old chap with the blood pressure of a flatulent balloon, it took him ages and left him in agony.

His wife Pompeia Paulina attempted to share his fate but Nero told her to stop being so dramatic and ordered her wounds bandaged up. She survived.

With his death taking forever, Seneca invited some friends over to watch him die. They had lunch as he tried in vain to bleed to death. Everyone suggested he should take poison and get in the hot baths to speed up the blood flow, so they finished lunch and went off to the bathhouse to watch the show there. In a world in which other people's perceptions of how noble and statesmen-like you carried yourself were everything, having an audience to watch you die a superb death kind of made sense. As long as you actually fucking died and didn't just lay there in the bath like a boiled sausage with a slow puncture.

All the poison did was make him vomit, so now things were even worse. He was bleeding to death incredibly slowly, and he was covered in puke. At least he was in the bath.

In the end, the audience became a little bored and some soldiers were invited to 'hasten' his end.

His body was cremated 'without the usual funeral rites', according to Tacitus, so probably around the back of the palace, on a bonfire.

Pliny the Elder

Almost 1945 years ago, on August 24th/25th, 79AD, the Roman *colonia* of Pompeii and Herculaneum were destroyed in the infamous eruption of Mount Vesuvius, an event witnessed by Gaius Plinius Secundus, Pliny the Elder, and his nephew (and later adopted son), Gaius Plinius Caecilius, Pliny the Younger.

The Elder was in charge of the navy fleet at Misenum in the Bay of Naples and the Younger was staying with him at their villa on the coast. The Younger relates what happened in an account to his friend, the historian Tacitus:

On the 24th August, in the early afternoon, my mother drew our attention to a cloud of unusual size and appearance... Its general appearance can be expressed like an umbrella pine, for it rose to a great height on a sort of trunk and then split off into branches, I imagine because it was thrust upwards by the fire blast and left unsupported as the pressure subsided, or else it was borne down by its own great weight so that it spread out and gradually dispersed. Sometimes it was white, sometimes blotched and dirty, according to the amount of soil and ashes carried with it

Immediately, the Elder mobilises the fleet to sail to the rescue, sailing straight into the danger zone and the looming clouds

Ashes were already falling, hotter and thicker, as the ships drew near, followed by pumice and bits of blackened stones, charred and cracked by the debris from the mountain.

They landed near the villa of a friend at Stabiae, some four miles south of Pompeii and picked up survivors. Attempts to leave were hampered by a 'contrary wind' and 'wild and dangerous waves'. Vesuvius was by now shooting 'broad sheets of fire and leaping flames'. Unable to leave, the Elder goes to bed.

> By this time the courtyard giving access to his room was full of ashes mixed with pumice so that its level had risen and if he stayed in his room any longer, he would never have got out... the buildings were now shaking with violent shocks and seemed to be swaying to and fro, as if they were torn from their foundations.

Early in the morning, the Elder rises

> But they were still in darkness at this time [from the eruption], blacker and denser than any night... he stood leaning on two slaves and then suddenly collapsed, I imagine because the dense fumes choked his breathing.

Pliny the Elder probably died from the effects of Carbon Dioxide poisoning from the volcano. His body was recovered on the 26th of August, 79, from where it had been buried in the pumice.
He was 56 years old.

Corbulo

Gnaeus Domitius Corbulo was the brother-in-law of Caligula and the father-in-law of Domitian. Above all, he was a general and a soldier. A soldier that was so achingly, straight-backed, hard-ass and military-like that when Nero, who had become as terrified of him as he was of everybody else, ordered him to commit suicide, he did so. Immediately.

When the messengers read out the command, he stood up, saluted, drew his weapon, strode forward, shouted the word 'Axios!', meaning "I am worthy", and fell on his own sword.

Some Christians

The Great Fire of Rome started on July 18th, 64AD and for six days ravaged the city. Nero's initial reaction, once he had rushed back to the city, was pretty good, considering he was a fucking moron. He organised relief for the citizens, saw to the reconstruction of the city and made sure the survivors were well taken care of. All that stuff about 'fiddling while Rome burned' is bullshit.

Firstly, he wasn't even in Rome when the fire started and secondly, the fiddle wasn't invented for another 1500 years. There are some reports that, on hearing the news, he played a lament on the lyre and given his reputation as a musician, you might have wanted to take your chances with the flames instead of listening to him wailing away.

However, he then went totally fucking mad again pretty quickly and public opinion soon began to turn against him, suggesting that he had set the fire himself so he could clear apartment blocks for his sparkling new playboy mansion, the *Domus Aurea*.

Nero needed someone to blame and, in the guise of a small and really annoying group of Jewish weirdos, he found one. Tacitus, in *Annals of Imperial Rome*, writes about it:

But neither human resources, nor imperial munifi-
cence, nor appeasement of the gods, eliminated sinister suspicions that the fire had been instigated. To
suppress this rumour, Nero fabricated scapegoats
- and punished with every refinement the notoriously

depraved Christians (as they were popularly called). Their originator, Christ, had been executed in Tiberius' reign by the governor of Judea, Pontius Pilate [this is the only mention in pagan Latin of this event]. But in spite of this temporary setback, the deadly superstition had broken out afresh, not only in Judea (where the mischief had started) but even in Rome. All degraded and shameful practices collect and flourish in the capital.

First, Nero had self-acknowledged Christians arrested. Then, on their information, large numbers of others were condemned - not so much for incendiarism as for their anti-social tendencies... Their deaths were made farcical. Dressed in wild animal skins, they were torn to pieces by dogs, or crucified, or made into torches to be ignited after dark as substitutes for daylight. Nero provided his gardens for the spectacle, and exhibited displays in the Circus, at which he mingled with the crowd, or stood in a chariot, dressed as a charioteer.

Despite their guilt as Christians, and the ruthless punishment it deserved, the victims were pitied. For it was felt that they were being sacrificed to one man's brutality rather than to the national interest.

Agrippina The Younger

Nero famously had his mother, Agrippina the Younger, murdered on March 23rd, 59AD. The reasons, apart from the fact that he had gone a bit bonkers by that stage, are quite complicated, but the circumstances in which she died are normally described as 'uncertain', which just means 'Some of this shit is clearly made up'. All of the accounts, however, are as bonkers as Nero was. There are three main accounts, one each from the big dogs of Roman history - Tacitus, Suetonius and Cassius Dio.

According to Tacitus, Nero considered the normal route of stabbing, poisoning or just strangling her, but all of these were far too obvious and would just make people mad at him. So he hatched a plot - a self-sinking boat. Of course.

Although she was aware of the plot, she still got on it and, on cue, a rope was pulled and a collapsing lead ceiling fell, which was supposed to crush Agrippina and sink the boat. Only it did neither. So the crew sank the boat themselves, instead.

Agrippina, undaunted, swam back to shore where she was met by a crowd of cheering onlookers. Nero, hearing the news, sent Anicetus, the trierarch Herculeius, and the marine centurion Obaritus, as well as an "armed and menacing column" to kill her. They broke into her bedroom and smacked her over the head with a club. She offered her womb instead with the instruction "Stab me here", indicating that she knew exactly who was behind this.

They took her up on the offer.

Suetonius' account says that Nero tried to poison his mother three times, attempts she pre-empted by taking the antidote in advance. Next, brilliantly, he rigged up a trap that would drop ceiling tiles on her as she slept, but she discovered the plan, presumably when a bunch of workmen turned up to install a falling ceiling tile trap in her bedroom. So again, Nero brings out the collapsing boat trick.

In this version, there's a deliberate collision between her galley and one of his captains who then offers her the trick boat to get back to shore. The boat fails to collapse.

The following day, Nero received word of her survival from her freedman Agermus. He then orders a guard to plant a weapon on Agermus and then immediately has him arrested on a charge of attempted murder, allowing him to implicate Agrippina in the plot.

Cassius Dio's account has a boat with a secret trapdoor which opens up while out at sea, pitching Agrippina into the waves. Again, athletically, she swims back to shore and so Nero has to resort to something more obvious and just sends an assassin to kill her.

Presumably during all this weird plotting, Nero either wasn't aware of how good a swimmer his own mother was, or it just didn't occur to him that simply having her stabbed to death would save him all the bother of inventing falling roof tile mechanisms and collapsing boats.

Petronius

Gaius Petronius Arbiter is normally the 'Petronius' credited with being the author of one the great Roman novels, *Satyricon*. As such, he became a well-known figure among the elite of Roman society and even though he was a courtier in Nero's imperial palace, he wasn't really a political player. However, being a big-time Charlie in the court of the mad king was enough to have the dread-eye turned upon you eventually, and Petronius invoked the jealousy of one Tigellinus, commander of the imperial bodyguard, who accused him of treason. Petronius knew the drill. You either did it yourself, or it was off with your head and into the Tiber with you.

He was arrested in 65AD but didn't bother waiting for a trial. Instead, he chose to take his own life. Tacitus records his suicide in the *Annals*:

Yet he did not fling away life with precipitate haste, but having made an incision in his veins and then, according to his humour, bound them up, he again opened them, while he conversed with his friends, not in a serious strain or on topics that might win for him the glory of courage. And he listened to them as they repeated, not thoughts on the immortality of the soul or on the theories of philosophers, but light poetry and playful verses. To some of his slaves he gave liberal presents, a flogging to others. He dined, indulged himself in sleep, that death, though forced on him, might have a natural appearance. Even in his will he did not, as did many in their last moments, flatter Nero or Tigellinus or any other of the men in power. On the contrary, he described fully the prince's shameful excesses, with the names of his male and female companions and their novelties in debauchery, and sent the account under seal to Nero. Then he broke his signet-ring, that it might not be subsequently available for imperilling others.

Pliny the Elder records that before he died, he smashed his flourspar (a green, glass-like mineral) wine-dipper, worth 300,000 sesterces because Nero had taken a shine to it. It's a bit strange that someone would lust after another man's wine-dipper and even stranger that some bloke owned 300,000 bucks worth of fancy glass wine spoon.

Galba

Galba's brief reign ended on the 15th of January, 69AD, although it never looked particularly solid at any point. Half of the army had declared for his rival, Otho, and Galba's various bribes to the rest had still to be paid. Galba responded by having all sorts of potential troublemakers executed, but he was surrounded by mutinous mutterings. He must have known he was in trouble. According to Suetonius, Galba wore a linen corset, remarking it was little protection against so many swords.

He was lured, alongside his heir, Lucius Calpurnius Piso Frugi Licinianus, to the Forum by a rumour, only to find a bunch of angry bastards who wanted their money. Galba tried to buy his life with the promise of payment, but he'd already promised payment and that had been bullshit, too. As the killers fell on him, he asked them to finish it quickly by beheading him.

One hundred and twenty people would later claim to have been there to attack Galba, and one man, a centurion in the Praetorian Guard named Sempronius Densus, tried in vain to protect him, armed only with a dagger. Plutarch takes up the story:

> No man resisted or offered to stand up in his defence, save one only, a centurion, Sempronius Densus, the single man among so many thousands that the sun beheld that day act worthily of the Roman Empire, who, though he had never received any favour from Galba, yet out of bravery and allegiance endeavoured to defend the litter. First, lifting up his switch of vine, with which the centurions correct the soldiers when disorderly, he called aloud to the aggressors, charging them not to touch their Emperor. And when they came upon him hand-to-hand, he drew his dagger, and made a defence for a long time, until at last he was cut under the knees and brought to the ground.

The assassins hacked Galba's corpse to pieces and paraded his severed head on a pole. Piso, meanwhile, legged it sharpish to the hypothetical safety of the Temple of the Vestal Virgins. Two assailants tracked him down, dragged him outside and killed him.

Otho had hoped to be named heir over Piso and when he finally got to Rome to take over, Tacitus remarks how Otho "studied the victim's [Piso's] severed head with peculiar malevolence, as if his eyes could never drink their fill."

The one hundred and twenty people who tried to claim the credit for killing Galba and Piso, expecting to be rewarded, were later executed by Vitellius, whether they were there or not. That'll teach them.

Vitellius

Aulus Vitellius was Emperor from April until December of 69, until Vespasian, or more correctly Vespasian's agents, turned up in Italy at the head of a massive army and 'persuaded' the Senate that Vitellius had lost. By killing everyone.

Vespasian's men entered Rome and the defenders that were left put up a brave if utterly futile struggle, throwing sticks, stones and roof tiles at the invaders.

Fifty thousand died.

Vitellius was finally tracked down hiding in his bedroom and initially, the soldiers didn't recognise him, so he pretended to be someone else. When they figured out who he was, he begged for mercy, pretending that he had some vital information for Vespasian and that he should be held until the new Emperor could arrive in Rome. Vespasian's men were not in the mood for clemency. Suetonius tells us what happened next:

> Nevertheless, he was dragged half-naked into the forum, with his hands tied behind him, a rope about his neck, and his clothes torn, amidst the most contemptuous abuse, both by word and deed, along the Via Sacra; his head being held back by the hair, in the manner of condemned criminals, and the point of a sword put under his chin, that he might hold up his face to public view; some of the mob, meanwhile, pelting him with dung and mud, whilst others called him " an incendiary and glutton." They also upbraided him with the defects of his person, for he was monstrously tall, and had a face usually very red with hard-drinking, a large belly, and one thigh weak, occasioned by a chariot running against him ... while he was driving.

They dragged him to the Gemonian Stairs, where he was tortured. His last words were "Yet I was once your Emperor!" Which was pushing it a bit. He was Emperor for eight months. Then he was hacked to pieces, his head stuck on a spike and paraded around town, and his body dragged by a hook and thrown into the Tiber. I told you a lot of people ended up in the Tiber.

His brother and son were murdered also, because fuck them too, although they did let his wife fish the pieces out of the river and give them a burial.

Otho

Marcus Salvius Otho himself was also only around for a very short time. He lost his job at the first Battle of Bedriacum and his successor, Vitellius, effectively lost his job at the second Battle of Bedriacum.

Although he wasn't totally defeated at Bedriacum, he saw the writing on the wall and was aware that his defeat had been his own stupid fault.

He took to his bed on the 15th of April, 69AD, making a speech in which he bid everyone farewell and saying how what he did, he did for the greater good of Rome. He then stabbed himself once in the heart with a dagger he had hidden under his pillow.

Otho was a close companion of Nero and despite the fact that Nero was utterly bonkers, he was wildly popular among the people and so was Otho. Soldiers threw themselves on his funeral pyre. His death went down as heroic and noble, a man sacrificing himself to end the civil war and bring about peace.

Which might have been true, or more likely, he just read the tea leaves and saw that his future involved a rather gory a trip down the Gemonian Stairs, dinner with, or rather for, the dogs and a watery grave.

Titus Flavius Sabinus

Titus Flavius Sabinus was the brother of the Emperor Vespasian. He was in Rome during 69AD, the Year of the Four Emperors and his influence was important, both as a stabilising force on the city and as an agent of his brother, who was amassing his own plans in the east.

After the death of Otho, Sabinus directed the urban cohorts to swear allegiance to Vitellius, predominantly to prevent further bloodshed. At the same time, his son, also called Titus Flavius Sabinus, directed his troops to swear for Vitellius.

When Vespasian's plans became apparent, and Vitellius appeared to be losing, he offered to surrender to Sabinus. His troops, however, were having none of it and forced him to try to defend Rome

Sabinus ended up besieged in the Capitol with his family members, including his nephew Domitian. The troops burned the Capitol and in the ensuing chaos, his family escaped. Sabinus, however, was caught and dragged before Vitellius, who, to be fair to him, with his brother's army only days away, tried in vain to stop the soldiers from lynching him. He couldn't.

Sabinus was cut to pieces, and the bits were thrown down the Gemonian Steps before ending up in the Tiber. When Vespasian's agents took the city, Sabinus, or what they could fish of him out of the river, was buried with honours.

Presumably, hacking the brother of the bloke who is about to become Emperor to death didn't strike them as a really bad idea for some reason, but to be fair to Vespasian, he showed great restraint and didn't simply have half the city slaughtered as revenge. Half the city was already dead, mind.

Vespasian

The Emperor Vespasian was a big bloke with a sardonic wit and the rough-around-the-edges, traditional values of the Italian countryside he was raised in.

His no-nonsense, anti-bullshit persona was in marked contrast to the flighty drama queen antics of the Julio-Claudians he had superseded and he was particularly dismissive of their eagerness to turn each other into gods at the drop of a hat. It was precisely this bucolic, unprepossessing nature that allowed him to go under the radar for most of his career.

He was an accomplished if unspectacular soldier and an efficient administrator. He kept his head down when it mattered and tried, not always successfully to stay out of the Emperor's eyeline and not seem like a threat. When Nero needed someone to command several legions in order to quell rebellious Jews, Vespasian was the obvious choice. Nobody of his low breeding and apparent unimportance could ever pose a threat to the Emperor himself so leaving that amount of power in his hands wasn't really a risk.

Vespasian's long game worked perfectly and when Nero fell, the year-long civil war that ensued was the perfect moment to launch a bid for power. Assembling support in the east, he sent legions in his name to take Rome, meaning that he could, technically at least, claim to have taken power without spilling any Roman blood himself. He just got someone else to kill everyone.

On the 1st of July 69AD, the governor of Egypt, Tiberius Julius Alexander, declared Vespasian Emperor and the Mule Breeder, as he had been known, had completed the journey from country bumpkin to Emperor of the known world.

His death, in 79AD, was unexpected and brought on by his refusal to take seriously a fever and a bout of diarrhoea.

Taken suddenly by a 'violent spasm', he struggled to his feet, saying 'An Emperor ought to die standing'.

His blunt humour fits well with his character, as does his other attested last words, 'Oh no, I think I'm becoming a god'. However, if you read Suetonius' account a little more closely, these are not his final words, but something he says "when his distemper first seized him ..."

Crassus

Marcus Licinius Crassus, defeated by the Parthians at the Battle of Carrhae in 53BC, was not really in position to discuss terms with the victorious general Surena and yet the Parthians, perhaps out of curiosity, still agreed to meet him on the battlefield.

Crassus rode out to the Parthian camp when suddenly a young officer named Octavius, suspecting a Parthian trap, grabbed Crassus' reigns to pull him back. Making sudden moves in the middle of a surrender negotiation is probably a stupid idea and in the ensuing fight, Crassus and his men were slain.

As a souvenir, the Parthians took his head and a later story, mirroring that of the fate of Valerian, tells that they poured molten gold into his mouth, mocking his lust for wealth.

Crassus' head turns up again in another story during the feasting at the wedding ceremony of the Parthian king Orodes II's son. The guests were watching a performance of Euripides' Greek tragedy *The Bacchae* when a certain actor of the royal court, named Jason of Tralles, took the head and sang the following verses:

We bring from the mountain
A tendril fresh-cut to the palace
A wonderful prey.

Crassus' head was then used as a prop.

Titus

Titus died on the 13th of September, 81AD, apparently in the same rural villa as his father, Vespasian. Titus is another in a long list of people for whom the exact cause of death remains unclear, but he had a fever and was young, only 41 years old. Nobody was expecting his death.

However, and it's a big however, this is Titus, the man who led the Roman attack on Jerusalem during the First Jewish-Roman War in 70AD. This is the man who destroyed the Temple, fulfilling a Biblical prophecy and in the history of both Judaism and Christianity, this dude is a major bad guy. In secular history, he was a pretty good ruler, very much in the same vein as his father.

On his death, Domitian became Emperor and Domitian was a bully and a tyrant, unlike either his brother or father. Domitian's reputation as one of the 'baddest' of the early Emperors is enough to have influenced the works of people such as Tacitus, who writes with anger born of this tyrannical regime.

As such, the rumours that Domitian poisoned his brother were early and rife, although they must be tempered as being more reactions to Domitian than to any veracity of such claims. There's no evidence that Domitian poisoned Titus, it's just the sort of thing he might have done. Titus' last words were "I have made but one mistake" and what he meant by this is unclear. Speculation is that his mistake was not dealing with his younger brother whilst he had the chance.

The Babylonian Talmud attributes Titus's death to an insect that flew into his nose and picked at his brain for seven years, although this is an allegory relating to the biblical King Nimrod. Jewish tradition has Titus being cursed by God for destroying the Temple and dying as a result of a gnat going up his nose, causing a tumour inside his brain.

Aquillius

The First Mithridatic War between the Pontic king Mithridates VI and the Roman Republic began in 89BC. This Mithridates is not the famous Mithridates the Great, King of Parthia.

For the Romans, one Manius Aquillius had the idiot idea of trying to take on Mithridates with one single legion of auxiliaries which went about as well as could be expected.

Having lost, he then ran away to the island of Lesbos where he was captured, returned to the city of Pergamon, and paraded around on a donkey.

Not to be outdone by the Parthians and because they had fucking tons of the shit, Mithridates also executed Aquillius by pouring molten gold down his throat.

More Christians

The brazen bull, or Bull of Phalaris was a torture device said to have been a hollow bull, made entirely of bronze, with a door in one side into which the condemned were crammed. The whole thing was then set over a fire and the poor bastard inside roasted alive.

A series of pipes and tubes would allow steam to come from the animal's nostrils and steam pressure would cause the pipes to emit a bellowing sound as the prisoner cooked inside it, making it seem as though the animal had come alive.

Romans used this torture device to kill some Christians, notably Saint Eustace, who according to Christian tradition was roasted in a brazen bull with his wife and children by Hadrian.

The same fate befell Antipas of Pergamum during the persecutions of Domitian, who was roasted to death in a brazen bull in 92 AD.

This Gladiator

Gladiators didn't always fight to the death. A gladiator was expensive to train and worth money, so mindlessly slaughtering them all the time wasn't a very productive way of making a living. But they did die during fights, of course, sometimes even by accident. Some of the most common combats were simple boxing matches and those, too, often proved fatal. This funerary inscription records the death of a gladiator:

You see me, a corpse, passers-by. My civilian name [so not his athlete's name] was Apollonius... but now the soil of Nicodemia, the thread of destiny spun by the Fates, holds me fast to this ground. Eight times he won games, but in the ninth boxing match, he met his fated end. Play, laugh, passer-by, knowing that you too must die. Alexandria, his wife, erected this.

Domitian

Not to put too fine a point on it, but the Emperor Domitian was an absolute asshole. So, nobody was surprised when he was assassinated on the 18th of September, 96 AD—least of all his wife, Domitia or his niece, Flavia Domitilla, who were both among the plotters. The common people didn't really care; the army was angry because he had increased their pay, while the Senate, who both feared and hated him, cursed his name and struck it from the records.

Domitian had his cousin, Flavia's husband, Titus Flavius Clemens (a man of the most contemptible sloth, according to Suetonius), executed in 95 and adopted the dead man's sons as his own, which must have made dinner times a bit awkward.

According to Cassius Dio, the charge against Clemens was "atheism, for which offence a number of others also, who had been carried away into Jewish customs, were condemned—some to death, others to confiscation of property." Clemens had been a consul, so if even Domitian's nephew-in-law, who had held the highest elected office, wasn't safe, who the hell was?

This charge of converting to 'Judaism' really meant that Clemens had become a Christian. Flavia was also a Christian, and one of the earliest Christian cemeteries in Rome is named after her. In the Orthodox Church, she is St. Flavia Domitilla.

While her husband was murdered, she was family, so she was exiled to the island of Pandateria, modern-day Ventotene, 25 miles off the west coast of Italy. Which might sound lovely to you or me, but to the granddaughter of an Emperor, it might as well have been the Moon. This is where Domitian messed up because she was not going to take this lightly, uncle or not.

Flavia's steward, a man named Stephanus, was tasked with the deed. Concealing a dagger in his sleeve, he managed to get an audience with the Emperor. While the tyrant was perusing some documents at a desk, Stephanus pounced, stabbing him in the balls.

A struggle ensued, and the two men fell to the floor. Domitian, who was a big bastard, wrestled the knife free and stabbed Stephanus, killing him. Three more of Flavia's plotters, along with an imperial gladiator, then fell upon Domitian. Everyone had it in for him. They hacked him to death on the floor of his bed-chamber, threw his body on the back of a bier, and then burned it.

The name of the first Christian killed by the Romans isn't recorded, but the first Emperor assassinated in a largely Christian plot was Domitian.

Nerva

Nerva's death passed relatively uncontroversially which, in itself is unusual enough to include it in a list of unusual deaths. It is unusual because it was not very unusual. He was the first Emperor chosen solely by the Senate and the interesting thing here is that they, legally, had no obligation to do so. They could simply have resorted to ruling themselves, as a Republic, had they so chosen.

There were no pretenders to the throne and Domitian had no heirs. Instead, they chose the already elderly Marcus Cocceius Nerva as a safe pair of hands.

He died from the effects of a stroke on the 27th of January, 98AD. So little is known about the details of his brief reign partly because it wasn't very long, but mostly because those records don't survive.

He had named Trajan his heir before his death, ensuring a smoother transition than his own and Trajan dedicated a temple to the deified Nerva and apparently issued a set of commemorative coins to mark his transition to god status which were minted for 10 years, although no trace of either has ever been found.

Ultimately, by choosing Nerva, the Senate hoped to put in place a base level of standards for the Emperor that natural processes couldn't match. By choosing someone old, wise and childless, they hoped to ensure that no more Domitians found themselves next cab off the rank when it came to succession. This attempt at a meritocracy was a perfectly honourable idea that didn't work.

Trajan

Selinus was a small port city on the coast of Cilicia, modern-day Turkey. In 117AD, in ill health and on his way back to Rome, ostensibly to die somewhere important, the Emperor Trajan died there of natural causes, aged 63. He'd been frail for some time, as evidenced by the display of a bronze bust at the public baths of Ancyra, showing an aged and emaciated man. However, the attribution of this to Trajan is disputed.

Although it was widely acknowledged that Trajan wanted Hadrian as heir, he had yet to publicly declare it and it's possible that Trajan's death was kept secret for a few days by his wife Pompeia Plotina, presumably by popping him on ice or something, until she could suddenly and miraculously discover a letter that named Hadrian as successor.

This deathbed letter, when it was found, was signed only by Plotina and it was immediately deemed suspect. Trajan had been co-guardian of Hadrian and his sister, Paullina, alongside a man called Publius Acilius Attianus and rumour suggested Attianus and Plotina were lovers. They were both present when Trajan died, and both stood to benefit from Hadrian becoming Emperor. But the problem with this suggestion, notwithstanding there being zero evidence of it, is that it relies heavily on the old trope of Roman women either being witches, bitches or whores.

Plotina spent her whole life doing nothing that merited any sort of suspicion. She was a dutiful and above all (in historical terms) silent wife. Once her husband dropped dead and her signature turns up, suddenly she's on the same level as some of Rome's greatest Machiavellian matriarchs like Livia and Agrippina. Most likely, she just signed the letter because Trajan couldn't or she did it soon after his death in order to make sure his wishes were carried out. But that's not enough for some people. For some people, she also had to be an absolute bitch. In ancient history, women, who normally don't get much of a voice, tend to be shoe-horned into patriarchal narratives.

Hadrian's Ear

The 'Townley Hadrian' is a remarkable marble bust of the Emperor Hadrian currently on display in the British Museum. It's named after Charles Townley who acquired the bust for £105 in March 1795 from an art dealer in Livorno.

It has long been of interest not only for the quality of the carving and the artistic merit but for highlighting two distinct pronounced creases running diagonally across the lobe of the ear. They are not disfiguring, but are an intriguing early genetic indicator that all may not be well with a person's coronary arterial system, suggesting that Hadrian died, in 138AD, from heart disease. The British Museum currently displays the bust alongside that of his lover, Antinous.

Antinous

As for Antinous, in early October 130AD, Hadrian and Antinous assembled at Heliopolis to sail upstream along the River Nile. The retinue included officials, the governor of Egypt, army and naval commanders, as well as literary and scholarly figures.

At some point in October, around the time of the Festival of Osiris, Antinous either fell, was pushed or his body was thrown into the Nile, where he drowned. Hadrian was devastated. Although it is never explicit, Hadrian's marriage produced no children and was an unhappy and distant one, and Antinous was very probably Hadrian's lover.

The exact circumstances of his death have produced all sorts of speculation, some of it wild and baseless. Rumours began instantly that the Emperor's young lover was murdered to protect the royal integrity, but Hadrian's assumption was that he died by accident and it seems the likeliest cause. The *Historia Augusta* records it:

> During a journey on the Nile he lost Antinous, his favourite, and for this youth he wept like a woman. Concerning this incident there are varying rumours; for some claim that he had devoted himself to death for Hadrian, and others – what both his beauty and Hadrian's sensuality suggest. But however this may be, the Greeks deified him at Hadrian's request, and declared that oracles were given through his agency, but these, it is commonly asserted, were composed by Hadrian himself

Marcus Aurelius

Marcus Aurelius seemingly suffered from several health issues, the nature of which is ambiguous. He may have had stomach ulcers and complained of sleep problems and poor appetite. However, some of this can be put down to his stoic attempts at pain management rather than as an indicator of general poor health. It might be that lots of people suffered from the things Marcus did, but they are highlighted in his case simply because he tried to find ways to deal with them that didn't involve rubbing bat turds in his eyes or something weird. And that he was Emperor, of course

He died at the age of 58 on 17th March 180, of unknown causes in his military quarters either in the city of Vindobona

(Vienna) or near Sirmium (Sremska Mitrovica). This is at the end of what was known as the Antonine Plague which itself is a pretty mysterious illness, but was probably smallpox.

Cassius Dio gives a very brief account of his death in which he refers to the 'the disease from which he still suffered' and how his physicians make a decision about the Emperor's future that reflects on how unwell he actually was at the end. This would tend to suggest that he was suffering from smallpox right at the end.

> Now if Marcus had lived longer, he would have subdued that entire region; but as it was, he passed away on the seventeenth of March, not as a result of the disease from which he still suffered, but by the act of his physicians, as I have been plainly told, who wished to do Commodus a favour. When now he was at the point of death, he commended his son to the protection of the soldiers (for he did not wish his death to appear to be due to Commodus), and to the military tribune who asked him for the watchword he said: "Go to the rising sun; I am already setting." After his death he received many marks of honour; among other things a gold statue of him was set up in the Senate-house itself. This then was the manner of Marcus' death.

Antoninus Pius

Antoninus Pius turned 70 years old in 156AD and by this stage, he was a frail man existing on a diet of dry bread and wearing a corset in order to hold him upright in his seat. As his closest advisors began to die around him, the Emperor became increasingly wraith-like and gaunt. By March 5th, 161AD, Antoninus was at his estate at Lorium, in Etruria, about twelve miles outside of Rome. He ate a meal of alpine cheese, which he vomited in the night and he awoke with a fever.

Sensing the end, he summoned his council and gave instructions to pass his legacy to Marcus Aurelius. When the tribune of the night watch came to ask for the password, he responded, "aequanimitas" (equanimity). It's a common trope in the death of Emperors for the night watch to come in at the moment of death and ask for the evening's password, only for the Emperor to give some wonderfully apt response. Which tends to suggest that they are made up. Either way, he rolled over, went to sleep, and never woke up again.

Lucius Aurelius Verus

A big chunk of Marcus Aurelius' reign was as co-Emperor alongside his adoptive brother, Lucius Aurelius Verus.

Verus died in January or February of 169AD, returning from campaigning against the Macromanni. The cause of death isn't recorded, but it was likely the Antonine Plague again. Maybe as many as 10 million people died from it.

The Macromannic Wars are ostensibly the war portrayed at the start of the movie *Gladiator*, although for some reason in that bizarre film, they chose to depict the Macromanni as being dressed like cavemen, in furs, rather than in the armour and equipment of the Roman auxiliary units some of them had once been.

Marcus Aurelius, despite a few quibbles with his brother, was heartbroken by his death and accompanied the body back to Rome where he ordered games to be held in his memory and deified him.

Commodus

Marcia Aurelia Ceionia Demetrias was the concubine of the Emperor Commodus. Commodus is the Emperor from the movie *Gladiator*, although he wasn't murdered in the arena by a grumpy Australian. He was killed in a plot hatched in part by Marcia.

When she found a list of people Commodus intended to have executed, she discovered that she, the prefect Laetus, and Eclectus, among others, were on it. The three of them plotted to get their revenge in first. Cassius Dio takes up the story:

For these reasons, Laetus and Eclectus attacked him, after making Marcia their confidant. At any rate, on the last day of the year, at night, when people were busy with the holiday, they caused Marcia to administer poison to him in some beef. But the immoderate use of wine and baths, which was habitual with him, kept him from succumbing at once, and instead he vomited up some of it; and thus suspecting the truth, he indulged in some threats. Then they sent Narcissus, an athlete, against him, and caused this man to strangle him while he was taking a bath. Such was the end of Commodus, after he had ruled twelve years, nine months, and fourteen days. He had lived thirty-one years and four months; and with him the line of the genuine Aurelii ceased to rule.

Pertinax

On the 28th of March 193, Pertinax was at home, minding his own business of minding everyone else's business when an angry mob turned up at the gates. Two hundred soldiers, angry at having been promised 20,000 sesterces a man, but only receiving 12,000 each, wanted answers as to where their money was. Crucially, they were armed.

A bolder and perhaps more brutal Emperor would simply have set the guard on them. He had the entire city night watch on hand, plus a contingent of cavalry and turning up with swords to shout at the Emperor should have been an instant death sentence. But Pertinax was a noble sort of chap and so instead of killing them, or running away, or even just hiding, he chose to try and win them over.

The angry mob either broke into the palace, or was let in, and Pertinax, along with his chamberlain Eclectus, went to meet them, hoping to rely on his presence as Emperor and his wit, reason and logic.

"I got this" said Pertinax. He did not, it turns out, have this.

At first, it went rather well. The soldiers were sheepish and couldn't look him in the eye. They sheathed their swords and shuffled about uneasily, unsure of what to do next. It had all rather got out of hand and all they wanted was their money. Sorry about this, boss. But one man wasn't having it. Cassius Dio takes up the story:

> ...but that one man leaped forward, exclaiming, "The soldiers have sent you this sword," and forthwith fell upon him and wounded him. Then his comrades no longer held back, but struck down their Emperor together with Eclectus. The latter alone had not deserted him, but defended him as best he could, even wounding several of his assailants... ... The soldiers cut off the head of Pertinax and fastened it on a spear, glorying in the deed. Thus did Pertinax, who undertook to restore everything in a moment, come to his end. Rather prudently, Pertinax had refused to give either his wife or son official titles which spared them from also being slaughtered in the aftermath.

Didius Julianus

With Pertinax in pieces, the Praetorians announced that the next Emperor would be chosen by auction. The man who offered the most money would be installed as ruler. I'm not sure about you, but by this stage, I might consider offering the Praetorians money *not* to become Emperor.

The winner of the auction was Didius Julianus, not that it did him much good. With Septimius Severus threatening to come down to Rome and kick his teeth in, Julianus spent two months lolling about the palace trying to save his own arse.

He was inevitably assassinated on the June 2nd 193AD, whilst reclining on a couch. His only words were, "But what evil have I done? Whom have I killed?"

Septimius Severus became the sole Emperor without further bloodshed. His first task was, wisely, to dismiss the entire Praetorian Guard and refill it with his own loyal soldiers. He then had all the soldiers who murdered Pertinax executed.

Septimius Severus

Several Emperors and generals had tried, over the decades, to deal with the problematic tribes north of, and sometimes south of, the line that was eventually drawn by Hadrian's Wall. Some, like Agricola, had been quite successful, but the problem was always that once up there, it was hard to justify a significant cultural or military presence in what is now Scotland. There simply wasn't enough up there to balance up the enormous cost. We'll talk more about this later in this book.

The locals were a boisterous bunch as well, which didn't help much, and Septimius Severus had taken it upon himself to finally be the one to bring them in check. But was really just a matter of principle by this stage. The Caledonii weren't behaving and that was annoying. Severus told his men:

Let no-one escape sheer destruction, no-one our hands, not even the babe in the womb of the mother, if it be male; let it nevertheless not escape sheer destruction.

And it was going swimmingly, to be fair. He retraced the steps of Agricola, reopening old forts and supply routes, despite being old a frail and having to be carried up and down rain-sodden glens in a litter.

In late 210AD, he grew perilously sick and retired to Eboracum, modern-day York, where he died on the 4th of February, 211, apparently with a little help from his son, Caracalla. Cassius Dio tells us the following:

At all events, before Severus died, he is reported to have spoken thus to his sons (I give his exact words without embellishment): "Be harmonious, enrich the soldiers, and scorn all other men." After that, his body, arrayed in military garb, was placed upon a pyre, and as a mark of honour the soldiers and his sons ran about it; and as for the soldiers' gifts, those who had things at hand to offer as gifts threw them upon it, and his sons applied the fire. Afterwards, his bones were put in an urn of purple stone, carried to Rome, and deposited in the tomb of the Antonines. It is said that Severus sent for the urn shortly before his death, and after feeling of it, remarked: "Thou shalt hold a man that the world could not hold."

Asking your sons to, if I can paraphrase "trust each other, pay the soldiers well, and fuck everyone else" is all well and good, but Severus wasn't saying this because his sons, Caracalla and Geta, were a good team. He was saying it because he suspected that as soon as he was dead, one of them, at least, would be at the other's throat. All three of them had reigned for a while as joint Emperors and the boys were supposed to carry on this arrangement between them

The major problem with this was that one of them was fucking Caracalla.

Geta

Severus' wife, Julia Domna, was one of the most formidable women in ancient Roman history and it was through her sheer force of will that Caracalla and Geta didn't just tear each other apart the instant Severus died.

They both travelled back from Britain apart, lived apart, and even divided the imperial palace in two, with two sets of officials and servants. They only ever met with their mother present and under heavy guard. Caracalla was desperate to get rid of his younger brother and tried to assassinate him during Saturnalia on 17th December, 211.

Julia Domna had enough and demanded the two boys appear alone in her chambers. No guards, no officials, no generals or Senators, and very definitely, no weapons.

The three of them, two naughty boys who wouldn't stop fighting and their mother would sort the problem out once and for all.

On the 26th of December, 211, Geta turned up first, on his own as required, sat down and waited with his mother for his brother to come.

Caracalla never came.

But the centurions he had sent instead were right on time. Cassius Dio takes up the story:

> ...but when they were inside, some centurions, previously instructed by Antoninus [Caracalla], rushed in a body and struck down Geta, who at sight of them had run to his mother, hung about her neck and clung to her bosom and breasts, lamenting and crying: "Mother that didst bear me, mother that didst bear me, help! I am being murdered." And so she, tricked in this way, saw her son perishing in the most impious fashion in her arms, and received him at his death into the very womb, as it were, whence he had been born; for she was all covered with his blood, so that she took no note of the wound she had received on her hand. But

she was not permitted to mourn or weep for her son, though he had met so miserable an end before his time (he was only twenty-two years and nine months old), but, on the contrary, she was compelled to rejoice and laugh as though at some great good fortune; so closely were all her words, gestures, and changes of colour observed. Thus she alone, the Augusta, wife of the Emperor and mother of the Emperors, was not permitted to shed tears even in private over so great a sorrow.

Caracalla

Right now you're probably hoping Caracalla gets a taste of his own medicine, right? Well, let's find out. On the 8th of April, 217AD, Caracalla was at a temple near Carrhae in what is now Turkey, on his way to kick-off with the Parthians, who had it coming. The temple was built to mark the spot where, in 53BC, seven whole legions of Rome's finest men under the command of the statesman Marcus Licinius Crassus had been obliterated by the lightly armed archer cavalry of the Parthian general Surena. Twenty thousand Romans, including Crassus, died.

Caracalla popped behind a tent for a piss where he was joined by an ordinary soldier named Justin Martialis. Martialis wasn't happy. The shifts had recently been changed and he'd been given the short straw. Again. Early watch all week. Up all night on his own with the dogs and The Moon. He'd also applied directly to Caracalla for the rank of centurion and been turned down.

The Praetorian prefect, Marcus Opellius Macrinus had been in Martialis' ear for weeks, telling him what a shit Caracalla was. How he had it out for him, personally. How he should do something about it.

And as they stood there, taking a piss, he did something about it. He drew a knife and stabbed the Emperor once, in the heart. He died almost instantly. The bodyguards rushed in and hacked Martialis down where he stood, both of them in an open toilet behind a campaign tent in a field in Turkey.

With the full backing of the army, Macrinus declared himself Emperor three days later, not a piss stain nor a drop of blood on him. On hearing of Caracalla's murder, and with plotting in the air, Julia Domna took her own life. At least she hadoutlived the little fucker.

Macrinus

Julia Domna's elder sister, Julia Maesa, had a grandchild called Sextus Varius Avitus Bassianus and although this kid was only 14 years old and the chief priest of a weird Syrian sun god called Heliogabalus, who was worshipped via a polished black meteorite, the little scrap posed a serious threat to Macrinus' tentative grip on power. Particularly given that the entire female side of the Severan family, Julia Maesa and her daughters Julia Soaemias and Julia Mamaea had it in for him for usurping Caracalla. It also helped that Julia Maesa was jaw-droppingly rich and willing to spend it on armies.

The kid was a favourite of the Legio III Gallica who were stationed in Syria and liked to pop around to watch the priest do their strange meteorite rituals. Julia Maesa saw an opportunity and started a rumour that the kid was the illegitimate child of Caracalla. On the 16th of May 218AD, they duly declared Sextus Varius Avitus Bassianus Emperor and Macrinus' days were numbered.

A force under the command of the kid's tutor, Gannys, met Macrinus' forces on the 8th of July at the Battle of Antioch. As soon as it started going badly, Macrinus fled back into the city, only to find the streets in turmoil and his welcome exhausted. He took off in the direction of Rome allowing Bassianus to enter Antioch as the new and undisputed Emperor of the Roman Empire.

Rather stupidly, in an effort to reinforce his legitimacy, Macrinus had made his own 10-year-old son, Diadumenianus, co-Emperor. Neither of them would make it back to Rome.

Macrinus got as far as Chalcedon before someone spotted and caught him. Diadumenianus had been sent to the care of the Parthian king Artabanus IV and was caught and executed before he even got there. On hearing of his son's death, Macrinus tried to escape and was nearly successful until he injured himself. He was then taken to Cappadocia in Turkey where he was beheaded. The heads of father and son were then sent to the new Emperor as trophies. In time, Sextus Varius Avitus Bassianus became known by the name of the god they worshipped: Elagabalus.

Severus Alexander

Severus Alexander at least managed to last a few years. His downfall came via his failings as a military commander and his over reliance on the advice of his mother - those Severan ladies again!

Where he died isn't entirely clear. Some reports put it in Britain, some in Gaul, but the most likely location, considering it came about with regard to the war against the German tribes was in Germany itself.

Early in 235AD, Alexander was in Germany trying to solve the problem of the barbarians first-hand. His mother persuaded him that the best course of action was to sue for peace, which the troops took as a great slight. There were all sorts of bad omens in the air, according to the *Historia Augusta*:

> When he was praying for a blessing for his birthday the victim escaped, all covered with blood, and, as he was standing in the crowd dressed in the clothes of a consideration, it stained the white robe which he wore. In the Palace in a certain city from which he was setting out to the war, an ancient laurel-tree of huge size suddenly fell at full length. Also three fig-trees, which bear

the kind of figs known as Alexandrian, fell suddenly before his tent-door, for they were close to the Emperor's quarters. Furthermore, as he went to war a Druid prophetess cried out in the Gallic tongue, "Go, but do not hope for victory, and put no trust in your soldiers." And when he mounted a tribunal in order to make a speech and say something of good omen, he began in this wise: "On the murder of the Emperor Elagabalus". But it was regarded as a portent that when about to go to war he began an address to the troops with words of ill-omen.

The story then takes a more bloody turn:

He had lunched, as it happened, in his usual way at a general meal, that is to say, in an open tent and on the same food that was used by the troops — for no other kind of food was found in the tent by the soldiers when they tore it to pieces. And as he was resting after the meal, at about the seventh hour, one of the Germans, who was performing the duties of guard, came in while all were asleep; the Emperor, however, who alone was awake at the moment, saw him and said, "What is it, comrade? Do you bring news of the enemy?" But the fellow, terrified by his fears and having no hope that he could escape, seeing that he had burst into the Emperor's tent, went out to his comrades and urged them to kill their rigorous prince. Whereupon a great number in arms quickly entered the tent, and after slaying all who, though unarmed, resisted, they stabbed the Emperor himself with many thrusts. Some relate that nothing at all was said and that the soldiers merely cried out, "Go forth, depart," and thus slaughtered this excellent man.

His mother, Julia Mamaea, was in the same tent with Alexander and died with him. Their bodies were returned to Rome and buried in a mausoleum that can still be seen in the Piazza dei Tribuni, in the Quadraro area in Rome, as a large earth mound. A sarcophagus, which apparently contained their remains, is now in the Palazzo dei Conservatori Museum in Rome. With their deaths, the Severan dynasty was over.

Maximinus Thrax & Some Gordians

Emperor Maximinus Thrax met his end in June of 238AD, during a mutiny sparked by dissatisfaction among his own troops. After a reign marked by relentless military campaigns and severe financial demands on the Empire, Maximinus' tyrannical rule fostered deep resentment. The final blow came when the Senate, fed up with his reign, declared him a public enemy and supported the revolt of Gordian I and II in Africa. Although the Gordians were quickly defeated, the Senate remained opposed to Maximinus, supporting the elevation of Pupienus and Balbinus as co-Emperor.

Maximinus marched towards Rome with his army, intending to crush the rebellion, but his progress was stalled at the city of Aquileia, which resisted his siege. Facing a prolonged and demoralizing stalemate, his soldiers grew increasingly disgruntled. The combination of hunger, exhaustion, and bitterness led them to turn against their leader. In a swift and brutal act, they murdered Maximinus along with his son, Maximus, in their tent. Their heads were severed and sent to Rome as a symbol of the end of his oppressive rule. His death marked a critical turning point in the Year of the Six Emperors, briefly stabilizing the Empire amidst its ongoing turmoil.

Gordian I was joined as co-Emperor by Gordian II. Both of them were called Marcus Antonius Gordianus Sempronianus Romanus, only II was I's son.

They didn't think of 'Gordian Junior', apparently.

Either way, both of them lasted a matter of weeks, arguably the shortest reign of any of the imperial set-ups. Gordian

II led a rag-tag bunch of poorly trained soldiers against the forces of Maximinus Thrax at the Battle of Carthage in April of 238, lost and was killed. On hearing the news, Gordian I hung himself with his own belt, the first Emperor to take his own life since Otho in 69AD. At least he got to be called 'Max Thrax', which is cool as fuck.

Elagabalus

Elagabalus proved to be wholly unsuited to the role of Emperor. Too young, too fragile and too controversial, their reign barely made it into adulthood. A lot of the more controversial reports of their behaviour must surely be the result of writers hostile to their memory, but even so, some of it caused uproar across Roman society.

Not least of which were the religious extremities they introduced, including installing the black meteorite of their god in a dedicated temple in Rome. The elites of society and, crucially, the Praetorian guard, found their overtly foreign behaviour completely unacceptable and when Julia Maesa began to sense the hostility, she knew that she had to act to preserve the family line and that more than just Elagabalus needed dealing with.

Firstly, she persuaded Elagabalus to adopt their more sober and acceptable cousin, Severus Alexander, as heir, even though that kid was only thirteen years old, too. Apparently, they couldn't find any grown-ups to put in the role of ruling the known world.

All that did, of course, was to cause Elagabalus to try and assassinate Alexander, which they tried to do several times. In order to try and gauge the public mood themselves, Elagabalus invented a rumour that Alexander was either dead or dying.

When the furious Praetorians demanded that Elagabalus produce their cousin to prove he was alive, the Emperor and their mother were quick to bring him to the Praetorian camp.

On presentation of Alexander, the guard began cheering wildly and an outraged Elagabalus demanded the arrest and execution of everyone who had cheered their cousin and therefore slighted themselves. Which didn't go very well. Cassius Dio explains what happened:

> ... so he made an attempt to flee, and would have got away somewhere by being placed in a chest, had he not been discovered and slain, at the age of eighteen. His mother, who embraced him and clung tightly to him, perished with him; their heads were cut off and their bodies, after being stripped naked, were first dragged all over the city, and then the mother's body was cast aside somewhere or other, while his was thrown into the river.

Pupienus & Balbinus

Unlike being called 'Max Thrax', being called 'Pupienus' is *not* cool as fuck, but he and Balbinus spent the next ninety-nine days sitting at opposite ends of the Imperial Palace, glowering at each other like sulky teenagers in adjacent bedrooms, whilst around them the Praetorians plotted to go up to their rooms and chop them into pieces.

Pupienus became aware of the Praetorian threat and begged Balbinus to call for the Batavian bodyguard. Balbinus, believing that this was a trap, refused and the two began to argue just as the Praetorians burst into the room, seized them and dragged them back to the Praetorian barracks where they were chopped into pieces in the bathhouse.

Let that be a lesson to you, sulky bedroom teenagers.

Another Gordian

Having run out of names and people who were old enough to tie their own sandals, the 13-year-old Gordian III became the next Emperor with his neck on the chopping block

His death in February 244 AD remains shrouded in mystery, with conflicting accounts describing his demise. Gordian spent much of his reign battling external threats, particularly the Sassanian Empire in the East. In 243 AD, he led a successful campaign against the Sassanids, but the following year, the situation took a grim turn.

The Roman army, under the command of Gordian and his Praetorian Prefect, Philip the Arab, engaged in a critical battle, the Battle of Misiche, near the Euphrates River. It is unclear whether the young Emperor was killed in combat or fell victim to a conspiracy led by Philip. Some sources suggest that Gordian was murdered by his own troops, possibly at Philip's instigation, as Philip sought to usurp the throne.

Gordian's body was later found on the battlefield, and Philip, now Emperor, quickly moved to secure his power. To legitimize his rule, Philip had Gordian deified, presenting his death as a noble sacrifice for the Empire.

Philip

In April 248 AD Philip led the Empire in the celebration of the 1,000th birthday of Rome which according to the Empire's official Varronian chronology was founded on the 21st of April 753BC by Romulus. It being Rome, the celebrations were spectacular, with secular games in the Colosseum in which more than 1,000 gladiators, one for each year, were slain alongside hundreds of exotic animals including hippos, leopards, lions, giraffes, and one poor old rhino.

It took a few months, until September of the following year to be precise, for Philip to be added to the pile of dead bodies. Philip met his death during a battle near Verona,

Italy, amidst a revolt led by the ambitious Gaius Messius Quintus Decius.

Decius, who had been sent by Philip to quell a rebellion on the Danube frontier, was proclaimed Emperor by his troops, forcing a confrontation with Philip. Determined to defend his position, Philip marched his forces north to confront the usurper.

The two armies clashed near Verona, where the battle ended in defeat for Philip, and he was either killed in combat or murdered by his own soldiers who saw the tide turning in favour of Decius.

His son, Philip II of course, who had been given the title of Caesar when he was seven years old, disappears at the same time, aged around 12, likely killed by our old chums the Praetorians.

Gracchus

Tiberius Sempronius Gracchus was a politician famous for his agrarian law reforms. No! Wait! Don't go! I'm not going to bore you with agrarian laws reforms, don't worry.

In 133BC the electoral *comitia* was counting the votes for the tribunes for the following year. Tiberius and his mob seized the Capitoline Hill in a January 6th style attempt to dictate the result. At a senate meeting, Tiberius' first cousin Publius Cornelius Scipio Nasica Serapio, the *pontifex maximus* (chief priest), attempted to incite consul Publius Mucius Scaevola to intervene and use force to stop Tiberius from getting re-elected. Scaevola refused and so Scipio Nasica took matters into his own hands.

With a rallying cry of *"qui rem publicam salvam esse volunt me sequatur!"* (Anyone who wants the community secure, follow me!), the traditional cry used to rally passing soldiers to your aid, he led a crowd of bloodthirsty volunteers to attack the *comitia*, with 'his toga drawn over his head'.

This symbolic gesture, *capite velato*, is a symbol of *pietas* (piety) and the individual's status as a *pontifex*, *augur* or priest. It mirrors the requirement of some religions to have one's head covered during religious rites.

Capite velato is such a Roman display of piety that it is probably behind the Apostle Paul's instructions (1 *Corinthians*, 11:4) that:

Any [Christian] man who prays or prophesies with his head covered dishonours his head.

With his official hat on, he was able to spin what he was about to do as a religious rite, rather than just a brutal attack. The mob set about Tiberius and his entourage, who didn't fight back. They were beaten to death with stones, fists, furniture, anything that was lying about, and their bodies were - you guessed it - thrown into the Tiber.

Not the Same Gracchus

In 121 BC, the politician Gaius Gracchus was jeered during a sacrifice by one of the ceremony's attendants. This was not only rather rude but also broke the convention of silence during religious rites. Gracchus' entourage responded by stabbing the noisy bugger to death with their styluses. Carrying weapons was strictly forbidden during such occasions, but carrying sharp pens was fine.

That alone would have been worthy of mention among these pages, but the Senate then urged the consul Lucius Opimius to attack Gracchus and his mates. They fled to the temple of Diana on the Aventine hill where Opimius, offering a bounty of the weight of Gracchus' head in gold, set about the attack. With his entourage killed, Gracchus fled across the Tiber and was caught at which point he was either killed or more likely took his own life.

The person who got his head scooped out the brains
and filled the empty skull with molten lead before claiming
his reward.

Not the Same Cleopatra

Cleopatra Selene II was the only daughter of Greek Ptole-
maic Queen Cleopatra VII of Egypt and Roman Triumvir
Mark Antony. The actual Cleopatra and Antony. Those ones.

After Antony and Cleopatra's defeat at the Battle of
Actium in 31 BC, and their suicides in Egypt in 30 BC, Selene
and her brothers were brought to Rome and placed in the
household of Octavian's sister, Octavia the Younger, their
father's former wife. She ended up married to King Juba II
of Numidia and so a queen in her own right and a powerful
and magnificent one, too.

She died, aged 35, probably of natural causes and was
buried in The Royal Mausoleum of Mauretania, which still
stands in Algeria today. The year of her death is normally
given as 5BC although no account of the exact date exists.
Instead, the date is calculated from a poem written by Crina-
goras of Mytilene. It goes like this:

The moon herself grew dark, rising at sunset,
Covering her suffering in the night,
Because she saw her beautiful namesake, Selene,
Breathless, descending to Hades.
With her she had had the beauty of her light in common,
And mingled her own darkness with her death.

Which suggests that she died during a lunar eclipse. Lunar
eclipses occurred in 9, 8, 5 and 1 BC and 5BC is the more
likely year of her death. Just in case you're wondering, the
mausoleum is empty. It might never have held the bones of
the King and Queen at all, merely serving as their memorial.

Not the Same Herod, Either

King Herod Agrippa, is the king named Herod whose death is recounted in *Acts* 12 (12:20–23). His daughter, Julia Drusilla, appears at Felix's side, during St. Paul's captivity at Caesarea – the *Book of Acts* 24:24 reports that:

> Several days later Felix came with his wife Drusilla, who was a Jewess.

Her son, Marcus Antonius Agrippa, is one of the few named people known to have died during the eruption of Mount Vesuvius in 79AD that destroyed Pompeii and Herculaneum.

Josephus reported that he was at Herculaneum when he died 'with the woman'. This might mean his wife, although it's not certain if he was even married, or it might mean Drusilla herself.

Chapter Two

ON BRITAIN

Strange Cousins

Egypt might have been the weird cousin that the Empire kept locked in the attic, but Britain was the muddy-booted, tousle-haired, shamanic, twigs-in-their-beard madman who spent all Christmas with his face pressed against the drawing-room window, begging to be let in, only to run away bellowing like a stag should you open the door and offer them a sausage roll. Britain might, on occasion, be allowed into the kitchen to warm its frozen hooves by the range, but in no circumstances ever must Britain be permitted into the cleaner and more civilised areas of the house.

It's little surprise then that the Romans took so long to commit to a full invasion of the islands, and no wonder that they were part terrified of and part covetous of the British islands, what with their reputation for magical otherworldliness and riches beyond imagination.

Britain has always been a fascinating province for students studying Roman history. It is a place that was at once fully committed to the *Pax Romana*, the 'gift' the Romans gave or forced upon, depending on who you asked, those they conquered, and, at the same time, fiercely resistant to Roman rule. Added to that, the nature of the British tribes meant that some of them were on board before the Romans even showed up, others lined up nicely afterwards, and others never bent the knee.

This is true of other provinces, of course, but few did so with such determination. Gaul resisted for a long time before finally becoming fully subdued, and its tribes united. Two thousand years later, the tribes of Britain are still not fully united, even if larger parts of the island labour under the name of the 'United Kingdom'. There are streets in Britain that are not fully united, let alone constituent countries. The Romans built a huge fuck-off wall across the middle of the country for a reason, and to this day, those on either side of it revel in the division it still brings.

Added to this is the very clear set of circumstances that brought about the end of Roman Britain. The 'fall' of the Roman Empire is a fascinating subject and one that takes academicians whole careers and vast tomes to fully explain and, as such, it is far too broad a subject for a compendium such as this. However, the end of Roman Britain can be used as an example of what happened during the collapse of Roman rule in the West.

It is also true that as a proud Welshman, Roman Wales holds a place dear in my heart, and so I ask that the reader indulge me as I ramble on about it for a while. The Roman town of Carmarthen, with its unusual and romantic surviving amphitheatre is where I first fell in love with Roman archaeology and history, and as Roman Britain forms the backbone of my knowledge on this subject, it would be a bit daft to leave it out. The following is a concise wander around the landscape of Roman Britain.

Come with me.

Invasion

People didn't think much of Tiberius Claudius Caesar Augustus Germanicus - Claudius to you - when he first became Emperor. Caligula had left no heir, and the Senate toyed, briefly, with the idea of just doing away with the whole 'Emperor' nonsense and reverting to being a republic again before the Praetorians dumped Claudius on the throne and persuaded everyone, presumably with the aid of something very sharp, that their best interests were served by going along with it.

He would turn out to be a competent and efficient ruler in the end, but he was a slight chap with a stammer, and he probably wasn't in the most robust of health, although his physical limitations have been somewhat exaggerated by those who sought to sully his name in the years following his reign. He was the sort of bloke who rattled around inside his armour. So, what he needed was some ass to kick and who better to provide that ass than the Britons? Julius Caesar had a go, two goes in fact, before popping back over the Channel in time for the winter break and a nice rest somewhere drier, which, knowing Britain, was just about anywhere. He would probably have gone back and finished the job, too, had it not been for the escalation of events elsewhere, particularly in Gaul and that matter with the stabbing.

Claudius was well aware that by invading Britain, he would be following in Caesar's footprints and standing on those particularly broad shoulders could do him no harm either in the eyes of the Senate, the army or the people.

Nothing was left to chance. This time, there would be no retreat in Winter. This time, they wouldn't rock up to the shores of Gaul, as Caligula had done, peer timidly across the sea at the white cliffs of Britain, pick up some shells and go home again.

The bridgehead in Gaul was carefully organised by the procurator of Northern Gaul, Graecinius Laco and they called for the experienced governor of Pannonia, Aulus Plautius, to head an invasion force of four legions plus auxiliary. About 40,000 men in total. Even then, the myth of the strange, magical kingdom, Rome's Mordor, which was the dark realms of the British islands, struck fear into the hearts of the men, and they refused to embark. It took Claudius' freedman, Narcissus, a rich and powerful right-hand man of the Emperor, to persuade them.

'Io Saturnalia!' they cried, an allusion to the annual festival dedicated to the god Saturn when slaves dress in their master's clothes.

The force was split into three parts, although where they landed is a subject of great debate. If it can be narrowed down for certain, it not only serves an immense historical purpose, illustrating the very point at which the future of Britain changed forever, but some enterprising chap will put up some sort of facility to part fascinated tourists from their money. The archaeology seems to suggest that Richborough in Kent was one of the landing points, and Chichester around the coast in Sussex might have been another. Military buildings dating to the invasion period have been discovered at nearby Fishbourne, where the client king Cogidubnus (or Togidubnus, depending on how you read it) lived in an enormous palace built for him by the Romans. He was certainly benefiting from Roman largesse and must have offered his support to the invasion in return. The invasion seems to have moved at pace and with no resistance through the area nominally held by the Atrebates tribe which suggests they at least stood aside or again offered direct help.

The legendary British tribal leader Caratacus and his brother, the King Togodumnus of the Catuvellauni are defeated in a series of skirmishes before staging a major battle at a river crossing, probably on the Thames. After the defeat, Togodumnus is killed in a smaller skirmish and the Romans dig in, the major part of the first stage complete. With the forward base set and the locals quietened, Plautius called for Claudius to lead the march on the Catuvellaunian capital, Camulodunum, modern-day Colchester.

The people conquered by the Romans came from a variety of ethnic groups. The people right at the very north, the Caledonians, appear to have been there since time immemorial, but those further south were descendants of what we now call the Celts who migrated through northern Gaul in the late Iron Age. The relatively recent arrival of most of the southern tribes might explain the apparent power struggles that were going on before Roman intervention.

Unlike Gaul, where everyone seemed to get along quite happily, the Britons were still spitting mad at each other. The coinage of the age shows that allegiances and tribal makeup are constantly shifting, and archaeology shows an abundance of hillfort construction and other demonstrations of power and military prowess. These inter-tribal fights not only aided the Roman invasion, they might have gone some way to triggering it.

Caesar's intervention of 55-54BC was followed by planned invasions by Augustus in 34, 27 and 26BC, but instead, the Romans satisfied themselves with forming client relationships with the major tribes of the south. Both Augustus and Tiberius managed to avoid committing any physical resources to Britain as the inter-tribal squabbling intensified. But whilst those rulers had a power base back home to rely on, Claudius was keen, if not a little desperate, to get over there and make a name for himself. His foray into Britain was the last time he left Italy, and he spent a total of 16 days on the island. More for show than for anything else, he brought elephants, although the sight of them must have served to freak out the natives a bit, and they also helped to emphasise the Hellenistic - and thereby totally alien nature - of the invading army. He was there for the fall of Camulodunum, which was clearly considered, if only by the Romans, as the capital of Britain, but there's no suggestion he was involved in any military sense.

The fragmentary inscription on an arch erected in Rome in 51AD records that eleven British kings surrendered, one of whom was a king from all the way up in Orkney. It was assumed for a long time that the British tribes, when they weren't leathering ten bells out of each other, led somewhat independent existences. Recent archaeological developments, including the stunning news that the Altar Stone at Stonehenge came from all the way in northern Scotland, suggests instead that this was a closely interconnected society with a communication network that could summon kings from Orkney to bend the knee to Claudius in Essex without the Romans having to go up there and threaten to stab them.

> To Tiberius Claudius Caesar, son of Drusus, Augustus Germanicus, pontifex maximus, holding the tribunician power for the eleventh year, consul five times, acclaimed imperator ... times, father of his country, the Roman senate and people [dedicated this] because he received the surrender of eleven kings of Britain conquered without any reverse and because he was the first to subject to the sovereignty of the Roman people barbarian tribes across the ocean.

That these kings surrendered as one suggests things about British society that paint a whole different picture than the traditional one of tribes glowering across valleys at each other from hillforts. Perhaps some among these eleven saw the writing on the wall and simply persuaded the others that capitulation was better than annihilation, particularly when chaps like Cogidubnus didn't seem to be doing too badly out of the whole thing. Perhaps they were all part of some wider alliance that we're not aware of because not all the locals were so accommodating, of course, including lots of them between Orkney and Essex. Out west remained wild for some time.

However it happened, news spread fast, and we mustn't discount that this surrender was just seen as a political move on the part of the Britons rather than some sort of complete loss. They would certainly have known who the Romans were and what their reputation was, even if the sight of them was alien. Memories of what the Romans did at Carthage and Corinth would have been at the forefront of the Britons' dealings with them. More pertinently, perhaps, given the nature of the tribes' more recent heritage, the annihilation of Vercingetorix's huge forces at Alesia by Caesar in 52BC would have been a terrible reminder. Rome might have been a completely different culture, but it was one the Britons were very aware of and in contact with. As such, they were well aware that the Roman war machine was not to be taken lightly, and the wiser leaders would surely have known this. That the Romans took and then sacked Camulodunum only served to sharpen the Britons' senses.

The whole thing was re-enacted back home in a display in the Campus Martius in Rome, complete with a burning city and kneeling kings. A coin was struck showing Claudius with an arch inscribed DE BRITANN[IS]. An arch was built at Boulogne to commemorate the departure of Claudius and his triumphant return. Reliefs were erected at Aphrodisias and Cyzicus in distant Asia Minor. Everyone knew that Britain had fallen, and everyone knew that Claudius had taken it. As a PR exercise, the whole thing couldn't have gone any better.

Colchester was re-established as a proper Roman town with a big fortress for the 20th Legion and a smaller fort a few miles away near a royal residence. The fort was either there to protect or intimidate the leader of the Trinovantes - maybe a little of both.

From there, the army split into three, marching north, north-west and west. The western force, consisting largely of the 2nd Legion, was under the command of Vespasian, who became Emperor in 69. His men fought thirty battles, took the Isle of Wight and more than 20 *oppida* (a defended town, including hillforts) and subdued two powerful tribes who are unnamed but were likely the Durotriges and the Dubunni.

Less is known about the other two assault forces, as the history is either lost or has yet to be discovered, but they appear to have made steady progress along the lines of what is now Watling Street and Ermine Street, suggesting that these later major Roman arterial routes were already substantial highways (down which, Orkney kings hurried, one assumes). As they went, they established friendly client kings around them, whose rulers were nominally independent but controlled by the alliances they agreed with the Romans. One such buffer zone was established in the area around Chichester, where a partial inscription from the town that was then known as Noviomagus (New Market) refers to a chap known as Tiberius Claudius Cogidubnus. He has the Roman 'trinomina' (three names) of a Roman citizen, and the nomen Claudius suggests that his citizenship was granted by the Emperor himself. He has the title of Rex Magnus Britanniae, 'Great King of Britain', and may have ruled substantial parts of south-eastern Britain and several tribes. The palace at Fishbourne mentioned earlier is normally attributed to him, at least at the time it was being constructed.

Another famous client king was Prasutagus, who is known from coinage but about whom not a lot is known apart from he was King of the Iceni who lived in what is now Norfolk. He was the husband of the rebel queen Boudica and it was his death that kicked off events that led to her going completely postal on the Romans. We're going to hear a lot about her, believe me.

Of the eleven who surrendered, one was likely another Queen, Cartimandua of the Brigantes of northern England and southern Scotland - the areas that were later bisected by Hadrian's Wall. The *oppidum* built at Stanwick in Northamptonshire appears to have served as a regional warehouse distribution centre for everything from wine to building materials, and this might have been Cartimandua's regional capital. Another might have been the anonymous royal buried with great riches in about 50AD on a conspicuous hillside outside Verulamium. The grave contained a rich bounty of grave goods, most of them ritually broken, and sat in an enclosure into which a large Romano-British temple was later inserted. Who it was is the subject of debate. Maybe Adminius, a son of Cunobelinus, another King of the Britons and brother of Caratacus and Togodumnus.

This juxtaposition of British royalty, the Roman war machine, and the new towns following in the wake of the Roman march north could mean only one thing.

The Romans were here, and they were staying.

Despite the acquiescence of the eleven kings (or queens), the occupying forces weren't taking any risks. The extent of forts and military outposts in south-eastern Britain isn't clearly defined, ostensibly because a lot of the archaeology remains buried under the most populated parts of Britain, but must also indicate that this area was largely pacified, or was compliant, relatively quickly. But there is a great military road peppered with forts that runs between Exeter and Lincoln (with an extension that runs up to the Humber River) known as the Fosse Way. You can still follow the majority of its virtually straight line through the country to this day. The 320km of road is a great example of military planning, serving as a superhighway right through various territories, friendly and, one must assume, enemy.

The major fortress at Isca Dumnoniorum (Exeter) has a later foundation (around 55), but its construction and position echo earlier invasion roads, which deliberately bypass existing centres of occupation and were probably instigated by Plautius himself. The Fosse Way essentially marks the earliest boundary of Roman expansion. This practice of road building to demarcate expansion and then building another and then another, consolidating the land behind it as you go, is echoed elsewhere in the Empire.

In the middle of 47AD, Aulus Plautius was recalled to Rome, where he was given a ceremonial 'ovation' - Claudius got the formal triumph, of course - and by this time, the road and all its military stations and forts had been completed. It seems obvious then that Plautius was charged with taking the invasion to at least this point and its completion marked the end of his service. It serves as his crowning glory.

All this suggests, of course, that the whole area was firmly under Roman control, which was far from the case. The first thing the new governor, Ostorius Scapula, does is disarm everyone in the area of control, ally or not. This immediately causes trouble, notably among the Iceni, who are to show up later in this story with a vengeance. They kick off a rebellion, although who leads it isn't clear. It couldn't have been Prasutagus, who we mentioned earlier, because he wouldn't have been allowed to remain in power to die and signal Boudica's rebellion of 60/61. Whoever it was, they were promptly crushed. This must have led to an increased military presence in the area that couldn't have done anything but inflame the tensions that were to overspill later with Boudica.

Even the Romans might have struggled to justify the invasion of Britain as 'they just fancied the place and so took it', even though, in effect, they just fancied the place and took it. Rolling up and punching everyone into submission is fine, but Rome was a society of laws and rules, and as such, drumming up some sort of reason to be there was essential, if only to placate those Senators back home who insisted on such boring things as following the law.

The British tribal leader Verica, who, from his coinage, would appear to have been king of the Atrebates, gave them one when in around 42AD, he gets himself thrown out of Britain and appears in Rome, cap in hand, wanting to know what the Romans are going to do about it. He had the title *rex*, which would make him a client king of the Romans, and he appears to have lost bits of his kingdom to Tiberius Claudius Cogidubnus, who we met earlier, over a period of a few years until the area he controls shrank to almost nothing.

All this gives the Romans the perfect opportunity to give the invasion a sheen of legitimacy. Ordinarily, they might just have sent Verica on his way with an armful of coins and a dismissive shrug. Sending a bunch of legions across the sea to beat up his enemies for him is, in theory at least, precisely the sort of support they should have offered, but as we saw from earlier, Cogidubnus also appears to have been a Roman friend and so intervening would have meant picking a side. Invading the whole damned island under the pretence of keeping the peace is another matter. What happened to Verica isn't clear, but he would have wanted his land back. He clearly didn't get it, so he probably stayed in Rome as he would have been an old man by this stage anyway.

Cassius Dio gives an account of the invasion in which he directly says that it was launched not for the glory of Claudius but for Verica, whom he refers to as 'Bericus'.

Aulus Plautius, a senator of great renown, made a campaign against Britain; for a certain Bericus, who had been driven out of the island as a result of an uprising, had persuaded Claudius to send a force thither… So they [Roman forces] put into the island and found none to oppose them. For the Britons as a result of their inquiries had not expected that they would come, and had therefore not assembled beforehand. And even when they did assemble, they would not come to close quarters with the Romans, but took refuge in the swamps and the forests, hoping to wear out the invaders in fruitless effort, so that, just as in the days of Julius Caesar, they should sail back with nothing accomplished.

Plautius, accordingly, had a deal of trouble in searching them out; but when at last he did find them, he first defeated Caratacus and then Togodumnus, the sons of Cynobellinus, who was dead. (The Britons were not free and independent, but were divided into groups under various kings.) After the flight of these kings, he gained by capitulation a part of the Bodunni, who were ruled by a tribe of the Catuellani; and leaving a garrison there, he advanced farther…

Shortly afterwards Togodumnus perished, but the Britons, so far from yielding, united all the more firmly to avenge his death. Because of this fact and because of the difficulties he had encountered at the Thames, Plautius became afraid, and instead of advancing any farther, proceeded to guard what he had already won, and sent for Claudius. For he had been instructed to do this in case he met with any particularly stubborn resistance, and, in fact, extensive equipment, including elephants, had already been got together for the expedition.

When the message reached him, Claudius entrusted affairs at home, including the command of the troops, to his colleague Lucius Vitellius, whom he had caused to remain in office like himself for a whole half-year; and he himself then set out for the front. He sailed down the river to Ostia, and from there followed the coast to Massilia; thence, advancing partly by land and partly along the rivers, he came to the ocean and crossed over to Britain, where he joined the legions that were waiting for him near the Thames. Taking over the command of these, he crossed the stream, and engaging the barbarians, who had gathered at his approach, he defeated them and captured Camulodunum, the capital of Cynobellinus. Thereupon he won over numerous tribes, in some cases by capitulation, in others by force, and was saluted as imperator several times, contrary to precedent; for no man may receive this title more than once for one and the same war. He deprived the conquered of their arms and handed them over to Plautius, bidding him also subjugate the remaining districts. Claudius himself now hastened back to Rome, sending ahead the news of his victory... The Senate on learning of his achievement gave him the title of Britannicus and granted him permission to celebrate a triumph.

All of this paints a somewhat rosy picture of the Roman invasion, which couldn't be further from the truth. Ostorius faced a serious escalation in open warfare against the more belligerent locals including Caratacus who had escaped defeat during the initial invasion and was now off in Wales riling up the locals, particularly the Silures of south-east Wales and the Ordovices of the mountainous central regions.

Before he could deal with those, he had to deal with the Deceangli in the north. The results here in Wales are interesting, with the north remaining largely 'uncivilised' and Roman presence there mostly military in nature whilst further south, eventually, the locals become enthusiastically Roman, with villas and towns such as Carmarthen being built.

The Demeteae of Carmarthen appear to have been rather willing to accept the incoming culture, and the transition into Roman ways seems smooth as a result. This suggests that the transition was a two-way process because the Romans could, if they had felt like it, very easily have 'domesticated' the northern tribes, too. That this didn't happen would suggest a lack of will on both sides. They didn't want to become Romans, and the Romans didn't see the benefit in forcing them to. As long as everyone remained happy with that status quo, then a string of forts was enough to keep the peace, and everyone could get on with their lives. Significant mining operations in the north made the Roman presence viable, and the military presence was as much to protect those interests as to subjugate the population.

Before that, however, Ostorius was forced to intervene in trouble with the Brigantes and the nominally pro-Roman Queen Cartimandua. Not all of her subjects were big fans of her relationship with the Romans, and Ostorius had to send men in to support a valuable ally, a move that was to reap benefits later on.

Dealing with Caratacus, the Silures, and the Ordovices would require legionary support, so in 49, the 20th Legion's fortress was turned into a *colonia*, a town for retired soldiers who were given an allotment of land. They could also serve as a reserve force in an emergency and as a way of establishing a beachhead of Roman civilisation, law, and culture among the British. It also gave Roman elites somewhere to establish themselves. It gave the 20th somewhere to operate out of and somewhere to fight for. It gave them ownership of the British project.

The Silures took a lot of crushing before they would behave. The Romans tried the normal, violent methods, they tried persuasion, probably in the form of bribery and they tried offering peace. The locals weren't interested. *Non atrocitate, non clementia mutabatur*, as Tacitus put it - Neither cruelty nor clemency could change them.

In the end, the old-fashioned methods worked. Where the decisive battle was isn't clear, but it was a final victory and the Silures were sufficiently cowed to the extent that they soon became some of the most enthusiastic of converts, with the magnificent town of Venta Silurum (Caerwent) built for them and all sorts of sycophantic inscriptions praising the Emperor being raised.

Caratacus flees again, this time north to the lands of the Brigantes. He was obviously expecting some form of refuge, presumably because the anti-Roman factions among them were so strong, but Cartimandua fulfilled her diplomatic obligations and handed him over to the Romans. This caused more trouble between the Brigantes who were wedded to the old ways and those loyal to Rome.

Caratacus (and his family) were then taken to Rome and paraded as a captured chieftain and great military adversary. He reportedly spoke to the Senate, asking them why, with such a magnificent city, they still coveted the Britons' meagre huts. It was a speech that apparently so impressed the Senate that they gave him a pardon and allowed him to live out his days in Rome as a free man, which sounds rather implausible. These great rhetorical speeches are, of course, not the words of the people they are assigned to, and the whole story sounds like political spin. That they would even allow a prisoner to stand before the Senate and ramble on is improbable and that he would say something so amazing that they simply forgave him and set him up in a villa for life even more so. Instead, this sounds like a Roman angry at the decline in Roman moral standards using Caratacus as a mouthpiece to voice their discontent. Caratacus probably ended up being quietly strangled and tossed in the Tiber when they were done parading him about, just as they did with Vercingetorix a few generations earlier. Even if the story is only partly true and Claudius saw some political judiciousness in pardoning him, the speech is still likely fiction.

When Ostorius died prematurely in 52, he and Plautius had achieved a huge amount in just ten years. Mining operations, including lead and silver, were already underway by 49, helping to defray the astronomical cost of the operation. Urban centres apart from Colchester were developing strongly in the same period; Verulamium was given municipal status, granting its citizens the so-called 'Latin' rights under Roman law. This status was not far short of full citizenship, and those who held official duties in such a municipium would gain full rights. Londinium was founded around 50AD - dendrochronology from a wooden drain found in London dates to 47AD. It was probably an entirely new settlement established by overseas traders to exploit the lucrative new markets that the invasion had opened up.

The new guy, Aulus Didius Gallus, arrived in 52; he was met with the news that a legion had been defeated by the Silures. No further information about this battle is known, and no legions seem significantly affected, which suggests that the defeat was not particularly calamitous and that the term 'legion' might refer to a smaller unit. His five-year governorship saw little further expansion and again, this might have been a deliberate plan to simply consolidate power. He was called on again to send a legion into the Brigantian regions to support Cartimandua in the split that now saw her consort, Venutius, championing the increasingly strong anti-Roman factions in what had become the strongest tribal power in Britain. The trouble was quelled, but it was a problem contained rather than solved.

When Nero became Emperor in 54, the new Emperor apparently toyed with the idea of abandoning the new province. That idea didn't last long because by 57, a new governor, Quintus Veranius, was pushing into Wales, and he was surely operating under higher instructions when he did so. He would hardly just have arrived in the province and decided to expand off his own back. His campaign came to a crashing end when he dropped dead within a year of arriving, and the task of completing the job was left to Suetonius Paulinus, who was to become a central figure in the early days of Roman Britain.

He was a good appointment. An Italian from Pisaurum (Pesaro on the Adriatic Sea) who had served in Mauretania Caesariensis, where he was the first Roman to lead a force over the Atlas Mountains. Fighting rebellious sorts in upland areas is what he was good at, and this experience did him well in Wales. Beginning in 58, within two years, the job was largely finished, with only the Druid stronghold on Mona (Anglesey) remaining as any form of resistance. Tacitus provides us with a famously vivid account of the scene the Roman army faced as they attempted to cross the narrow straits between the mainland and the island. This account comes from Tacitus' own father-in-law, Julius Agricola, who, as a young officer, was seconded to Paulinus.

> Flat-bottomed boats were built to contend with the shifting shallows and these took the infantry across. Then came the cavalry; some utilised fords, but in deeper water the men swam beside their horses. The enemy lined the shore in a dense armed mass. Among them were black-haired women with dishevelled hair, like Furies, brandishing torches. Close by stood Druids, raising their hands to heaven screaming dreadful curses. This weird spectacle awed the Roman soldiers into a sort of paralysis. They stood still - and presented themselves as a target. But then they urged each other (and were urged by the general) not to fear a horde of fanatical women. Onward pressed their standards and they bore down their opponents, enveloping them in the flames of their own torches. Suetonius garrisoned the conquered island. The groves devoted to Mona's barbarous superstitions he demolished.

Some possible archaeological confirmation of the cult's activities on Anglesey are provided by the collection of artefacts found in Llyn Cerrig Bach, including swords, shields, trumpets, horse fittings and a slave chain. These items represent a considerable accumulation of wealth, ritually deposited in the lake suggesting people came from far and wide to deposit them there.

While Suetonius was there, cleaning up the resistance and putting the remaining Druidic sites to the torch, he received word that something major was afoot back in the Iceni homelands and that affairs were escalating at an alarming rate.

Boudica

Boudica, who for most of British history has been known as 'Boadicea' due to some misreadings of ancient manuscripts in the 18th and 19th centuries was the wife of King Prasutagus and as we have seen, they cannot have been part of the Iceni rebellion of 47AD or they would have been very quickly, and brutally dealt with there and then. Their base has never been satisfactorily identified, which probably suggests the whole tribe would wander around their territory in what was mostly the modern county of Norfolk, perhaps travelling from site to site on a seasonal basis.

At this time, large proportions of their territory would have been marshy bog, which doesn't take well to a sedentary lifestyle - growing crops is hard in a swamp - but is fantastic for evading one's enemies, particularly when you know the winding ways through the reeds, and they don't. Areas of what now appear to be low-lying mounds, barely even hills, would have been distinct islands at the time and moving between these was a tactic that Alfred the Great employed to some success when he wasn't burning cakes. It's not the sort of area the Romans would feel at home in, particularly in a military sense. So engaging Prasutagus as a client king made absolute sense.

The client king relationship might appear at first to be of equally mutual benefit, but Rome would always weigh the odds in their favour, and their relationship with Prasutagus was no different. The very first thing such an agreement offers the Roman opportunist is the chance to engage in one of the few occupations that was seen as befitting of the Roman gentleman. Such tawdry business as trading is not something a senator or other noble would be seen, directly anyway, getting their hands dirty with. Lending money, on the other hand, was a noble and fine profession for such an elite luminary and as such, the Romans, apparently with Seneca the Younger to the fore with his fat little fingers twitching, lent Prasutagus an exceedingly large amount of money. Prasutagus was a king and kings find the lure of tons of gold hard to resist, even when they're not entirely sure how they are going to pay them back.

The other problem arises from the pretty standard clause in such deals which required half the kingdom to be handed over to the Romans on the death of the client. When Prasutagus died then, Boudica suddenly found herself with half a kingdom and a whole bunch of Roman moneylenders standing there with their hands out, looking rather threatening at the same time. What's more, she now only had half a kingdom to pay them back with. No wonder then, she felt unable to complete the deal, and with the addition of a particularly tyrannical procurator, Decianus Catus, who seemed very keen on creating misery through ruthless taxation, tensions were soaring. The last straw was the rape of Boudica's daughters and her own humiliation by flogging, and the Iceni rose in revolt.

The details of the events leading up to the revolt come from two sources, Tacitus and Cassius Dio. Tacitus has the advantage of writing much closer to the events, some 50 years after they happened and, as mentioned earlier, a future father-in-law in Britain at the time, albeit a few hundred miles away at the time. Cassius Dio is writing hundreds of years later, but partly using Tacitus as a source as well as the official records of the Empire. Dio's reasons for the revolt are pretty clear:

An excuse for the war was found in the confiscation of the sums of money that Claudius had given to the foremost Britons; for these sums, as Decianus Catus, the procurator of the island, maintained, were to be paid back. This was one reason for the uprising; another was found in the fact that Seneca, in the hope of receiving a good rate of interest, had lent to the islanders 40,000,000 sesterces that they did not want, and had afterwards called in this loan all at once and had resorted to severe measures in exacting it.

What these 'severe measures' are, he doesn't say, but later on, in a speech he attributes to Boudica (but is all him), he adds:

"Why is it that, though none of us has any money (how, indeed, could we, or where would we get it?), we are stripped and despoiled like a murderer's victims?"

But apart from that, the tales of rape and flogging don't appear, or they are incidental to the financial problems. In Dio's story, this revolt is all about money. Tacitus, on the other hand, has a story wholly without any mention of money issues:

As a beginning, his widow Boudica was flogged and their daughters raped. The Icenian chiefs were deprived of their hereditary estates as if the Romans had been given the whole country.

The differing accounts can largely be explained by the relevant author's narrative focus. Tacitus is writing at a time when Rome is going through, in his eyes at least, a sharp decline in moral standards. The Republican values he aspires to have all but disappeared, particularly under the rule of Domitian under whom he served as a senator and who held the Senate in an iron grip of terror.

His writings serve as a reaction to this moral decline. They are protests against the way Rome is going and warnings that they need to change their ways of perish. It's no coincidence that he was writing *Annals of Imperial Rome* at the same time an unknown author was writing the Biblical Revelation with its apocalyptic vision of the future of Rome. Both are works of their time and place and both have the same message - change or die.

In Tacitus' account, it's necessary to have two sets of Romans - the good ones, played in this particular scenario by people like Agricola and Suetonius Paulinus and the bad ones played by those who rape Boudica's daughters and disrespect the Iceni.

Cassius Dio, writing at a completely different time, doesn't have the same message to send and so his story either ignores the crimes of the Romans to make his side seem better, or they never existed to report on in the first place. It's a much more sober reflection on what happened. Does this then necessarily mean it's the more accurate account? That would be impossible to say, although reaching that conclusion would appear to make sense. However, Tacitus can reasonably say that he was able to talk to a direct witness for his account and therefore his account is more accurate. Either way, what happened next was a quite staggering amount of bloodshed.

> The Iceni gained support from the neighbouring Trinovantes whose resentment at the treatment they had received from the veterans at Camulodunum saw them fit to burst. Together they marched on what had once been a royal British centre and was now just a hated symbol of Roman oppression.

Camulodunum had yet to receive any form of defence and was a sitting duck. It was quickly overwhelmed, and the occupants slaughtered. The last survivors held out for two days in the temple of the Divine Claudius, the vaults of which still stand under the Norman castle.

The Ninth Legion, under Quintus Petilius Cerialis Caesius Rufus attempted to relieve the town but was defeated, probably in an ambush. The entire infantry was massacred, but the commander and his cavalry made it back to base and sheltered behind their defences.

By now, Suetonius Paullinus was racing back from Wales as fast as he could. He had the 14th Legion, some of the 20th and a few auxiliary troops, maybe 10,000 men in total. He tried to call up the 2nd Legion from their base at Exeter, but their commander, Poenius Postumus, refused to budge. The reason for his reluctance isn't clear; he was an experienced soldier with no previous record which might suggest cowardice on his part. It might have been he suspected a trap, the same sort of trap that Cerialis had fallen into, and it might also have been that on receiving word of Cerialis' defeat and Decianus Catus' decision to flee to safety in Gaul, he thought he might be the only significant Roman force left in Britain and that it was prudent to sit tight and wait for reinforcements. Either way, when he learned of the eventual outcome, the shame was too much, and suicide was his only option.

The rebels then turned their attention to London, with even more devastating results. Paulinus had arrived by now but took one look at the undefended town and decided he couldn't save it. The townsfolk begged him to stay and fight, but to do so would have been crazy. He offered anyone who wanted to leave passage out of the city and then left it to its fate.

The Britons tore the place apart, slaughtered everyone they found, and burned the place to the ground. Then they turned their attention on Verulamium and ripped that town to shreds, too. Seventy thousand died. Tacitus describes the killing:

> For the British did not take prisoners, or practice other war-time exchanges. They could not wait to cut throats, hang, burn and crucify.

Suetonius Paullinus knew he couldn't just let the rebels continue on their rampage and despite being massively outnumbered - Tacitus says 80,000 rebels, Dio puts it as much as a staggering 250,000 - he knew he would have to face them eventually.

He chose the battlefield well, with his back to a small defile and forests protecting his flanks. The peripatetic rebels had brought everything, and everyone, with them and the wagon train of animals, children, old people, supplies and general hangers-on had arranged themselves at the far end of the battlefield to watch the rebels crush the Romans once and for all. Tacitus has Boudica make a famous rhetorical speech which is, of course, nothing to do with what she might have said - after all, how could they have heard her across the battlefield, speaking in a language none of them could understand - and all to do with what Tacitus wants to say:

> Boudica drove around all the tribes in a chariot with her daughters in front of her. "We British are used to women commanders in war" she cried "I am descended from mighty men! But now I am not fighting for my kingdom and wealth. I am fighting as an ordinary person for my lost freedom, my bruised body, and my outraged daughters. Nowadays Roman rapacity does not even spare our bodies. Old people are killed, virgins raped. But the gods will grant us the vengeance we deserve! The Roman division which dared to fight is annihilated. The others cower in their camps or watch for a chance to escape. They will never face even the din and roar of all our thousands, much less the shock of our onslaught. Consider how many of you are fighting - and why. Then you will win this battle, or perish. That is what I, a woman, plan to do! - let the men live in slavery if they will"

All stirring stuff and the sort of thing that has made Boudica the poster girl for rebellious barbarian queens and a genuine British hero ever since. The myth of Boudica comes almost entirely from what amounts to a few paragraphs from *Annals*, as does the image of her as a righteous avenging warrior driven to rebellion by the evils of Roman rapacity. What else could someone do when faced with such provocation but rise up and defeat those who had offended and oppressed her people in such a manner? It's even more remarkable and telling that this view of her has nothing to do with her at all. It's the Roman view of her. It's the bad guys' view of her. The Romans created the heroic Boudica entirely themselves, which goes some way to explain the narrative Tacitus is trying to convey. Dio has a speech, too, equally as stirring, and this is largely based on Tacitus' account, albeit slightly more sober. Neither of them can be accurate.

The battle was brutal. The overwhelming numbers of the Britons were mitigated by their ability to get to the Roman front line. The Britons charged, and the first wave smashed against the Roman line, which held. Ultimately, with Roman discipline in place, the Britons could only physically fight one-on-one, and in that respect, they were no match for the Romans. 250,000 men are fine if you can use them, but when 249,000 of them are standing around in the background, shouting and looking angry because they couldn't get past their own men to the Roman line, they were meaningless.

The Romans hurled javelins and waited until the Britons started to fall. When the time was right, they moved into wedge formations and drove into the Britons, who, unable to press home the only advantage they had, began to panic. Faced with the advancing Roman death machine, they scrambled to get away, only to run into more of their own men, charging relentlessly forwards. And the Romans went to work. Hacking, slashing and stabbing, they chewed through the Britons, who by now were hemmed in by their own wagon train and had just become a huge, teeming, terrified target for the Roman army.

Tacitus says 80,000 Britons died, including all the women, children, old people and even animals from the wagon train. It was carnage on an unimaginable scale.

If we believe Dio's numbers, the dead might have numbered over a quarter of a million. It's slaughter unmatched until the charnel fields of The Great War. Tacitus says Boudica drank poison and died. Dio says she disappeared.

One person who didn't disappear was Suetonius Paulinus who, over-excited by victory and out for revenge, goes on something of a rampage across the country. Catus' replacement, Gaius Julius Alpinus Classicianus whose tomb was broken up and used in the construction of London's medieval walls, was rediscovered, and is in the British Museum, has to manufacture a charge of losing some ships against Suetonius so he can be sent back to Rome. His replacement was the rather more sober Publius Petronius Turpilianus.

Paulinus at least seems to have been celebrated for his efforts when he gets back to Rome, and a man with the same name, either himself or a son, is consul for the second time in 66AD. He reappears in the year 69, the Year of the Four Emperors, on the side of Otho. He is captured by the future Emperor Vitellius, who pardons him. After that, he is lost to history.

Boudica's destruction was total, and her defeat was complete. She not only lost, she lost everything, including nearly all of her tribe. Yet still, she became an iconic figure in British history. That her name became synonymous with victory is strangely poignant. Perhaps she represents a victory of the soul rather than a victory per se.

What became certain, however, was that in the nearly 120 years between Julius Caesar first setting foot in Britain and Suetonius Paulinus' men obliterating every last remnant of the Iceni rebellion, even if more rebellions were to come, Britain had been brought fully within the Roman world and the path of the country changed forever. Before, there had been remarkable prehistoric achievements on the islands, but now, with the written word to the fore, the country had entered a new phase that was to eventually form it into the nation it is today. Moreover, when the United Kingdom began its own expansionist and *colonial*ist practices, it was to spread those ingrained Romanised values of law, culture, society and education around the world with it. America today, for example, runs on a legal system that is borrowed from the British, and the British borrowed it from the Romans. Many of the basic legal structures that Americans enjoy, such as the right to not have to bear witness against oneself, are rights that were written into Roman law and, subsequently, British law 2,000 years ago. If the Romans were the progenitors of Western society, the British were the ones who carried Roman ways to the Earth's furthest corners. Whether they wanted it or not.

Grim Up North

For most of the lifetime of Roman Britain, the northernmost border lay along the Tyne-Solway isthmus that was definitively delineated by the construction of Hadrian's Wall. By the time the Welsh tribes were brought under control in the 70s, it was the only frontier and after dealing with the Welsh, Julius Agricola pushed north, presumably to complete the conquest of the whole island. His gains lasted less than a decade, and the later Antonine push could only muster another 18 years. There were plenty more excursions into what is now Scotland, but they were either reacting to or punishing behaviour by the Caledonii. All these forays appear to have gone up the eastern side of Scotland, and Agricola probably got no further, at least with his main forces, than the Great Glen, except maybe by sea. Tacitus tells us he reached the very end of the island, but there's no archaeological evidence that he spent any time that far north or that he took a significant force of men with him. Neither is it clear what is meant by 'the end' of the island.

In his biography of his father-in-law, Tacitus lays out some of the techniques Agricola employed when enforcing Roman provincial administration in Britain, particularly as he pushed into the north.

Agricola fully understood the temperament of the province [of Britain], and he was aware from the experience of others that little is gained by conquest if it is followed by injustices. He therefore determined to root out the causes of war. Starting with himself and his retinue, he kept his household in check - a thing as difficult for many as governing a province. He transacted no official business through his freedmen or slaves. No personal feelings, no recommendations, no pleas induced him to take centurions or soldiers on his staff; in each case, he regarded the best man as the most reliable...

The augmentation of tributes and contributions he mitigated by a just and equal assessment, abolishing those private exactions which were more grievous to be borne than the taxes themselves. For the inhabitants had been compelled in mockery to sit by their own locked-up granaries, to buy corn needlessly, and to sell it again at a stated price. Long and difficult journeys had also been imposed upon them; for the several districts, instead of being allowed to supply the nearest winter quarters, were forced to carry their corn to remote and devious places; by which means, what was easy to be procured by all, was converted into an article of gain to a few.

By suppressing these abuses in the first year of his administration, he established a favourable idea of peace, which, through the negligence or oppression of his predecessors, had been no less dreaded than war. At the return of summer he assembled his army. On their march, he commended the regular and orderly, and restrained the stragglers; he marked out the encampments, and explored in person the estuaries and forests. At the same time he perpetually harassed the enemy by sudden incursions; and, after sufficiently alarming them, by an interval of forbearance, he held to their view the allurements of peace. By this management, many states, which till that time had asserted their independence, were now induced to lay aside their animosity, and to deliver hostages. These districts were surrounded with castles and forts, disposed with so much attention and judgment, that no part of Britain, hitherto new to the Roman arms, escaped unmolested. The succeeding winter was employed in the most salutary measures. In order, by a taste of pleasures, to reclaim the natives from that rude and unsettled state which prompted them to war, and reconcile them to quiet and tranquillity, he incited them, by private instigations and public encouragements, to erect temples, courts of justice, and dwelling-houses. He bestowed commendations upon those who were prompt in complying with his intentions, and reprimanded such as were dilatory; thus promoting a spirit of emulation which had all the force of necessity. He was also attentive to provide a liberal education for the sons of their chieftains, preferring the natural genius of the Britons to the attainments of the Gauls; and his attempts were attended with such success, that they who lately disdained to make use of the Roman language, were now ambitious of becoming eloquent. Hence the Roman habit began to be held in honour, and the toga was frequently worn. At length they gradually deviated into a taste for those luxuries which stimulate to vice; porticoes, and baths, and the elegances of the table; and this, from their inexperience, they termed politeness, whilst, in reality, it constituted a part of their slavery.

The Wall

It's hard to know exactly what the Romans' relationship with the tribes north of the frontier was like. Certainly, they traded with them, and the idea of those tribes as being mystical shadow warriors, flitting in and out of the realms of existence and appearing to be like some sort of shamanistic alien nation is the result of modern hyperbole. These people were Brittonic-speaking Britons, much like everyone else on the island, and in that respect, they were no different than the tribes the Romans encountered in Wales or England. They might seem more warlike, but all the information we have about them comes from the Romans, and all that information is only recorded in relation to warfare. They didn't write down stories about how much they traded with them or friendly encounters, just the ones where they got into fights with them. The Romans loved nothing more than a *casus belli* to justify aggression and glory, and Caledonian 'aggression' might be translated as nothing more than moving troops about in response to Roman activity. If you're one of the Caledonii, then preparing for a scrap might be seen as prudent when several thousand heavily armed Romans turn up on your borders. That the Romans then took this as the pretext for a fight is impossible to judge, but it's likely the Romans were as much provocateurs as defenders.

Had the Romans really wanted to conquer Scotland, of course, then they would have and could have. The problem was that they saw it almost as launching another full-scale invasion, similar to the one they launched in 43. Establishing all the conditions for that invasion had been hugely expensive, and the complex client relationships built with the southern tribes had gone a long way in smoothing that invasion. These weren't conditions they had in Scotland, and such a military campaign would have needed the resources of several legions, especially at first. Such legions require support, so more legions would have had to have been moved to Britain first to provide the logistics and also to replace those now pushing north. The south still required garrisoning.

In all, the Romans might have ended up with eight legions in Britain simply to take Scotland and, to be frank, Scotland wasn't worth that much trouble. The lack of client king relationships meant that they would have had to fully commit the resources of the Roman state machine, and that required money. Such things could be justified if there was money to be made from being in the region. Wales had copper, tin and gold. Parthia had huge amounts of gold. These were places that were worth being in. By comparison, Scotland appeared to have a lot of rain and some inhospitable, if glorious, countryside. The only possible thing the Romans could have exported out of Scotland was glory, and they had plenty of that from elsewhere. It came as little surprise then when Hadrian slammed the brakes on expansionism and decided to draw the frontiers where they were.

The *Historia Augusta* tells that Hadrian built his wall to separate Rome from the barbarians and it certainly separated stuff alright. Modern Scots are quick to claim that the Romans built it to keep them out, but most of it is built slap bang in the middle of what was probably Brigantian territory, and this would make sense. Trying to put up such an immense fortification right on the edge of, or in, enemy territory would have been incredibly difficult, whereas the more compliant Brigantes, even if they were constant troublemakers throughout the Roman period, was whole degrees easier. But neither Hadrian's nor the later and further north Antonine Wall was impenetrable, and neither were they meant to be. Attacking such a wall en masse, particularly at a point where it was most weakly defended, would have only necessitated the use of a few ladders, and there was always the option to simply take to the sea and go around the bloody thing. So, separation is not a primarily military one, even if it does serve some defensive purpose. The separation is as much about a statement of intent as anything else. In drawing the line on the map right there, the Romans can then point to everything they own and say this is the

Roman Empire. It's a full stop at the end of the expansionist sentence. It's the Romans finally whipping the rabbit out of the hat and going 'Ta-da!' It's the 'The End' message at the final reel of a movie.

It's also a giant statement of folly. Hadrian was an enthusiastic builder, and the Romans loved nothing more than a grand statement piece. Romans engineered things sometimes simply to show that they could do it, and what better way of intimidating the locals, be they Brigantes or Caledonii, or of impressing the folks back home than an immense wall snaking across Rome's northernmost border.

Lastly, like all frontiers, it serves to control an area. It's easier to exercise control over the area with a big-ass wall than it is to drop in all those legions we talked about earlier. Frontiers control movement, and the myriad of milecastles and forts along its length serve both as watch points and control centres. The gates through the milecastles were originally wide enough to allow loaded wagons to pass through, suggesting the Romans at least expected a lot of trade (and hence money) to pass through them. Some of the milecastles had their gates narrowed in later years, and some were blocked completely. These narrower gateways were only passable by single-file pedestrians which means they were perhaps only used by people moving livestock from summer to winter pastures. It could be that the gateways were only ever designed for military purposes and the narrowing of the gates simply reflects more peaceful times.

Forts along the wall were built north and south of the main line, with most of the satellite forts to the south. This compares to most front lines, with the logistics and support units based some way behind the front, but some of these forts are reinforced themselves at later dates and are very heavily defended in the first place, so they must have been defending against someone if only unhappy Brigantes who, at times, couldn't seem to decide who's side they were on.

Even if the frontier wasn't generating the income such a customs post might expect to, it was still heavily manned, both with men on the wall and with support troops in the forts within reach. There were, probably, more troops in this area of Britain than anywhere else, and this might seem like they are constantly prepared for, or preparing for, war. Such wars never seem to arrive, at least on the grandest of scales, even if there is a steady supply of people to bash over the head over the centuries. If the Scots are arriving to fight, they are doing so in skirmishes and coming by sea; likewise, if they're coming to trade. And vice-versa, of course, with the occupants of Roman-controlled Britain travelling north to trade. We know from other frontiers, particularly in Germany, that regulation of movement into the Empire was strict. People couldn't simply come in as they pleased, and if they did come in, they had to be unarmed and under guard only during the daytime and, naturally, on payment of a fee. No wonder so many people probably just sailed around the coast. In some cases, they were only allowed to trade in certain markets where one assumes, they could be fleeced a little harder than the locals. They might also have extended taxation north of the border - a protection racket to stop villages mysteriously burning down when the Romans weren't around to 'protect them' or just a flat-out bribe to leave them alone. The problem is that the archaeology that might indicate trade, particularly north of the border, isn't known or never existed so the extent of it is either unknown or was primarily in one direction only. Evidence for the movement of people from the north into Roman areas is also scant. There's only one known Caledonian, a chap by the name of Lossio Veda, south of the wall. He erected an altar at Camulodunum, and as it was dedicated to Mars Medocius and Victory, he was probably a soldier.

There are named Caledonians who remain north of the wall; however, none more famous than the Chieftain Calgacus, who makes a superb and stirring rhetorical speech at the battle of Mons Graupius in which he wonderfully denounces Roman imperialism. It's from Tacitus' biography of Agricola and the speech is all Tacitus at his pomp, of course, laying it on thick against the facets of Rome he finds so distasteful. As a Senator, Tacitus can hardly denounce the *Pax Romana* in his own words, so he has this Scottish Chieftain do it for him. It's one of the most famous speeches in Roman history:

> Whenever I consider the causes of this war and our present straits, my heart beats high that this very day and this unity of yours will be the beginning of liberty for all Britons.... Now they have access to the farthest limits of Britain; there are no more tribes beyond, nothing but waves and rocks, and, more deadly than these, the Romans, whose oppression you have sought in vain to escape by obedience and submissiveness. Plunderers of the world, now that there are no more lands for their all-devastating hands, they search even into the sea. If the enemy is rich, they are rapacious, if poor, they lust for dominion. Not east nor west has sated them; alone of all mankind, they covet riches and poverty with equal passion. They rob, butcher, plunder, and call it "Empire"; and where they make a desolation, they call it "peace."

It's magnificently biting stuff. Tacitus looked Rome and the Empire straight in the face and let it have both barrels. The *Pax Romana* was Rome's gift to the barbarians, more so than culture or drainage or education or any of the other 'what have the Romans done for us' things trotted off the list, and to have a Senator, no less, describe the greatest gift as 'desolation' is a devastating critique. This Calgacus fellow, whoever he was, was up against Agricola at Mons Graupius, wherever that was (and attempts at pinning down which mountain was the scene of this battle have always been fruitless), and whatever speech he even did give in real life did him no good at all. Agricola wiped the floor with him without even having to engage the legions. The auxiliaries took care of him.

Vindolanda

The fort of Vindolanda, located near modern-day Hexham in Northumberland, just south of Hadrian's Wall, which it pre-dates, was established around 85AD as part of the Roman frontier system in northern Britain. Initially a wooden structure, the fort was built to guard the strategically important Stanegate road, which connected Corbridge to Carlisle. It served as an auxiliary fort, with the first structure probably being a small wooden fort, which appears to have been built by the 1st Cohort of Tungrians from what is now Belgium. This was replaced after a decade or so by a larger, still wooden fort put up by the 9th Cohort of Batavians from the low countries.

The commander of the fort around 100AD, when the fort was repaired, was a chap by the name of Flavius Cerialis. The style of his name suggests that he was a second-generation (or more) Roman citizen, but his rank (prefect), his connections with other Roman administrators, his relatively luxurious family life in the commander's house, and the literacy he and his family possessed all show him to be fully integrated into the wider Roman world. This man is a proud and successful Roman and a career soldier appointed to an important, yet not particularly major, Roman fort on the frontier of the Empire. The army was full of people like him, some of whom appear fleetingly in the accounts of people of far, far higher rank than him, but about him and his family, we know quite a lot. His wife was called Sulpicia Lepidina, and she was friends with the wife of the commander of a nearby but unknown fort. The commander of that fort was called Aelius Brocchus, and his wife, Lepidina's friend, was called Claudia Severa. Severa was also an educated and literate woman, and the reason we know this is because, incredibly, we have her handwriting.

In around 100AD she had her scribe write a birthday invitation to her 'sister' Sulpicia Lepidina, at Vindolanda. The use of the term 'sister' in the letter doesn't imply they are family. She is using the term in a sorority context.

Romans would send letters written in ink on thin veneers of pine or oak, two at a time, which would then be clasped together and bound through holes into an 'envelope' using leather or string. The receiver would then simply discard the letter into a 'midden' or rubbish dump once it was read. The conditions in the middens first uncovered during excavations in the 1970s at Vindolanda have preserved hundreds, even thousands of these letters, giving us a remarkable view into Roman life. These conditions are so unlikely that this medium-sized fort south of Hadrian's Wall has provided some of the most stunning archaeological artefacts in the Roman world. Everyone loves gold and swords and shiny things, but in comparison, what has become known as the Vindolanda Tablets are on another level.

Papyrus survives in desert conditions, and some other examples of written records have been discovered elsewhere, but there is nothing on this scale and nothing with this incredible level of detail. They contain what would appear to be rather mundane, everyday writings. Requests for socks, missives about poor roads, military orders, letters from home, letters to home. These snapshots of Roman life are simply unavailable to historians elsewhere. We have the musings of Senators and nobles like Tacitus and Seneca, but outside of examples like the graffiti on the walls of Pompeii, we hear almost nothing of the small people in society. At Vindolanda, there is a seemingly inexhaustible supply of them. They've been excavating them from the anaerobic, damp, northern soil for more than 50 years and still, they keep coming.

History and archaeology are, at the end of the day, the exploration of ancient human life and golden helmets are dazzling and spectacular and lure people into museums, but nothing has the romantic pull that these postcards from the past do. History sometimes seems to exist at arm's length. With the Vindolanda tablets, not only is that history brought alive, we get to realise that even though 2,000 years separate us, these ancient people were just like us. The Vindolanda tablets humanise the past. Here is what she had the scribe write to Lepidina:

Claudia Severa to her Lepidina. Greetings. On 11 September, sister, for the day of the celebration of my birthday, I give you a warm invitation to ensure that you come to us and make the day more enjoyable for me by your arrival, if you are present. Give my greetings to your Cerilais. My Aelius and my little son send him their regards.

What's even more remarkable is that at the bottom right of the postcard, Severa herself has added a personal message in what is clearly her hand.

I shall expect you, sister. Farewell, sister, my dearest soul, as I hope to prosper, and hail

The writing then goes back to the first hand, the scribe:

To Sulpicia Lepidina, (wife) of Cerialis, from Cl. Severa.

The Vindolanda Tablets also contain a fragment from another letter written in Severa's hand. These two letters are almost certainly the oldest extant writing by a woman in Latin found anywhere in the world and possibly the oldest known handwriting by any woman in any language anywhere.

Although the names of these two women make it unlikely they were actual sisters, they share a very close bond. They are more than just professional acquaintances - army wives who meet on formal occasions. She uses the term *iucundus* 'delightful' or even 'delicious', which is incredibly personal in this context. She could have just used 'pleased' or 'happy'. She misses her and cannot wait to see her again. There's almost a frisson of sensuality in there, although perhaps not in a sexual sense. The prose crackles with excitement.

There are elements of the writing in her own hand (*sperabo te soror, vale soror anima, mea ita valeam, karissima et have*) that allude to the fourth book of *Aeneid* in which Virgil describes Anna as Dido's *unanimam sororem* or 'sister who shares a soul'. This doesn't necessarily mean that the two women were familiar with the *Aeneid*, but it would seem likely and other letters in the archive directly quote from the *Aeneid* suggesting that it was an influence on the people involved. *Aeneid* was sometimes used in writing exercises and that these two mothers are influenced by it suggests that their children, probably with the mothers as tutors, have been using it in school, just as children were doing all over the Empire.

In contrast with these romantic and artistic personal touches, she uses the term *sollemnem natalem* and as the first word suggests, it refers to a 'solemn' and formal occasion, rather than just a happy-go-lucky birthday bash. These celebrations are held in accordance with the rules concerning religious rites and this is an annual, formal ceremony. No matter how formal this party is, however, it's clear these two are going to have an absolute ball together.

Vindolanda is not the only site in Roman Britain, let alone the Roman world, where writing tablets have been found, but the majority of those have been of the 'stylus' type that would contain a wax substrate, obviously long lost, into which writing was incised. The advantage of these was that they could be easily erased and reused. The disadvantage is that the writing doesn't survive. Even on Hadrian's Wall other writing tablets have been found and they are known from sites in London where the same specific anaerobic conditions exist. That so many of them exist at Vindolanda is something of a mystery. The sheer number of them cannot be satisfactorily explained by earlier archaeological excavations in other locations simply missing them. The early days of archaeology, when gentlemen antiquarians would dig recklessly through what they considered rubbish in search of gold and treasure, discarding the artefacts that today's archaeologists find invaluable, are responsible for the loss of a lot of material, but even they would have noticed several thousand wooden tablets if they existed elsewhere. There is always the perennial fall-back that these things exist elsewhere, but they are yet to be found.

The Bloomberg Tablets from London are wax tablets but some can still be translated via the faint scratches left by the styli on the wooden surface. They appear to have been made from recycled barrel staves and are the same 'diptych' type construction as those from Vindolanda. There are a number of tablets that are of interest.

> To his Crispinus. Since Grattius Crispinus is returning to ... and ... I have gladly seized the opportunity my lord of greeting you, you who are my lord and the man whom it is my very special wish to be in good health and master of all your hopes. For you have always deserved this of me right up to the present high office (?). In reliance on this ... you first ... greet (?) ... Marcellus, that most distinguished man, my governor. He therefore offers (?) the opportunity now of ... the talents (?) of your friends through his presence, of which you have, I know, very many, thanks to him (?). Now (?), in whatever way you wish, fulfil what I expect of you and ... so furnish me with friends that thanks to you I may be able to enjoy a pleasant period of military service. I write this to you from Vindolanda where my winter-quarters are (?)

You'll see that a lot of the text is reconstructed which a less generous person might suggest means 'made-up', but in reconstructing texts, they are cross-referenced with other known styles and examples and, ultimately, Latin is a very structured language and there are only so many things the original, lost, text can say.

The above tablet, number 225, is considered to be a draft of a letter from the commander, Cerialis, to Crispinus. Tablet 227, where the name of Cerialis is to be found in the nominative, is written in the same hand, as are several others. The form of this letter is rather unclear and haphazard which again suggests this is written by Cerialis rather than a professional scribe who would have been able to bash this into some sort of better shape. It cannot be proved for certain, but this is almost certainly the hand of Flavius Cerialis himself. The 'Marcellus' referred to is L. Neratius Marcellus, the governor of Britain from 101 to 104AD. The writing, notably, doesn't include the name of the sender, which is highly unusual, although it makes sense if we read it in the context of Cerialis quickly jotting down a draft letter.

Another great example of the Vindolanda tablets, number 343, is perhaps most famous for the very familiar, even across 2,000 years, complaint about the state of the roads. That part could have been written yesterday.

Octavius to his brother Candidus, greetings. The hundred pounds of sinew from Marinus - I will settle up. From the time when you wrote about this matter, he has not even mentioned it to me. I have several times written to you that I have bought about five thousand modii of ears of grain, on account of which I need cash. Unless you send me some cash, at least five hundred denarii, the result will be that I shall lose what I have laid out as a deposit, about three hundred denarii, and I shall be embarrassed. So, I ask you, send me some cash as soon as possible. The hides which you write are at Cataractonium - write that they be given to me and the wagon about which you write. And write to me what is with that wagon. I would have already been to collect them except that I did not care to injure the animals while the roads are bad. See with Tertius about the 8½ denarii which he received from Fatalis. He has not credited them to my account. Know that I have completed the 170 hides and I have 119 modii of threshed bracis. Make sure that you send me cash so that I may have ears of grain on the threshing-floor. Moreover, I have already finished threshing all that I had. A messmate of our friend Frontius has been here. He was wanting me to allocate (?) him hides and that being so, was ready to give cash. I told him I would give him the hides by 1 March. He decided that he would come on 13 January. He did not turn up nor did he take any trouble to obtain them since he had hides. If he had given the cash, I would have given him them. I hear that Frontinius Iulius has for sale at a high price the leather ware (?) which he bought here for five denarii apiece. Greet Spectatus and … and Firmus. I have received letters from Gleuco. Farewell.

This letter consists of two complete diptychs which have been folded in the normal way. The surfaces of both are smeared by offsets, indicating that the ink was still wet when the leaves were folded. Octavius was a little impatient. If we assume that Octavius wrote this himself, which is a pretty safe assumption given that he seems to be struggling with financial issues and scribes cost money, then the form of the letter says something interesting about him. The usual two-column format in which these letters are written is there, but with a difference. The letter begins in column 1 on the right-hand portion of the first diptych and continues with column 2 on the left-hand side. Likewise, the letter then continues on the right-hand side of the second diptych and then the left. The logical explanation for this is that he was left-handed and is writing in this manner so he can read what he has just written. Again, if a scribe had written this, it wouldn't be in this unusual format.

The writing style is colloquial with occasional phonetic misspellings, and Octavius uses a variety of financial idioms and technical terms that are known from other examples in the Empire, which suggests that this mixture of the formal and the informal was a common way of writing business letters. If we think of it in modern terms, a contractor, say, sending an order to a building supplies merchant, might use quite informal and even, at times, vulgar language to communicate with the merchant, but for clarity, the exact details of the order would be written with technical precision to ensure that the correct items arrive.

The sums of money and goods these two are talking about are considerable: Candidus is asked for 500 denarii, and Octavius has laid out 300, which is a year's salary to an ordinary soldier of this period. It seems logical that these two are involved in the supply of goods on a military scale. A modus was a dry measure that corresponded to about 8.7 litres or nearly 2 gallons, and they're talking about shifting 5,000 of them full of grain. They're talking about hides in their hundreds and these can only have come from tanneries of military scale. The letter refers to the hides at Cataractonium, modern-day Catterick, and there is archaeological evidence from there for a large tannery operating in the period around the end of the first century AD. Catterick, incidentally, is still a major army town to this day.

Unfortunately, there's not enough evidence in the names to tell us much about the identities of the two men. Either or both of them could have been civilians dealing with the military and in Octavius' case, this would seem the likeliest explanation. There are several mentions at Vindolanda of people called Candidus, but it's a common name. He might have been a freedman, tasked with the details of military logistics.

On the back of the right-hand side of the second diptych is written the abbreviation 'Vindol'. The assumption is that the absence of a fuller address means the letter was either delivered by hand by someone who knew the recipient or that it was part of a larger bundle of letters. It also indicates that the second diptych was stacked on top of the first.

Tablet 164 contains a very famous description of the locals from a Roman soldier's point of view. And it's not a particularly glowing tribute to them.

... the Britons are unprotected by armour (?). There are very many cavalry. The cavalry do not use swords nor do the wretched Britons mount in order to throw javelins.

The first thing that jumps out is the term 'wretched Britons'. The actual phrase used here is *Brittunculi*, whereas for the word 'Britons', the author has used the more normal *Brittones*. *Brittunculi* is nominally the diminutive form of *Brittones*. They are calling them 'Little Britons', but it is also very derogative. It's an insult. A more modern way of expressing it might be 'nasty little Britons'. The best guess is that this is an internal military report which describes the fighting qualities of the native Britons with particular reference to cavalry. It's obviously not very positive. It might be a report in advance of the recruitment of locals that we know happened in the time of Agricola, thanks to Tacitus. Are the nasty little Britons even worth recruiting? The really interesting thing is that the literary sources provide almost no evidence for native British cavalry at all. They tell us about the charioteers, the *essedarii*, who would ride into battle with javelin throwers on the back who would then leap off the chariot and engage the enemy on foot, a bit like paratroopers in modern battles. But about regular cavalry, almost nothing is known. Tacitus mentions them in his biography of Agricola at the Battle of Mons Graupius:

> The plain between resounded with the noise and with the rapid movements of chariots and cavalry.

Otherwise, British cavalry is only known from such snippets. It would seem that if this text was referring directly to the *essedarii* then it would have been more specific. What this text does show us is that for some Romans, there was a distinct difference between occupier and occupied. Between them and us. Overt racism is virtually unknown in the Roman world - we modern humans invented that ourselves - but cultural snobbery, particularly against barbarians, is common. It's probable that whoever wrote this is referring to Britons who were either in open conflict against the Romans or who were not citizens. It might not have been a blanket term for any Briton, just those who were either the enemy or not yet Roman.

The following text is written on the reverse side of two of three leaves of a triptych, containing a rather mundane order for some wheat. Both sides appear to have been written by the same person, and the fact that the wheat side covers all three leaves and this text only covers two, would lead us to conclude that the wheat side is the original and that this side was used as a draft. The text is startling:

> ... he beat (?) me all the more ... goods ... or pour them down the drain (?). As befits an honest man (?) I implore your majesty not to allow me, an innocent man, to have been beaten with rods and, my lord, inasmuch as (?) I was unable to complain to the prefect because he was detained by ill-health I have complained in vain to the beneficiarius and the rest of the centurions of his unit. Accordingly (?) I implore your mercifulness not to allow me, a man from overseas and an innocent one, about whose good faith you may inquire, to have been bloodied by rods as if I had committed some crime.

The writer is appealing to someone who he refers to using the term *maiestatem* or 'majesty'. Clearly, this is not an ordinary person, but someone of elite status and in this respect it is unlikely to be anyone else than the governor of Britain himself, especially as he points out that he has already appealed to the prefect, the *beneficiarius* (a junior officer) and the centurions. It seems unlikely that he would skip the governor and appeal directly to the Emperor. In protesting his innocence, he asks that he should not be beaten as if he were a common criminal. Whether this means he has already been beaten or he is expecting to be beaten and is looking for protection is not clear. This outrage at his treatment and his description of himself as *hominem trasmari-*

num, a man from overseas, make it clear that he thinks he shouldn't be treated in the same way as a common *Brittunculus*. The reference to trade and the account of wheat on the front indicates that he is probably a trader, and a citizen, who has followed the army across the sea.

He is complaining about being victimised by a member of the military and might even be imprisoned in the fort. The legal standing of this is uncertain because whilst Centurions were certainly able to beat the leather out of soldiers, they were not really allowed to detain and beat citizens, especially ones who appear to have had no trial. The doubly intriguing thing is that this text was found amongst the barrack blocks of the fort, implying that this is where it was written and, presumably, from where the author didn't get the chance to send it.

Tablet number 890 appears rather mundane on the face of it. Julius Verecundus writes to Audax about the transport of a wagon full of vegetables and about the wrong key to a box which Audax has sent.

> Iulius Verecundus to Audax, greetings. As soon as it will have been possible, send in the morning(?) part of the load which I have today dispatched to you (plural) with two loose horses ... lest it be damaged by the conveyance in which the greens will be brought, that is the shoots both of cabbage and of turnip, and send them. Also you sent another key with the box than you should have done, for this is said to be (the key) of the little storeroom ...

What makes this interesting is less the missive about turnips and cabbages and the wrong key and more about the tone of this interaction. Verecundus doesn't use any personal touches in his letter. The 'greetings' is a standard opening that would be attached to any letter, but he does not add *suo*, meaning 'my', to Audax's name, which would personalise it. Like writing "Audax, hello" at the start rather than the more normal "My Dear Audax, hello". In the original Latin, he uses the imperative '*Mitte*', which is abrupt and not a request at all. He is not asking; he is ordering, which would be fine in a military sense, but neither of these men is a soldier. The word '*audax*' is an adjective used in a pejorative sense meaning 'overly bold', as in the origin of the word 'audacious'. A modern person might translate it as 'Cocky' or even 'Smart Ass'. The whole thing begins to make sense when you turn it over and look at the address on the back, which reads:

To Audax, the slave of Verecundus.

The text of tablet number 154 is a report of the numbers of the First Cohort of Tungrians, the cohort who built the original wooden fort at Vindolanda. It dates to somewhere around 92-97AD.

An auxiliary unit, by convention, should be made of 10 centuries of 80 men, each with its own centurion. It has long been accepted that this 80 men per century figure is true, but there's no actual positive proof that this is the case. The numbers from the text of this tablet also seem to indicate that this isn't the case. The text is hard to follow, so a summary of it looks something like this:

Line 3 Total	752	inc. 6 centurions	
Absentees:			
Line 5 *Singulares*	46		
Line 7 *Coria*	337	inc. 2 centurions (?)	
Line 9 *Londinium*	1	centurion (?)	
Line 10	...	6	inc. 1 centurion
Line 12	...	9	inc. 1 centurion
Line 14	...	11	
Line 15	...	1	
Line 16	...	45	
Line 17	Total	456	inc. 5 centurions
Present:			
Line 19	296		inc. 1 centurion

Of whom there are:
Line 25   Unfit 31
Line 26   Healthy   265   inc. 1 centurion

The total figure of 752 men is close enough to the figure of 80 men in 10 centuries, given that some of them would have died or been discharged and have yet to be replaced, but as you can see from the total, they had an operating number of centurions at 6. The cohort is an infantry one, so one would expect there to be 10 centuries, but for cavalry units, there is evidence that they consisted of 6 centuries of around 150 men in each. How this difference came about has never been satisfactorily explained, but here we can see that this cohort would have consisted of 6 centuries, with 130ish men in each. You can't, obviously, have a century without a centurion.

It might be that as the size of the unit fluctuated due to various factors, they simply maintained the unit size at whatever they had rather than send for more recruits to keep the numbers up. If they lost 130 men, say, they'd simply make do with one less century. We sometimes think of reinforcements being raced around the Empire to keep numbers at a certain level, but it appears from this sort of evidence that they might go years, even decades, without reinforcing the unit and as long as it was operating efficiently, why bother? What's notable is that all this information, scant as it is, flies in the face of what the long-accepted norms were. It turns out that what we have always accepted as a fact about the structure of auxiliary units turns out to be probably wrong. We like to think of the Roman military as adhering to a very strict set of rules and these rules being applied universally across the Empire without fail, but evidence like this suggests that such blueprints are more like ideal scenario guidelines and the reality of life on the ground required them to make whatever ad hoc arrangements they needed to make things work. The 46 *singulares* [legati] are the Tungrians' contribution to the provincial governor's guard. They're the unit's 'best of the best', sent to, probably, the fort that stood at Cripplegate in London. The single centurion in Londinium is not with them; he is there on another matter, possibly on a diplomatic mission or carrying a special message.

The biggest number of troops, 337, are not at Vindolanda, surprisingly. This detachment, which outnumbers those left behind to guard the fort, is at Coris, which is likely to be the town now known as Corbridge, which was the most northerly town in Roman Britain at the time. The fort and town there have traditionally been known as Coria, and the origin of that name is likely explained by the name on this tablet. Why such a large number of the men are away from the main fort isn't explained and they appear to be under the command of only two centurions and, as the numbers on the tablet aren't particularly clear, possibly only one. Again this flies in the face of everything we've always assumed.

Of the next few entries, none of them has a clear location, although the unit of 45 men appears a reasonably large number, perhaps to man one of the fortlets along the road known as Stanegate. They can't be on Hadrian's Wall because it hasn't been built yet. The odd thing about this is that they have no centurion in command, so wherever they are and whatever they're doing, they're doing it without anyone in charge.

Finally, of the 296 men and one centurion left at Vindolanda, some 10% of them are unfit for duty. The text breaks these down into three categories - aegri - xv, uolnerati - vi and lippientes - x. Or sick -15, injured - 6, and 10 soldiers suffering from 'inflammation of the eyes.'

Brittunculi

Britain maintained a substantial army through most of its time as a province. In the early 2nd Century, this amounted to three legions, each around 4,800 strong and each consisting of Roman citizens. These were supported by more than 50 auxiliary units, originally drawn from Roman allies around the Empire. The theoretical strength of this army is more than 40,000 men, although, as we have seen, that total could have been as much as 25% below that number. It's unlikely to have been over-manned. At this theoretical peak, the total population of Britain is possible to estimate if you discount the highlands of Scotland, where archaeology is far too uncertain. Of course, such estimates are educated guesses, but guesses nonetheless.

With the advent of aerial photography and satellite imaging, we can get a wider snapshot of what the landscape looked like in the late Iron Age and through the Roman period and what we see is a flourishing of the population all through this period. Aside from the physical evidence for occupation on the ground, one can make assumptions about the growth of towns and villages from things like the place names. Auxiliary forts would generate their own civilian support centres known as a *vicus*. Essentially a small town that would grow outside the gates of the fort, with shops, taverns, craftsmen, prostitutes and places for soldiers' families to live (even if at some points they weren't legally allowed to have families), these places would sometimes grow into larger urban centres and outlive the lifetime of the fort itself. The names of these places still survive in suffixes such as '-wick' and 'wich', such as Norwich, Ipswich, Gatwick, Aldwych and even the Viking name for York, 'Jorvik'.

There are other indicators of population growth, too, such as the increase in drained soils for cultivation. These soils aren't draining themselves and even if the occupation isn't seen directly in the archaeological records, someone must have been doing this to grow crops. This reclaiming of land indicates the need to expand the agricultural footprint as the population grows.

The vast majority of this population were the native descendants of Iron Age Britons. Large numbers of soldiers, traders and, to a lesser extent, bureaucrats came into Britain, especially during the early phase of occupation, and some of these people died there and left their tombstones to be found. More came during the later phases and naturally gravitated towards the major urban centres, which became relatively mixed and cosmopolitan populations. However, the vast majority of Britons lived in rural areas.

Potter & Johns, (*Roman Britain*, 1992) have an interesting breakdown of the population, putting 83% of the population in the countryside. Although the spread of villas increased through the 2nd Century, these were the homes of relatively rich farmers or minor local nobles and the evidence for the continued occupation of traditional roundhouses and small communities carried on into this period. Essentially, people in the countryside just carried on like before. If you're a Norfolk turnip farmer, does it even matter who is in charge? The pigs still need feeding, and the turnips need whatever it is that turnips need, and the affairs of kings and nobles mean little to you even if now some bloke in toga turns up once a year and threatens to bash you over the head unless you give him some of your turnips.

This also means that their spoken language would neither have been Latin nor Greek, but whatever Brittonic tongue they were using before the Romans turned up and demanded everyone's turnips. It has always been tempting to think of the 'Celtic fringes' as being the areas of Britain where the native Britons were driven to following the invasion and hence these being the areas where the languages that developed from Brittonic - Welsh, Cornish, Cumbric and so on - went on to thrive. The reality must be something different because the rural population of the Romanised areas must also have been speaking Brittonic, too. Instead, these 'fringe' areas are simply the areas where Roman influence is at its weakest and when the subsequent Anglo-Saxon influencers came into the country, the newcomers simply stuck to the hypothetically more affluent areas already populated by the Romans. Again we see the ghost of Brittonic languages in the place names, even in areas we consider to be heavily Romanised.

Areas such as the south-west and Wales were conquered and then the majority of Roman influence simply moved on. The locals in these areas were either convinced to behave themselves or accepted the new status quo, and, as a result, those areas were lightly garrisoned, or the Romans pulled out altogether. In some areas, a military presence might have been left behind to supervise and protect mining interests or to protect trade routes from brigands and the constant threat of Irish pirates. It's intriguing then to consider a nominally Roman town in Wales such as Carmarthen, which came complete with a forum and an amphitheatre that you can still visit today, as being Roman but populated and run almost exclusively by Romanised locals who looked after themselves. Carmarthen is in the middle of one of the highest percentages of Welsh-speaking populations in the country today, and it would be cool to think that they have been like that all the way back to Roman times.

Major towns account for 120,000 people, smaller towns, which are quite numerous, around 220,000. The army, as we saw earlier, had about 40,000 and the same amount in the attached *vici*. The rural population would have been about 2,000,000 giving a total figure of around 2,500,000. Compare this to the estimates from Domesday, compiled in 1086, which would suggest a figure of around 1.75 -2.25 million. When we consider the growth of towns, the only real model we have in Britain is that from the Industrial Revolution, which saw a sky-rocketing of urban populations as the nature of the industrial and agricultural landscape changed. But the same picture doesn't apply to Roman Britain where, if anything, the rural population undergoes as much a revolution as the urban one. The populations of towns certainly grew, and people would have been drawn from the countryside to boost those numbers, but urban populations were also swollen by people from around the Empire, the followers of the army and their own population. Britons remained, unless they were throwing things at the soldiers, largely happy in the fields with their turnips.

The population would have included wealthy individuals, free peasants and slaves, evidence that is mainly derived from inscriptions. As we have seen, members of the British tribal elite were given citizenship by the Emperor. The free

Britons could have joined the army, done their 25 years of service and retired as citizens although, at first, they wouldn't have served in Britain or probably settled there afterwards. Although the cream of the British tribal crop would have either been openly hostile to the Romans or become part of the Roman elite, there were levels of lower nobles and landowners who either profited from the Roman occupation through the incoming villa economy or who remained in their *castra* and ran their own affairs.

The word '*castra*' is an interesting one when it comes to subsequent place names. The Latin word for 'fort' is '*castrum*', and this term is applied only to a Roman military site. This word is where we get the English word 'castle' from, as well as the Welsh word '*castell*'. The plural of *castrum* is '*castra*'. However, this word is also used in a singular sense to mean 'camp'. A camp is any military site that is not Roman in nature, so that would include native defensive enclosures, hillforts and the like.

There are several examples, both in England and Wales, of place names with the suffix '-castles' (or '*castellau*' in Welsh) and yet the local archaeology only ever shows one site. This has often been put down to mistranslations or misspellings being carried over into modern times, but the common factors in these instances are the presence of an Iron Age or Romano-British defended site and some nearby Roman activity. This suggests that the Romans came along and simply named the native site a '*castra*'. Subsequent people have then translated this without realising the context of its use as a singular, not plural, term and translated it as 'forts' and hence 'castles'.

The End

The Roman Empire came to an end on Friday, March 16th, 567AD, at around 3:30 in the afternoon, when a janitor called Maximus (or perhaps Minimus, it doesn't really matter) tripped over the power cord running the forum whilst mopping up blood and wine, shutting down the city and bringing a thousand years or more of glorious history to a low humming end. Plunged into sudden darkness, people simply shrugged off their togas and made their way wearily back out into the Latin countryside, where they invented Italy, pizza, semi-naked weather forecasters and disappointing beer.

At this point, you might have begun to suspect that I may be making some of this up. And you'd be right. But there are several questions one has to ask when talking about 'the end' of the Roman Empire: When did it end? Did it end? What caused it to end? Who caused it to end? Is there anything left of it? To which the answers are 'It didn't', 'No', 'Nothing', 'Nobody' and 'Yes'.

The question of why the Roman Empire came to an end has occupied the entire careers of scholars for centuries. It kept Edward Gibbon in whatever Edward Gibbon enjoyed for his whole life so if we were to go into every instance of what happened, the rest of this book would be about nothing else. What we can do, however, is look at what happened to Britain at the end of the Roman period because it serves as a microcosm of the wider picture, plus it happened, relatively speaking, pretty suddenly.

Everything kicked off in 406AD with a meteorological disaster in Germany which caused the Rhine to freeze over. The Alans, Vandals, Sueves and other tribes that had been squashed up against the natural barrier by the advancing terror of the Huns jumped at the opportunity to flood across into the safety of northern Gaul.

Due to its unique geographical location, Britain had always been susceptible to being cut off from the Empire. Bad weather, which is not unknown in Britain, was a factor and the physical barrier of the sea was always a problem, but if the Empire was to lose Gaul or even just the northern part of it, then it would lose contact with Britain at the same time. And vice-versa.

Although they had run away from the Huns, which sounded like a sensible idea, the invading German tribes were still strong enough to cause mayhem across northern

Gaul, and as a result, the unthinkable happened, and Britain became cut off.

Communication with the Empire was cut off at the same time, which then raised the problem of neither side of the new German lines being aware of what was going on on the other side of it. This was less of a problem for the southern side, which had the rest of the Western Empire to deal with, but on the northern side, there was virtually no news of what was going on at all. For all they knew, the entire Empire had been overrun by barbarians.

It was in this context then that by the end of 406, Britain had raised no less than three new Emperors of its own, all of them technically usurpers, even if they were raised with the best of intentions. For all Britain knew, they now were the Roman Empire, and if so, they'd better have an Emperor to run it. The third of these new Emperors was raised directly to deal with the problem of the German invasion of Gaul, or at least to break through the lines and go and see what was going on.

The first and second new Emperors were raised for matters unknown, perhaps for the same reasons or perhaps in response to another threat faced from elsewhere. There was nobody in charge, even if it was to repel angry Picts or those annoying new Angle fishermen from Denmark who were bobbing around the place. The first of the new guys, Marcus, was a soldier of some rank and his brief reign ends at the hands of his own men. The second, Gratian, held the rank of *municeps*, or town councillor, so he wasn't of elite rank, although this rank might also apply to a wealthy landowner as much as an urban official, so the possibility is that he was the descendant of a British tribal leader who was given citizenship and hence a man of ancestral rank. A man with an old family of some repute. In any event, he ends up being strangled and thrown into the Thames (the Tiber was too far away).

The army then raised up another Emperor, a Christian military leader called Flavius Claudius Constantinus, allegedly because he had a lucky name, which can't have done much for his own self-esteem if you're only getting the job because you're called 'Lucky Bob' or something. Constantine III, as he became known, must have been a man with some respected military reputation, particularly given his later actions, which makes one wonder why they didn't just make him Emperor to begin with. He renamed his two sons Julian and Constans, thus appealing to both pagan and Christian supporters as well as aligning himself to the dynasty of Constantine the Great with whom he clearly sought to identify.

Constantine set off for Gaul, taking with him all the mobile elements of the provincial army. At first, he had some success, establishing himself in the north, bashing Germans and making a name for himself. Around this point, he realises he has a problem because far from a widespread barbarian invasion, he discovers that not only is the Western Empire going strong and the German invasion limited to northern Gaul, but the principate is very much still going strong and the current office holder, Honorius, is now fucking pissed that some uppity British Christian ne'er-do-well is now claiming to be Emperor as well. Honorius has his own problems to deal with and Constantine III is the last thing he needs. The British might have sent him with the best of intentions, but now he is very unwelcome.

Constantine advanced south and set up his rule as far as Spain. Setting up his base in Arles, in southern Gaul, he proclaimed Constans co-Emperor in 408, clearly by this stage trying to forge himself a dynasty. In 411, he is besieged by Honorius to whom he is eventually forced to surrender after taking the precaution of ordaining himself and his son as priests. Nobody would execute a priest, so he thought, and although this might be the case, nobody had thought to tell Honorius, who promptly has them strangled and thrown in the Rhone, neither the Tiber nor the Thames being within reach.

With the death of Constantine, Britain was left without any effective imperial government and no mobile army. Some of the forts and borders were still manned, but this was a skeleton force. Whilst Constantine was in Gaul having fun, the later historian Zosimus and the *Gallic Chronicle* recorded an attack in 410 ascribed to 'barbarians from across the Rhine', presumably the infamous Saxons. This is repelled by the islanders themselves, presumably using the scant forces left behind plus whatever forces could be mustered among the warbands of British tribal leaders who had been left behind.

Constantine's forces in Gaul had by now either been assimilated into Honorius' army or were stragglers being hounded around Gaul by the Emperor's men. At this point, whatever Roman government, the supporters and administration of the now 'traitor' Constantine, that is left in Britain is expelled by the people as a show of loyalty to Honorius. After all, they can legitimately claim that the only reason Constantine was ever raised to the position of 'Emperor' was to save the Empire from the barbarians. How were they to know that Honorius was in charge still? It's a very good point, and by throwing out the last remnants of his supporters, they are effectively reinforcing their loyalty to the Empire and to Honorius. This action just goes to show how wafer-thin the veneer of Roman bureaucracy was, that the people can effectively put them on some boats and sail them off into the sea with little effort, particularly when there's no longer a standing army to bash them over the head should they try. Britain is very loudly and very obviously trying to reincorporate itself back into the Empire, particularly with the looming threat of more Saxon invasions. The Saxons, fair play to them, have spotted the weakness and are keen to press the advantage before the Romans return.

Honorius, famously, is having none of it. He has other usurpers to fight off - in Spain, for example - and other barbarians putting pressure on his borders, and the last thing he can afford right now is to send a couple of legions to Britain to protect them from the Saxons. He sends word to Britain, telling them to 'Look to your own defences'.

Which, to be fair to them, they do.

The earlier Saxon incursions are likely repelled partly with the aid of .. well, the Saxons. 'Saxon' is a generalised term for all sorts of tribes and some of them were perfectly happy to work for whoever would pay them and Saxon mercenaries are thought to have settled in Britain after helping to fight off other Saxon invaders. It's not a biggie then to re-employ these mercenaries to fight off further incursions and suddenly Britain has the beginnings of a post-Roman army. All it then takes is for the tribal leaders left behind to form themselves into warbands and suddenly Britain no longer needs the mechanism of the Roman state. Suddenly, at least in historical terms, they find that they can defend themselves against invaders and that nobody is going to come along and take their turnips anymore.

Suddenly, Britain no longer needed Rome at all.

Cultural Bully Boys

The commonly accepted narrative is that Rome turned up with some elephants and a bunch of men with pointy things, whacked people over the head until they behaved and then went about distributing olive oil in great big jars and togas out of the back of a wagon. These views are probably based on how we understand the term 'invasion' in a modern context. We immediately think of cultural and historical reference points such as the German Blitzkrieg of World War II or D-Day.

The latter wouldn't be too far short of the mark when it came to the Roman invasion as they likely did land in numbers, across probably two or three sites and then force their way inland. In some areas, the Blitzkrieg method can also work. The Romans moved quickly to establish bridgeheads and take strategic targets and set up administrative centres that allowed the logistical machine to follow established supply routes. But the idea that everyone they encountered then somehow 'turned Roman' as the *Pax Romana* was rubber-stamped on British society is misleading, as is the idea that 'Romanisation' was a homogeneous spoonful of jam that could be universally spread on any metaphorical piece of toast it came across.

The impact of Rome differed in the various areas of Britain as two cultures came into contact with each other. Then, as it is now, Britain was a culturally diverse place, and whilst archaeology has begun to demonstrate that British (and to a certain extent continental European) society was linked by common ideas such as the construction of megaliths in the years before the invasion, the idea of these people being 'Britons' is largely a Roman construct. They may just as easily have seen themselves as Iceni, for example, and the notion of being in any sense 'British' might have been alien or, at most, secondary. Even in modern times, the concept of being 'British' might come well down a list of someone's national identities. Someone can be Welsh before they are British, even if being British is, technically, at least, their actual status. It's a distinctly British thing to identify in a series of ever-specific demonyms. Someone might be British on a wider level, but ask them where they're from and they're a Pontypool lad who is Welsh and just happens to be British. So the idea that the Romans simply rolled up and told that Pontypool lad that he was now a Roman is both unrealistic and, to the Ponty boy at least, utterly meaningless.

Going back to the Blitzkrieg, the Nazis may have taken France in a matter of days, but that didn't mean that all the French people suddenly became Germans. Some of the French did become enthusiastic adopters of the new regime, and Vichy influenced bootlickers. But others, famously, did not and formed resistance warbands to fight back. In places such as Paris, the intermingling of the Nazi hierarchy and the locals was more seamless than it was in the *départe-ments*, where relationships could be openly hostile. Where these two cultures interacted the most freely is where the evidence of that interaction is most obvious, and this interaction is similar to that found in the archaeological record of Roman Britain.

All this is a long way of saying that the impact of Rome on Britain depended on where you were in Britain.

In northern England, the picture is largely of defended civilian settlements and military sites, but, with a couple of exceptions, there are no villas. The hierarchical impact of Rome in the area immediately south of the Wall is military. Go beyond the Wall and into what is now southern Scotland, and the hierarchy becomes civilian again with small settlements of roundhouses and farm sites overlooked by *brochs* (stone towers) and hillforts. The cultural impact of Rome is there on these sites, in the form of pottery and metalwork, but it is uncommon. That is either a reflection of the economic status of the site - they weren't high status enough to have an abundance of such material - or that the cultural interaction wasn't as strong, or both. Compared to the settlements immediately to the south of the Wall, these settlements are more commonly defended and have fewer associated field systems. There are several possible explanations for this. The obvious one is a question of safety. The military impact south of the Wall might have made agriculture easier to practice in that area, but agriculture was present in similar areas around Britain where modern farming might see the topography as unsuitable, such as upland moors, and where the military impact was less obvious.

It's easy to assume that people south of the Wall were farmers because it was good land and the people felt safe enough to settle down because the Romans were there to guard them, but people were also farming in upland areas of Scotland, Wales and south-west England where the land wasn't particularly good and there was no military safeguard.

Instead, what we might be looking at is the economic impact of the military presence, including the Wall. There were a lot of men on that Wall, whatever reason they were there for, and these soldiers attracted other people to them in order to serve their needs. All those people need to eat, and all those people have money to spend, so industry, including farming, grows to fill those needs. That the area north of the Wall has fewer farms might be less a reflection of the safety of the area or the soil conditions and more to do with the fact that people can get along with everything they need by trading with the economically strong Romanised area immediately on their borders. That there is no great archaeological evidence for the economics of this trading - coins, for example - might just be a reflection of the trading system. Perhaps they used a bartering system, exchanging animal hides for grain, for example? Further north, there is evidence of quite extensive grain farming (barley, mostly), so they could have farmed stuff if they wanted to, but if the neighbours have lots of wheat but no deer hides, and you have deer hides but no wheat, why bother getting up in the morning to plant seeds all day?

Immediately, we can begin to see how a military presence has affected two different cultures on its borders. One has grown to exploit that influence - and we might call this area more 'Roman', and the other has simply learned to adapt to its presence while remaining relatively 'un-Roman'. If you then extrapolate this to Britain as a whole, you can begin to see why the 'Celtic fringes' remained what we often describe as 'un-Romanised'. The cultural influence of Rome is there; it's just not there in a way that is obvious in the archaeology. When you ally this apparent absence in the archaeological record to the historical record of people like Caratacus and the resistance of the Silures, it's possible to draw a narrative where the central parts of England were all full of toga-wearing, dormice-eating cultural fascists, surrounded by hostile, naked, blue-faced Celts constantly trying to kill them, a picture a lot of Britons would still recognise today. It's a picture painted with a very broad brush.

In the south-west, the situation is much the same as in southern Scotland, with roundhouses and farm settlements (although the Brochs are uniquely Scottish), and almost no villas west of Exeter. In Wales, there are villas, but they all exist along the fertile south, in the corridor that also contains the towns of Carmarthen and Caerwent, but not in the middle or north where the military presence remains noticeable well into the 4th Century. In both of these places, however, the archaeological evidence for Romanisation is much stronger. It's not the traditional view of Roman culture we have - mosaics, villas and baths - but it is there. In other parts of Britain, the locals become more urban or more reliant on the villa system, but in places like Wales, the cultural impact is present in the archaeology, but the hierarchy remains rural and civilian. These are very different examples of how Roman culture interacts with local British culture.

So, on one hand, we have British people building villas, living in urban centres and farming; on another, we have the locals remaining largely distant from any Roman influence yet relying on the economic impact of the military presence. In the south-west we have people staying largely distant from the Romans and getting on much as they had before Rome arrived and in Wales, they maintain the previous way of life, but the interaction with the Romans is more obvious. It's different horses for different courses. The idea of a cookie-cutter Roman culture suddenly doesn't look so clear-cut.

Another way to look at the military presence is not as a catalyst for change but as one that stifles it. Further south, the change is more urban in nature, and the hierarchy is one of Romanised settlement. Who is to say that the more northerly areas wouldn't have developed in the same way had the army not been there in numbers to cream off the prime agricultural product for its own needs or to influence development in a certain direction? The relative absence of villas means that although the land was being extensively farmed, the cultural influences that come with the villa model aren't present. While farming wasn't, in any way, 'state-run', like some great Maoist idealistic model, it seemed more industrial in nature than anything else, and this doesn't allow room for the villa model to thrive.

Villas require a strong agricultural base, of course, but their absence in some areas of Roman Britain doesn't necessarily mean that the conditions weren't right for them to thrive. Simply saying that because there were no villas must mean that villas weren't suitable for that area is putting the cart before the horse. If the military is acting like a brake on villa development in the north, then in other areas, the lack of villas might not be because the land wasn't fertile enough. Areas such as Norfolk and Suffolk, where the Iceni were from, are today some of the best arable land in Britain and even accounting for the fact that a lot of this land was reclaimed from its boggy nature in the post-Roman period, the relative lack of villas in that area is notable. So if the land is good enough, and the locals have been beaten into submission, as we saw earlier with Boudica, and the area is wealthy enough to support a large Roman *colonial* settlement at Colchester, where are all the villas?

The archaeology is tricky in this respect because, whilst there's plenty of it, the agricultural impact is somewhat muddied (if you'll forgive the pun) by all that land reclamation in the medieval period and beyond. The settlements in this area tended to be on higher ground or relatively higher ground - Norfolk is pretty flat - and these survive later agricultural activity, including the dreaded ploughing. The farmland does not. So we can't tell exactly what the model was like, but the military presence is relatively light, the soil is good and, of course, no villas. So they were farming there, one assumes, but in another form.

Villas grow as a consequence of wealth rather than being parachuted into the countryside to exploit wealth. They start out small and become bigger as the owners grow in wealth and status and are less about prime land being parcelled off for exploitation. As the economy grows and shrinks, so do the villas. It's one of the reasons the villa model disappeared entirely in the post-Roman period - the land is still suitable for farming and is farmed, but the economy has moved to a different model, and the villa as an expression of wealth is no longer part of the narrative. People are still wealthy, naturally, but they begin to express that wealth in other ways. In the Anglo-Saxon period, that might mean military might. Expressing your wealth via personal military power, especially with no Roman army around, becomes fashionable. In Medieval times, rich people built large manor houses and exploited peasant farmers. When things got really rich, they built castles. So the absence of villas in Norfolk might simply be because people are expressing their wealth in other ways than with villas.

While the farming landscape further north might fit the narrative of the Romans coming in and exploiting the resources of the invaded nation for their own needs - bully boy Romanisation if you like - the villa model is one that reflects the growing wealth of the economy that is a consequence of the cultural interplay between Briton and Roman. Villa owners don't start out as industrial farmers, although they may become them; they start out as influential or wealthy local Britons who begin to expand as their fortunes change. They move into bigger and swankier roundhouses and then, as the money flows in, to rectangular houses, which become small villas and then medium villas and then big ones with an army of slaves all picking turnips or whatnot.

All that might be happening in Norfolk is that those same wealthy and influential people are investing their money into other things that better represent their own cultural heritage. Again, the impact of Romanisation has been felt quite heavily; they're just not reading Livy in the bath and wearing a toga. I counsel against reading Livy in the bath whilst wearing a toga at the best of times, but you go nuts if you like.

Whilst major settlements pre-dated the Roman invasion, it's fair to say that the concept of urbanism as we know it was introduced by them. The Romans may have taken over native settlements at places like Colchester, but in the frontier region, all the urban developments are primarily related to the military presence. We have already talked about the growth of the *vicus*, but these sites are largely only there, at first anyway, because the army is there. They originally consisted of camp followers, either the families of soldiers or people aiming to make their fortune off the economy mentioned above. There's not much evidence to suggest that they attracted large-scale migration from rural contexts, although this must have happened to a certain extent. The growth of towns and cities during the Industrial Revolution can be explained by peasants moving to the cities as the economic model changed, but in Roman Britain, the occupants of the civilian settlements were largely descendants of the original occupants or people who had moved in with the army - immigrants. In this area, large towns such as Corbridge, which was later expanded with walls to become a *civitas*, the Roman concept of public unity by which a town is designated, are just as reliant on the military presence as the *vici* that grow up outside a fort's walls. In areas where the military is less prevalent, such as Carmarthen and Caerwent in Wales, those towns then go on to get market status, and this is the catalyst for growth that allows the villa model to flourish. Villas need somewhere to sell their turnips. Farms that supply turnips to the army don't.

What might be going on here is simply that the locals are picking and choosing to what extent they embrace Roman culture and, by extension, vice-versa. Cultural integration, no matter how aggressive it might outwardly appear, is nearly always a two-way street. The British Empire might be responsible for appalling behaviour in places like India, but Indian culture has also left a colourful, expressive and, above all, delicious mark on British culture. And not simply by cultural cuckooing, either - the world's most-eaten curry, the Tikka Masala, is not an Indian dish influenced by British tastes; it's a British dish influenced by Indian tastes. Similarly, the implementation of what might seem overtly Roman culture on Britain required as much bending from the Romans as it did grovelling from the Britons. The conclusion is that resistance to the villa model in Norfolk was less about trying to keep a cultural tsunami at bay or open hostility to Romanisation and more that neither side seemed particularly willing to go down that particular route. When Rome bangs heads with the locals, it does, of course, sometimes force itself upon the conquered. But in other instances, if there is no mutual eagerness to begin the process of cultural exchange, it just doesn't happen. As long as the locals kept the peace, the Romans might not see any particular need to make them wear togas and read Livy in the bath. The lack of a town in north Wales might simply be because the locals don't want one and if they don't want one, then the Romans are happy to garrison the area to protect trade routes and their mining interests and maintain the status quo. Compare that to areas of central England, where the villa model is prevalent and the economy booming and the locals might be more ready to jump aboard the Roman gravy train. And as the Romans are themselves keen to see the locals expand the villa model, they're happy to stop the gravy train and let everyone jump aboard.

The archaeological record throws up instances of Roman artefacts found in hoards, and whilst we must sound a note of caution in that we haven't found all the hoards that were ever buried, that some hoards contain noticeably more Roman finds than others might suggest that the people who buried them were either less exposed to Roman culture in the first place or didn't wish to express their local identity via such trinkets. Even where Roman culture was embraced, it might still have had a local flavour. Roman-style fibula brooches become fashionable, for example, but in some areas, they still retain a distinctive pre-invasion decorative style. Again, we are seeing cultural interplay rather than outright cultural fascism.

By the middle of the third century, the Romano-British elite had become, in comparison to somewhere like Gaul, very wealthy, and the villa model of the economy had hit paydirt, showing just how invested this class had become in the notion of a 'Romanised' identity. These people could legitimately be said to consider themselves Romans, at least in terms of citizenship, first and foremost. These were now people who were invested in the Empire not only in Britain but on the continent as well. They held official positions in public life that drew them away from the islands, as would commercial opportunities. Their peers were no longer local tribal chiefs, even if they still existed in places, but provincial officials from the four corners of the Roman world.

The third century saw an economic crisis around the Empire, which was exacerbated by outside attacks and internal strife. Although Britain was affected, its unique position, a bit like that of Egypt, isolated it from the worst of the instability. It was helped somewhat by the boom years Britain had enjoyed in the previous century and its relative newcomer status to the provinces. But the decline was there, all the same. Public altruism in the shape of municipal building projects fell off, and some public structures fell into disrepair. What public building occurred appeared to be restricted to necessary works such as town walls. However, around the end of the century, a period of stability was observed, and the most obvious signs of this are visible in the archaeological records in the form of villas.

The term 'villa' used to mean any large country building, although these days, the term is largely reserved for a big house with the associated working estate, a bit like a post-medieval British country house with its large landscaped grounds, associated farm and an estate covering hundreds of acres. The owners of this estate, by this period at least, might also be like the later landed English gentleman in that he may live most of the week in town at 'business' and spend the weekend at his place (or one of his places) in the country. In this respect, most of the villas are located in the south of England and within drunken staggering distance of the nearest town. The sophisticated Roman wants to be out in the sticks, like their supposed Etruscan ancestors, but near an urban centre like their elite cousins in Rome so they can go to the theatre and get shitfaced with the right people.

Part of this Romanised lifestyle is seen in the quality of their homes, especially when it comes to the sophistication of baths, underfloor heating and, most spectacularly, the mosaics and wall paintings that villas are famous for. It's these luxuries that mark these buildings out as the homes of elites rather than just extensive agricultural buildings (although those were also found on site). In these villas, the elite are finally able to express their new status as Romano-Britons and celebrate their unique cultural affiliations.

They are showing off, and the people they are showing off to are other Romano-Britons, not those from elsewhere in the Empire, even if, in doing so, they are embracing that wider world.

Villas are not saying "Look at me, I'm Roman now", they are saying "Look at me, I'm cosmopolitan now." These are still very British expressions of Romanism, but embracing the Graeco-Roman world. Roundhouses and hillforts and so yesterday, darling! The Romano-British have gone full hipster.

And nowhere was this cultural identity more clearly expressed than in the unique examples of Romano-British art.

Underground Art

Britain is a damp old place at the best of times. It's either always raining or about to start raining. As a result, the archaeology of the British Isles is unlike that of just about anywhere else. Whereas the archaeology of the Mediterranean contains lots of nice, low extant walls with lovely coloured wall plaster on them, British archaeology essentially consists of different shades of mud. The new discovery of extant ruins, especially Roman ones, that extend to any significant depth is almost unheard of. More common, where they escape the plough, are mosaics and they provide valuable evidence for evaluating villa life and the fourth-century art scene in Britain.

Most of them are relatively simple, although this doesn't necessarily mean they were cheap and nasty. Minimalism is an art form in any century. More complex geometric designs and those featuring figures were also popular, and while the latter was almost certainly more time-consuming to lay and therefore more expensive, that doesn't mean that the simpler designs necessarily are the work of inferior craftsmen or customers looking to get work done on the cheap. Even a simple design can still be part of a more elaborate overall pattern.

The adoption of mosaics as home decorations is part of the trend of the Romano-British adopting particularly Roman fashions. Nothing like it was known in Britain before the Romans showed up, so this is one area where the cultural exchange is totally in one direction. Having said that, although the Romano-British followed the changing face of mosaic fashion like everyone else, they also forged their own particular design niches. This sharing of ideas around the Empire was probably helped by the fact that the layers of these pavements, like medieval stone masons, were peripatetic, travelling to wherever the work was available. This, of course, includes moving across the continent and bringing fashions and ideas into and out of Britain. But there were also distinct British schools of design suggesting that craftsmen became well known for producing certain types of work to a certain standard.

This would suggest that they worked off some kind of pattern book, like a modern-day carpet salesman with a swatch full of samples (although no such book has ever been found). The salesmen would turn up with a roll of designs under one arm and a measuring device, size up the rooms, discuss which designs and figures you'd like and then discuss a price. A few days later, or 9 months if they're anything like modern-day 'craftsmen', two blokes would turn up and sit in the wagon outside for half the day drinking posca (watered-down sour wine) and complaining that they don't have the right tools and Maximus had to go 'back to the depot'. These design books must have changed as seasons and tastes changed and it's easy to imagine an excited salesman eagerly informing a client that the new designs from Gaul are in, or 'Have you seen what they're doing in Athens this year?' It gives the Romano-Britons the opportunity to share in the Empire's cultural values.

Romano-British mosaics show a knowledge of Graeco-Roman mythology, just like their counterparts in Africa or Spain, say, but just as in those areas, there are some distinct local characteristics. The Romano-British have something of a penchant for rather obscure myths but don't widely follow the continental fashion for subjects like the circus and the amphitheatre and in general they seem to steer away from the Roman preoccupation with the rural idyll. Romans saw their ancestry in their supposed Etruscan roots and the pagan, bucolic utopia of the peasant fantasy. This is clearly not how the British see their own origins, and such imagery is just reflective of a way of life the Romano-British are trying to move away from, not aspiring to get back to.

There are universal constants in terms of design, such as Orpheus and the beasts, but in Britain, these are treated in specific ways, such as at Woodchester, where the beats are circling each other in concentric rings. There are other examples where the art has been criticised, somewhat unfairly, as 'naive' or 'provincial', such as the Rudston Venus, which is a classical scene but done in a very un-classical way. For years, Romano-British art was seen as a poor cousin because of the distinctly 'folksy' nature of the interpretation. With more sympathetic eyes, they are uniquely beautiful in their own way and give a clear indication of a localised British re-evaluation of classical culture. They are not ham-fisted attempts at reproducing scenes seen elsewhere in the Empire; they are specifically British interpretations of them. A perfect example of the two-way exchange of cultural ideas.

What's really interesting about these uniquely Romano-British examples of art is that they also contain imagery that is very definitely not British. Lions are drawn in a style that usually represents amphitheatre scenes, North African-style chariots, fighting bulls and so on. The craftsmen who made these mosaics must also, one assumes, made them from pattern books and so someone has travelled across the Empire to either receive these fashion ideas or see the animals themselves and brought them back to Britain. These same craftsmen must then also have had these supposedly crudely made and drawn Venus figures in their pattern books, too. These are not the work of someone who was unskilled and 'provincial'; they are catering to a market that demands art in this style. Presumably, because it represents a very British cultural view of their place in the wider

Empire. People aren't making this stuff because that's all they can do; they're deliberately asking for it like that.

One issue when it comes to trying to evaluate the cultural meaning of these designs is that nobody wrote down what they were thinking about them. What did these designs actually mean to people? Were they simply decorative, or did the figures have more than a symbolic value? A religious value, say? This is true of all ancient art because it's not something that writers addressed in much detail. What we can say with some certainty is that the mythological subject matter of some of the images is long established in Graeco-Roman culture but relatively new in Romano-British culture. Do they then have the same meaning to some chap living in Londinium as they do to some chap living in Rome? Do these particularly new Romano-British ways of treating these scenes mean that the original meaning behind them has become muddied or even trite? Are they simply copying the designs with their own spin because it's trendy? Or do these represent a whole new mythology that is no longer uniquely Graeco-Roman? Some motifs lend themselves to a wide range of interpretations.

The Wild Hunt is a classic scene used on many mosaics. It harkens back to that rural idyll we were just talking about. It's a vitally important part of Roman culture to the extent that the Wild Hunt would be recreated in gladiatorial shows with a specialist gladiator called a Venator who would put on displays recreating the scenes and with animals performing circus tricks - like a more modern-day lion tamer. Take this scene to Britain, and it's obviously going to be something they can immediately associate with and recognise, but the symbolic meaning might be very different or totally absent. The idea of hunting means something, but not necessarily the Wild Hunt.

There are plenty of generic motifs for which the context is inarguably universal. The four winds appear everywhere around the Empire and in Britain too, blowing in their good luck, bringing fertility and changing the seasons. But there are also examples that show literary scenes and whilst they are less common, they show a familiarity with classical literature. We already saw the allusions to Vergil and the *Aeneid* in the writings from Vindolanda and there are pavements in Britain that show scenes from it, too. There are also Vergilian allusions in some wall paintings and in coinage, but the question remains to what extent these are expressions of an individual's literary sophistication or just a bit of pseudo-intellectual snobbery. Can't answer that question, of course, but it does show an appreciation of these themes, if nothing else. People know what they are, and who Vergil is, even if they have never read any of it. Like people who claim to love everything about Jane Austen but have never read any of it. And that's fine because in a way you can still live the Jane Austen aesthetic if you want to. You don't have to have read Jane Austen to appreciate Regency-style parasols and chintzy tea sets.

All the things you would expect to see on a Roman mosaic, any Roman mosaic anywhere in the Empire, are there in abundance in Britain, naturally. All the usual gods - Mars, Venus, Bacchus (normally found in dining rooms, as you'd expect) and scenes from mythology such as the rape of Ganymede, Orpheus and Bellerophon killing the Chimera. The latter is found at several sites around Britain but rather rare in mosaics elsewhere and whilst we can only guess why, there's nothing obvious that jumps out about that story that would suggest Romano-Britons would be specifically interested in it. Perhaps then, the salesman that had Bellerophon in his sample book was a particularly silver-tongued sort of a chap?

What is also noticeable is there are instances where particular scenes are grouped together in ways that they aren't elsewhere. This could just mean that people are picking things that look nice and throwing them together. Perhaps they have seen 5 different scenes at the villas of friends and decided to pick one of each of their own homes? Or it might be that these specific groupings have another cultural meaning. Sometimes the designs simply represent what the room was used for, like Bacchus in the dining room, or watery motifs in the bath and this is a useful way of interpreting villa layouts. So we might be seeing peculiar combinations of Mars and mermaids because they liked the Mars image and they're in the bath house.

Sometimes the images portray specific religious practices or beliefs and these religious symbols would obviously suggest an adherence to the relevant cult. But then again, people today wear crucifixes and use religious symbolism without expressing any following of the religion the symbols represent. Bacchus might appear because he's a rotund little drunk fellow or because people are following the Bacchic cult. We just don't know for sure. The preponderance of Orpheus in imagery well into the supposedly Christian era has led some people to suggest that there is a hidden Christian interpretation in all this imagery, but is that just putting the cart before the horse? One thing that is notable about Roman Britain is the lack of solid evidence for any Romano-British churches. Plenty of temples were built in the 4th Century but, as yet, nothing that anyone can say with any degree of absolute certainty is a church.

Having said that, there is one very famous example, at Hinton-St-Mary of Christian iconography that is irrefutable. In the centre of the wonderful mosaic found there, slap bang in the middle of what was probably a dining room with an annexe is a bust of who can only be Jesus, complete with the early Christian symbol of pomegranates and a Chi-Rho. It's early 4th Century and the Christ figure doesn't have a beard, for anyone interested in that sort of thing. It must be said that it is possibly a picture of Constantine, although this is unlikely because putting the Emperor's face on the floor for people to walk all over is not a very clever idea. Gods, however, appear all over mosaics and nobody seems to have much of a problem stomping all over them. To counter that, it would seem almost impossible these days that a good Christian would put an image of Christ on the floor for people to walk all over.

However, the rest of that mosaic is full of pagan imagery. Bellerophon is there again, this time riding Pegasus. The four winds are in the corners, huffing away and various other animal motifs. So, there's no particular reason to assume that the villa owner was Christian or at least exclusively Christian. We know that some people dabbled in Christianity, and the Roman way of approaching the tricky relationships with the gods didn't exclude the possibility that you have someone who adheres to gods old and new at the same time. The Christian message required preaching in order to convert the heathen, unlike the pagan gods, who could just be followed in pretty much any way you fancied, within reason. If there's nobody around to tell you that you're worshipping Christ in the wrong way, then people might just approach it as if He was any other god and throw him in the mixer with all the others.

Again, we have to consider that these were just nice things to look at, that someone chose out of a book and had no particular meaning other than an aesthetic one, but another possibility is that this is a form of cultural cuckooing. In its pre-Nazi form, the swastika was often used in architectural contexts either as a decorative motif or as a good-luck symbol. That doesn't mean that anyone in the building was a Hindu. It comes into use in Victorian Britain because of the Empire and *colonia*lism and this is reflective of the interchange between cultures in the Roman times, too. Jesus might be on the mosaic because, to the villa owners, he's just one of a series of mythological concepts that they have cherry-picked from around the Empire. They might even have picked up these symbols on their travels and brought them back home again as souvenirs, just as Victorian travellers did during the Grand Tours of the 19th Century when they came back laden with cartfuls of, obviously, Roman artefacts that enthusiastic Italian peasants had dragged out of fields to sell to these rich tourists, a little bewildered as to why these foolish foreigners would want to pay so much money for all this old junk.

It might just be that the British going abroad and coming back with everyone else's cultural symbols is something they've been doing for the better part of 2,000 years. That

Britain, a country forged by decorating itself with the culture of other nations throughout its entire history, should suddenly, and quite willingly, find itself more isolated from the world than at any point in the past few hundred years is somewhat bewildering, especially to the large number of modern Britons who find such deliberate isolationism shameful.

Whilst it's not surprising that extant walls are hard to come by in British archaeology, evidence of wall plaster is more common, if only in fragmentary form. It still gives us a picture of the vivid colours that decorated the insides of villas, from saffron yellow to deep vermillion reds, blues, green, and sullen gothic black. The walls themselves were painted with frescoes depicting similar scenes to mosaics or with panels decorated with complicated borders, swashes and architectural elements. Views of city or pastoral scenes were common, perhaps as *trompe l'oiel* replacements for views that didn't exist.

In the 16th Century, this style became known as 'grotesque'. Although since the 19th Century that word has come to mean something different, the rediscovery of the ruins of Nero's glamorous Domus Aurea in the middle of the 16th Century saw artists such as Michelangelo lowered into the murky underground depths of what were once, and still are, spectacularly decorated and appointed rooms, to marvel at the scenes. The spectacular ceilings of the Vatican Library, by Domenico Fontana, are 'grotesque', as is the Ceiling of the Piccolomini Library, Siena Cathedral, by Pinturicchio. The cave-like rooms of the buried Domus Aurea - grottos - inspired generations of Renaissance artists, just as they had inspired and beguiled the Romano-British centuries before. It's hard to evaluate the overall picture of the quality of the wall art because so little of it survives, but there's no reason to not paint the same broad picture if you'll forgive the pun, as with mosaics.

What is more surprising, perhaps, is the relative lack of sculptures that have survived from these villas, certainly in comparison to other places in the Empire. There's nothing that suggests Romano-Britians didn't have as many sculptures in their villas as elsewhere around the Empire (and nothing to suggest they did, of course), but their relative absence is something of a mystery. It's possible that, with no obvious local material to carve statues out of - no marble, for example - a localised industry in statue production never got off the ground in Britain. Hence, lugging great lumps of marble or even finished statues across the continent to Britain was either impractical or witheringly expensive. Romano-Britons might have found other ways of expressing themselves via art than statues. The statues that are known are more often associated with funerary monuments from temples, shrines or military sites, for whom the cost and practicality of moving or creating them might have been less prohibitive. Smaller figures associated with household shrines are better known, but the idea of a villa filled with the big old white marble statues one thinks of as being quintessentially Roman don't appear to be the British norm. If they had all been looted in the post-Roman period, where were they looted to? It's more reasonable to assume they were never there to begin with.

Of the figures that survive, we see what would be expected in a villa context. Bacchus appears again - the British liked a drink as much then as now - Diana represents hunting scenes and several unidentified busts that are probably familial in nature but might also represent some form of ancestor reverence. You can call that 'religious' if you wish.

In other forms of decoration, and displays of wealth, much more common is imported tableware, including fine samian ware, silver and glass. These are found broadly across many Romano-British sites, meaning that such imported ware was either an incredibly popular way of displaying one's wealth and cultural allegiance to the Empire or that it was imported in huge numbers to flood the market. You might say that imported pottery was Rome's most successful cultural influence on Britain - a sort of second and third-century Coca-Cola can. It's everywhere you look, in some quantity or another, even if people just have a few pieces. This either means that everyone wanted it or that there was so much of it that everyone ended up with some. Like Victorian blue and white china; you can't remember ever buying it, or how you even got it; it's just there in the cupboard. You probably got it from a grandparent, and it might be that this was how samian ware got into the possession of Romano-Britons.

Another option is that such tableware served perfectly as relatively expensive gifts between friends. Some of the artefacts found are from known manufacturers in Gaul, say, that were famous for their products. Sending your friend a dinner set made by Wedgewood still has a cachet today, and it would have been no different back then, either.

This boom in mosaic laying, imported tableware and wall decoration coincides with the decline in private patronage of public building works, which tells us something about the relationship between public displays of wealth and private ones. People are not destitute or bankrupt as they are able to invest considerable sums in their own homes, but the 'extra' money for public works is either not available or is being saved up for better days. This also coincides with the beginning of the increase in hoards and can be seen in the votive offerings from temples and so on. People would never go to temples to throw large amounts of money into the coffers - the offering of a penny or two is all that matters; in the same way, people toss coins into fountains, but it shows that money is still around; it's just not being spent in grandiose ways.

The most striking thing about the way all this is represented is that, even with localised British elements, the general style is very much Graeco-Roman in nature. Some three hundred years after the surrender of the eleven kings, the people of Britain are inarguably now Roman.

Chapter Three

BREAD AND CIRCUSES

The Games

Perhaps the one place where you'd find all the echelons of Roman society rubbing shoulders was at the games. Everyone went. Everyone. Even those people who were vehemently opposed to them went. And there were many who found the whole spectacle gaudy, excessive, noisy, uncouth, violent and morally bankrupt. But they still went because not going was worse than going and being outraged. If you didn't go, then people would want to know why, and sometimes those people were the sort you wouldn't want to offend by not being there. Either way, they were an integral part of Roman life, not only in the great arenas like the Colosseum but in the provinces, too.

Sometimes, the games were spectacular, like in 248AD, in the middle of a civil war, anarchy and an immense economic crisis, when the Secular Games were held to celebrate Rome's 1000th birthday. The following passage from the *Historia Augusta* gives a glimpse of the rampant expense that must have gone into organising them.

There were at Rome in the time of Gordian, thirty-two elephants (of which Gordian himself had sent twelve and [Severus] Alexander ten), ten elk, ten tigers, sixty tame lions, thirty tame leopards, ten *belbi* [hyenas], 1,000 pairs of gladiators belonging to the imperial fisc, six hippos, one rhino, ten wild lions, ten giraffes, twenty wild asses, forty wild horses and various other animals of this nature without number. All of these [the Emperor] Philip presented or slaughtered at the Secular Games. All these animals, wild, tame and savage, Gordian intended for a Persian triumph, but his public vow [to present them if victorious] proved of no avail, for Philip exhibited them all at the Secular Games and at the gladiatorial and circus spectacles when he celebrated Rome's thousandth anniversary in his own and his son's consulship.

One of the people who found the games repugnant but still went was Seneca, who was a bit of a prude at the best of times. Here, he tells us how horrible he found one trip to the games, but, as he says, he not only went freely to the show but sort of popped in as he was passing, so nobody had to twist his arm to force him through the door. His claim that he went expecting some 'fun and wit' is pushing the boundaries of plausibility a bit. He knows where he's going, and he knows he's not going to a theatre, so his feigned shock when he gets there to find people hacking each other to death with swords instead of men discussing philosophy over a game of backgammon has to be taken with a pinch of salt. It's almost as if he went there deliberately to be shocked or at least to pretend to be. It's spectacularly affected moral pear-clutching, which is apt considering it comes from his work *Moral Epistles*. This account gives some idea of the atmosphere and what the crowd were calling for. He clearly finds it all very uncultured and barbaric. While he sits there and watches, of course.

I chanced to stop in at a midday show, expecting fun, wit and some relaxation, when men's eyes take respite from the slaughter of their fellow men. it was just the reverse. The preceding combats were merciful by comparison, now all trifling is put aside and it is pure murder. The men have no protective covering. Their entire bodies are exposed to the blows, and no blow is ever struck in vain ... In the morning men are thrown to the lions and the bears, at noon they are thrown to their spectators. The spectators call for the slayer to be thrown to those who in turn will slay him, and they detain the victor for another butchering. The outcome for the combatants is death; the fight is waged with sword and fire. This goes on while the arena is free*. "But one of them was a highway robber, he killed a man!" Because he killed he deserved to suffer this punishment, granted ... "Kill him! Lash him! Burn him! Why does he meet the sword so timidly? Why doesn't he kill boldly? Why doesn't he die game? Whip him to meet his wounds! Let them trade blow for blow, chests bare and within reach!" And then when the show stops for intermission, "Let's have men killed meanwhile! Let's not have nothing going on!"

*By 'free', he means during an intermission in the schedule in which criminals are forced to fight

The spectacular games put on by Pompey in his second consulship (55BC) on the dedication of his theatre and the Temple of Venus Victrix were attended by the writer Cicero. In *Letters to Friends*, He writes that although the spectacles put on were incredible, the excess and the slaughter began to feel empty. The crowd had seen it so many times that, by the end, they began to feel nothing but sympathy for all the beings that were killed.

If you ask me, the games were of course most magnificent; but they would not have been to your taste;

that I infer from my own feelings ... For my feeling of
cheerfulness was extinguished by the spectacle of such
magnificence - a magnificence which, I am sure, it will
not disturb you in the least to have missed seeing. For
what pleasure can there be in the sight of 600 mules
in the Clytaemnestra, or of 3,000 bowls in the Trojan
Horse, or of the varied accoutrements of foot and horse
in some big battle? ...

There remains the wild-beast hunts, two a day for five
days - magnificent; there is no denying it. But what
pleasure can it possibly be to a man of culture, when
either a puny human being is mangled by a most powerful beast, or a splendid beast is transfixed with a
hunting spear? And even if all this is something to be
seen, you have seen it more than once; and I, who was
a spectator, saw nothing new in it. The last day was that
of the elephants, and on that day the mob and crowd
was greatly impressed, but manifested no pleasure.
Indeed the result was a certain compassion and a kind
of feeling that that huge beast has a fellowship with the
human race.

Juvenal's famously withering sarcasm about Rome's moral
decline is just the best-known of a series of descriptions
of the population's—of all classes—fervent enthusiasm for
actors, gladiators, and horses.

The people which once bestowed imperium, fasces,
legions, everything, now foregoes such activities
and has but two passionate desires: bread and
circus games.

The most essential features of the Roman games were chariot races, wild animal fights and gladiatorial combat. In the
latter, criminals and slaves equipped with various types of
weapons and armour were pitted against other gladiators
or wild beasts. The elite, including Emperors and Senators,

played a significant role in providing these lavish shows to keep the people happy and, hence, peaceful. Happy people forget to riot.

As many as fifty days of the year could be dedicated to the games, and in addition, there was a revival, in the Imperial period, of Greek-style athletic meetings, which had declined since the heyday of the Greek city-states. The exchange went the other way, with Roman-style games becoming more popular in the Hellenic world. Famous old festivals of the past were revived, and new ones were organised across the Empire. A new, Empire-wide athlete's guild, with Hercules as the patron god, was established, with imperial patronage and favour. The guild's members, all professional athletes, toured the Empire competing at various meetings and enjoyed extraordinary honours, privileges and wealth, including the right to pensions from their home cities as rewards for their victories.

Here, Fronto, the rhetorician and advocate, reminds us that not everyone gets the dole of free grain or bread but that everyone - and he means everyone - gets the free shows.

It was the height of political wisdom for the Emperor not to neglect even actors and the other performers of the stage, the circus, and the arena, since he knew that the Roman people is held fast by two things above all, the grain supply and the shows, that the success of the government depends on amusements as much as on serious things. Neglect of serious matters entails the greater detriment, of amusements the greater unpopularity. The money largesses are less eagerly desired than the shows; the largesses appease only the grain-doled plebs singly and individually, while the shows keep the whole population happy.

The Career of a Famous Charioteer

The following inscription comes from a monument to a charioteer called Diocles. It was erected by admirers and teammates, probably on his retirement at the age of forty-two after twenty-four years of driving in races. It's a very long inscription - he was very famous! - so only the start is replicated here.

There were four chariot racing 'stables' or teams called *factiones* known by their colours - Red, Blue, Green and White.

Gaius Appuleius Diocles, charioteer of the Red Stablem a Lusitanian Spaniard by birth, aged 42 years, 7 months, 23 days. He drove his first chariot in the White Stable, in the consulship of Acilius Aviola and Corellius Pansa [122AD]. He won his first victory in the same stable, in the consulship of Manius Acilius Glabrio and Gaius Bellicius Torquatus [124AD]. He drove for the first time in the Green Stable in the consulship of Torquatus Asprenas (for the second time) and Annius Libo [128AD]. He won his first victory in the Red Stable in the consulship of Laenas Pontianus and Antonius Rufinus [131AD]

Grand totals: He drove chariots for 24 years, ran 4,257 starts, and won 1,462 victories., 110 in opening races* In single-entry races** he won 1,064 victories, winning 92 major purses, 32 of them (including 3 with six-horse teams) at 30,000 sesterces, 28 (including 2 with six-horse races***) at 40,000 sesterces, 28 (including 1 with a seven-horse team****) at 50,000 sesterces and 3 at 60,000 sesterces.

Let's take a closer look. He averaged 177 races a year for 24 years, or an average of three to four races on each of the fifty circus days of the year.

*Before the races began, there was a grand parade through the streets to the circus itself. The teams would lead straight

into the stadium and immediately begin the race. These 'opening races' had a special distinction.
**These are races in which each stable fielded only one team of competitors and offered the biggest prizes. Obviously, each stable would field their star driver
***Later on, the inscription tells us that these two victories were won on a single day, which is apparently an unprecedented event.
****The inscription later tells us that this was "A number of horses never before this exhibited at the games"

Let's carry on:

> In two-entry races he won 347 victories, including 4 with three-horse teams at 15,000 sesterces; in three-entry races he won 51 victories. He won or placed 2,900 times taking 861 second places, 576 third places and 1 fourth place at 1,000 sesterces*; he failed to place 1,351 times. He tied a Blue for first place 10 times and a White 91 times, twice for 30,000 sesterces. He won a total of 33,863,110 sesterces. In addition in races with two-horse teams for 1,000 sesterces, he won three times, and tied a White once and a Green twice** He took the lead and won 815 times, came from behind to win 67 times, won under handicap 46 times, won in various styles 42 times, and won a final dash 502 times*** (216 over the Greens, 205 over the Blues, 81 over the Whites). He made nine horses 100-time winners and one a 200-time winner.

The rest of the inscription lists in great detail "His Records", naming record-holding drivers and horses and all the records he broke. It calls him the Champion of all Charioteers.

*Normally, fourth place would win you nothing.
**If you're counting as you go along, these are the six races you are missing

***The 'final dash' victories were the most highly regarded, which is why they are further broken down.

Religious Holidays

A papyrus roll found during the 1931/32 excavation of the Roman town of Europus on the banks of the Euphrates contains a calendar of the religious holidays celebrated by the garrison stationed there, and the animals that were to be sacrificed. It dates to around 224AD:

January 3 - Vows fulfilled and offered for the preservation of our lord Marcus Aurelius Severus Alexander Augustus [the Emperor Severus Alexander] and for the eternity of the Empire and the Roman people. To Jupiter, Best and Greatest, an ox; to Juno, a cow; to Minerva, a cow; to Jupiter Victor, an ox.... to Father Mars, a bull; to Mars Victor, a bull; to Victory, a cow....

January 28 - The Arabian, Adiabenic and very great Parthian victories of the deified Severus, and accession of the deified Trajan. To the Parthian Victory, a cow; to the deified Trajan, an ox....

June 26 - Our lord Marcus Aurelius Severus Alexander named Caesar [note how his name has changed slightly now] and clad in the toga of manhood [Alexander was only 13 when he became Emperor]. To the genius of Alexander Augustus, a bull...

July 11 - Birthday of the deified Julius [Caesar]. To the deified Julius, an ox.

September - Birthday of the deified Faustina [either the wife of Antoninus or Marcus Aurelius, or possibly both]. To the deified Faustina, public prayer.

September 23 - Birthday of the deified Augustus. To the deified Augustus, an ox...

There are a couple of interesting things here. Firstly, the nature of the animal sacrificed changes according to the gender and importance of the person being celebrated - a cow for a woman, an ox for a man, a bull for the really important ones. Secondly, this document is how we know the birthdays of some of the Emperors.

Religious Reforms

In the latter part of the 1st Century BC, Augustus instigated a wide series of reforms to Roman religion, the main reform being 'worship me, you bastards'. Oriental cults were banished, obsolete priesthoods, religious traditions and old rituals were restored and many of the temples that went with them were rebuilt.

> After he had finally assumed the office of pontifex maximus... he collected whatever prophetic writings of Greek or Latin origin were in circulation anonymously or under the names of irresponsible authors and burned more than 1,000 of them, retaining only the Sibylline Books and making a selection even among these; and he deposited them in two gilded cases under the pedestal of the Palatine Apollo...

Augustus had thus transferred the sacred oracular books from the temple of Jupiter on the Capitol, where they had been since the Republic, to the shrine of his new 'imperial' God, Apollo.

> ...He increased the number and prestige of the priests and their privileges, in particular those of the Vestal Virgins. Moreover, when there was occasion to choose another Vestal in the place of the one who died, and

when many had used all their influence to avoid submitting their daughters to the hazard of the lot, he solemnly swore that if anyone of his granddaughters were of eligible age he would have proposed her name. He also revived some of the ancient rites which had gradually fallen into disuse, such as the augury of safety...

The 'augury of safety' was annual ceremony in times of peace in which the priests would sit about and decide if it was worth praying for the safety of the Roman people, given that nobody was, presently, trying to strangle them and throw them in the Tiber.

...the office of flamen Dialis [a controversial priest of Jupiter who came with so many taboos that nobody wanted to do it], the ceremonies of Lupercalia, the Secular Games and the festival of the crossroads....

The festival of the crossroads was a cool street party for the lower classes held at street corner shrines. It had been outlawed by Julius Caesar, because he was a miserable bastard.

...at the Lupercalia he forbade beardless youths to join in the running and at the Secular Games he would not allow young people of any gender to attend any entertainment by night except in the company of some adult relative. He ordained that the protecting deities of the crossroads should be decorated with flowers twice a year, in spring and summer.

Lupercalia

Speaking of the Lupercalia, Plutarch briefly describes what the festival entails. It's about wolves and laughing and thongs. And milk. It takes place on February 15th

The Lupercalia, judging from the time of its celebration, would seem to be a feast of purification, for it is observed on the dies *nefatus* [a day on which it was improper to transact legal business or hold assemblies] of the month of February, which one may interpret to signify purification, and the very day of the feast was in ancient days called *Febrata*; but the name of the holiday has the meaning of the Greek *Lycaea* [Feast of Wolves] and it seems thus to be of great antiquity ... And we see the *Luperci* [Priests of Faunus] begin their course from the place where they say Romulus was exposed. But the actual ceremonies make the reason for the name hard to surmise; for there are goats killed; then two youths of noble birth are brought to the priests, some of whom touch their foreheads with a bloody knife, while others at once wipe it off with wool dipped in milk. The youths must laugh after their foreheads are wiped. Next, having cut the goats' skins into strips, the priests run about naked, except for something about their middle, lashing all they meet with the thongs; and the young wives do not avoid their blows, fancying that they will promote conception and easy childbirth.

Terminalia - February 23rd

When the night has passed, see to it that the god who marks the boundaries of the tilled lands receives his wonted honour. O Terminus, whether thou art a stone or a stump buried in the field, thou too hast been deified from days of yore. Thou art crowned by two owners on opposite sides; they bring thee two garlands and two cakes. An altar is built. Hither the husbandman's rustic wife brings with her own hands on a potsherd the fire which she has taken from the warm hearth. The old man chops wood and deftly piles up the billets, and strives to fix the branches in the solid earth; then he nurses the kindling flames with dry bark; the

boy stands by and holds the broad basket in his hands.
When from the basket he has thrice thrown corn into
the midst of the fire, the little daughter presents the cut
honeycombs. Others hold vessels of wine. A portion of
each is cast into the flames. The company dressed in
white look on and hold their peace. Terminus himself,
at the meeting of the bounds, is sprinkled with the
blood of a slaughtered lamb, and grumbles not when a
suckling pig is given him. The simple neighbours meet
and hold a feast and sing thy praises, holy Terminus;
thou dost set bounds to peoples and cities and vast
kingdoms; without thee every field would be a cause
of wrangling. Thou courtest no favour, thou art bribed
by no gold: the lands entrusted to thee dost guard in
loyal good faith.

So there you go. If you want to keep something or someone
out of your garden, you need to do some beseeching to Terminus. Get two cakes and a pig, some kids with honeycombs
and some wine. Make a day of it. Light up the barbecue.

Robigalia - April 25th

On that day, as I [the poet Ovid] was returning from
Nomentum [Mentana in Lazio] to Rome, a white-robed
crowd blocked the middle of the road. A flamen [priest]
was on his way to the grove of ancient robigo [mildew],
to throw the entrails of a dog and the entrails of a
sheep into the flames. Straightway, I went up to him
to inform myself of the rite. Thy flamen, O Quirinus,
pronounced these words: "Thou scaly Mildew! Spare
the sprouting corn, and let the smooth top quiver on
the surface of the ground. O let the crops, nursed by
the heaven's propitious stars, grow till they are ripe for
the sickle! No feeble power is thine: the corn on which
thou hast set they mark, the sad husbandman gives up

for lost. Not winds, nor showers, not glistening frost, that nips the sallow corn, harm it so much as when the sun warms the wet stalks; then, dread goddess, is the hour to wreak thy wrath. O spare, I pray, and take thy scabby hands from off the harvest! Harm not the tilth; 'tis enough that thou hast the power to harm. Grip not the tender crops, but rather grip the hard iron. Forestall the destroyer ... But do not thou profane the corn, and ever may the husbandman be able to pay his vows to thee in thine absence" So he spake. On his right hand hung a napkin with a loose nap, and he had a bowl of wine and a casket of incense. The incense, and wine, and sheep's guts, and the foul entrails of a filthy dog, he put upon the hearth - we saw him do it.

I wouldn't be trying this one, however. Take thy scabby hands off the filthy dogs!

Lemuria - May 9th

When from that day the Evening Star shall thrice have shown his beauteous face, and thrice the vanquished stars shall have retreated before Pheobus, there shall be celebrated on olden rite, the nocturnal Lemuria: it will bring offerings to the silent ghosts. The year was formerly shorter, and the pious rites of purification (februa) were unknown, and thou, two-headed Janus, wast not the leader of the months. Yet even then people brought gifts to the ashes of the dead, as their due, and the grandson paid his respects to the tomb of his buried grandsire. It was the Month of May, so named after our forefathers [maiores*], and it still retains part of the ancient custom. When midnight has come and lends silence to sleep, and dogs and all ye varied fowls are hushed, the worshipper who bears the olden rite in mind and fears the gods arises; no knots constrict his feet; and he makes a sign with his thumb in the middle

of his closed fingers [to ward off the evil eye, still practised in Italy today], lest in his silence an unsubstantial
shade should meet him. And after washing his hands
clean in spring water, he turns, and first he receives
black beans and throws them away with face averted;
but while he throws them away, he says "These I cast;
with these beans I redeem me and mine." This he says
nine times, without looking back; the shade is thought
to gather the beans and to follow unseen behind. Again
he touches water and clashes Temesan bronze [tiny
cymbals from Southern Italy] and asks the shade to go
out of his house. When he has said nine times "Ghosts
of my fathers, go forth!" he looks back, and thinks that
he has duly performed the sacred rites.

So if your house is haunted by black bean fancying ghosts of
your forefathers, you know what to do. Good luck!

*This explanation is a commonly accepted though incor-
rect derivation of the name of the month of May. It is actually
named after *Maia*, an old Italian divinity, later associated
with the Greek *Maia*, the mother of Mercury.

Saturnalia - December 17th

Saturnalia is the one Roman festival that everyone has heard
of and the one everyone thinks they know the most about.
The following poem, *Silvae* by Statius, commemorates a
celebration of the Saturnalia in the reign of Domitian. This
seven-day festival, which began every year on December
17th, involved lots of merry-making, drunken revelry, and
the exchange of gifts. Plus, famously, for one day only, slaves
were given the day off and changed places with their masters.

Hence, father Phoebus and stern Pallas! Away, ye
Muses, go, keep holiday; we will call you back at the

New Year. But Saturn, slip your fetters and come hither, and December tipsy with much wine, and laughing Mirth and wanton Wit, while I recount the glad festival of our merry Caesar and the banquet's drunken revel.

Scarce was the new dawn stirring, when already sweet-meats were raining from the line*, such was the dew the rising east wind was scattering; the famous fruit of the Pontic nut groves, or of Idume's fertile slopes [Palestinian dates], all that devout Damascus grows upon its boughs [Damson (Damascene) plums], or thirsty Caunus ripens [figs], falls, gratis, in a generous profusion. Biscuits and melting pastries, Amerian fruit [apples and pears] not overripe, must cakes, and bursting dates from invisible palms were showering down ... Let Jupiter send his tempests through the world and threaten the broad fields, while our own Jove sends us showers like these!

But lo! Another multitude, handsome and well dressed, as numerous as that upon the benches, makes its way along all the rows. Some carry baskets of bread and white napkins and more luxurious fare; others serve languorous wine in abundant measure ... Thou dost nourish alike the circle of the noble and austere and the folk that wear the toga, and since, O generous lord, thou dost feed so many multitudes, haughty Annona knoweth nought of this festival ... ** One table serves every class alike, children, women, common people, knights and Senators: freedom loosed the bonds of awe. Nay even thyself - what god could have such leisure, or vouchsafe as much? - thou didst come and share our banquet. And now everyone, be he rich or poor, boasts himself the Emperor's guest.

Amid such excitements and strange luxuries the pleasure of the scene flies quickly by: women untrained to the sword take their stand, daring, how recklessly,

men's battles! ... Then comes a bold array of dwarfs ...
They give and suffer wounds, and threaten death - with
fists how tiny! ...

Now as the shades of night draw on, what commotion
attends the scattering of largess! Here enter maidens
easily bought; here is recognised all that in theatres
wins favour or applause for skill or beauty. Here a
crowd of buxom Lydian girls are clapping hands, here
tinkle the cymbals of Cadiz, there troops of Syrians are
making uproar, there are theatre folk, and they who
barter common sulphur for broken glass [junk deal-
ers] ... Countless voices are raised to heaven acclaiming
the Emperor's Saturnalia festival; with loving enthusiasm they salute their lord. This liberty alone did Caesar
forbid them ... [that is, the liberty to call him 'lord'].

For how many years shall this festival abide! Never
shall age destroy so holy a day! While the hills of
Latium remain and Father Tiber, while thy Rome
stands and the Capitol thou hast restored to the world
it shall continue.

*Dainties were dangled on a rope stretched across the
amphitheatre, which people were free to help themselves to.

** That is, there is such an abundance that the usual grain
supply problems of Rome don't exist.

Buxom Lydian girls, fighting women, dwarves, drinking and
free figs. Happy Christmas, everyone!

Festival Days

The earliest form of the Roman calendar called the Calendar of Numa, is perhaps the oldest extant record of Roman
civilisation. It was established back in the old Etruscan

days and concerns the *fasti* - days on which there were no religious impediments to normal business. The whole thing is designed to ensure that forty-five religious festival days are observed. These are based on pre-Roman agricultural traditions.

The calendar was based on a 12-month lunar year of 355 days, with provision for an extra 'intercalary' month of 22 or 23 days every couple of years. This floating month was the main reason Julius Caesar brought about the reforms outlined in the Julian Calendar. Caesar did away with this month and rejigged everything into pretty much what we have now. The only major difference between the Julian and Gregorian calendars that we use today is the way leap years are calculated. Contrary to popular belief, Caesar didn't add months to the calendar; he took one away.

The month we now call July was called *Quintilis*, and August was called *Sextilis*, which is why September, October and so on are 7 and 8. March used to be the first month of the year, so *Quintilis* was the fifth. January became the first month in 153BC to coincide with January 1st being the date on which Consuls began their year of service.

The reason Caesar got rid of the extra month is that there appears to be no specific rule when it could be implemented. This meant that unscrupulous politicians could add the month to prolong the year-long service of either themselves or a political friend, or not have it in order to shorten that of a rival.

The year was divided into 8-day periods, which were not numbered but given letters from A to H, with each ninth day being a market day called *nundinue*. The months were divided into phases of the Moon as follows:

New Moon - *Kalends*
First Quarter - *Nones*, always the ninth day before the Ides
Full Moon - *Ides*

Each day had a religious significance attached to it. The symbols for the days are:

F - *Faustus*, a day on which you could conduct business in court.
C - *Comitialis*, a day on which comitia (public assemblies) could meet.
N - *Nefastus*, a day on which it wasn't allowed to transact business or hold meetings.
NP - Uncertain, but perhaps no legal business or meetings and a public holiday.
EN - *Endotercius, faustus* in the middle of the day, but *nefastus* in the morning and evening.

The infamous month of March, with its Ides, would then look something like this:

B Kalends NP, C - F, D - C, E - C, F - C, G - C, H Nones F, A - F, B - C, C - C, D -C, E - C, F - EN, G - NP *Equirria* [horse races in honour of Mars], H Ides NP, A - F, B - NP *Liberalia*, C - C, D - NP *Quinquatrus*, E - C, F - C, G - N, H - NP *Tubilustrium*, A QRCF*, B - C, C - C, D - C, E - C, F - C, G - C, H - C.

That looks complicated, but March 4th, for example, is E - C or 'Day E, *Comitialis*'. The day of Caesar's famous assassination, March 15th is 'Day H, Full Moon, NP'. OK ... maybe a little complicated.

*QRCF is *Quando Rex Comitiavit Fas* - when the king has dissolved the assembly - and the day is also *fastus*.

Lavish Spending

In his work *On Duties,* Cicero makes a plea for moderation:

There are, in general, two classes of those who give largely: the one class is the lavish the other the generous. The lavish are those who squander their money on public banquets, doles of meat among the people, gladiatorial shows, magnificent spectacles, and wild beast fights - vanities of which but a brief recollection will remain, or none at all ... I realise that in our country, even in the good old times, it had become a settled custom to expect magnificent entertainments from the very best of men in the year of their aedileship ... Still, we should avoid any suspicion of penuriousness. Mamercus was a very wealthy man, and his refusal of the aedileship was the cause of his defeat for the Consulship. If, therefore, such entertainment is demanded by the people, men of right judgment must at least consent to furnish it even if they do not like the idea. But in doing so, they should keep within their means, as I myself did.

Against Bacchanalia

In the early second century BC, the secret rites of the Hellenic cult of Bacchus spread rapidly from the south, up the Italian peninsula. It found converts among the lowest levels of society, including slaves, reaching Rome in around 186BC. Roman prudishness and revulsion at certain orgiastic practices played a big part in the Senate's decision to suppress the worst excesses of Bacchanalian rites. The pretend pearl-clutching apart, the main reason for the crackdown, was driven by the growth of secret societies associated with the cult. They then decided to dress the measures against the cult as a suppression of conspiracy against the State.

The following year diverted the consuls Spurius Postumius Albinus and Quintus Marcius Philippus from the army and the administration of wars and provinces to the suppression of an internal conspiracy ...

A nameless Greek came first to Etruria, possessed of none of those many arts which the Greek people, supreme as it is in learning, brought to us in numbers for the cultivation of mind and body, but a dabbler in sacrifices and a fortune-teller; nor was he one who, by frankly disclosing his creed and publicly proclaiming both his profession and his system, filled minds with error, but a priest of secret rites performed by night. There were initiatory rites which at first were imparted to a few, then began to be generally known among men and women. To the religious element in them were added the delights of wine and feasts, that the minds of a larger number might be attracted. When wine had inflamed their minds, and night and the mingling of males with females, youth with age, had destroyed every sentiment of modesty, all varieties of corruption first began to be practised, since each one had at hand the pleasure answering to that to which his nature was more inclined. There was not one form of vice alone, the promiscuous matings of free men and women, but perjured witnesses, forged seals and wills and evidence, all issued from this same workshop: like-wise poisonings and secret murders, so that at times not even the bodies were found for burial. Much was ventured by craft, more by violence. This violence was concealed because amid the howlings and the crash of drums and cymbals no cry of the sufferers could be heard as the debauchery and murders proceeded.

The destructive power of this evil spread from Etruria to Rome like the contagion of a pestilence. At first the size of the City, with abundant room and tolerance for such evils, concealed it: at length information came to the consul Postumius in about this manner ... Postumius laid the matter before the Senate, everything being set forth in detail; first what had been reported, then what he had himself discovered. Great panic seized the Fathers, both on the public account, lest these conspiracies and gatherings by night might produce something of hidden treachery or danger, and privately, each for himself, lest anyone might be involved in the mischief. The Senate, moreover, decreed that the consul should be thanked because he had investigated the affair both with great industry and without creating any confusion. Then the investigation of the Bacchanals and their nocturnal orgies they referred to the consuls, not as a part of their regular duties; they directed the consuls to see to it that the witnesses Aebutius and Faecenia did not suffer harm and to attract other informers by rewards; the priests of these rites, whether men or women, should be sought out, not only at Rome but through all the villages and communities, that they might be at the disposal of the consuls; that it should be proclaimed in addition in the city of Rome and that edicts should be sent through all Italy, that no one who had been initiated in the Bacchic rites should presume to assemble or come together for the purpose of celebrating those rites or to perform any such ritual. Before all, it was decreed that an inquiry should be conducted regarding those persons who had come together or conspired for the commission of any immorality or crime. Such was the decree of the Senate.

The consuls ordered the curule aediles to search out all the priests of this cult and to keep them under surveillance, in free custody for the investigation; the plebeian aediles were to see to it that no celebration of the rites should be held in secret. The task was entrusted to the triumviri capitales of placing guards through the City, of seeing that no night meetings were held, and of making provision against fire; as assistants to the triumviri, the quinqueviri uls cis Tiberim were to stand guard each over the buildings of his own district ...

Then they ordered the decrees of the Senate to be read and announced the reward to be paid the informer if anyone had brought any person before them or had reported the name of anyone who was absent. If anyone was named and had escaped, for him they would designate a fixed day, and, if he did not respond when summoned on that day, he would be condemned in his absence. If anyone was named of those who were at that time outside the land of Italy, they would fix a more elastic date if he wished to come to plead his cause. They next proclaimed that no one should venture to sell or buy anything for the purpose of flight; that no one should harbour, conceal, or in any wise aid the fugitives ...

But so numerous were the persons who had fled from the City that, since in many instances legal proceedings and causes were falling through, the praetors Titus Maenius and Marcus Licinius were compelled, through the intervention of the Senate, to adjourn court for thirty days, until the investigations should be finished by the consuls. The same depopulation, because at Rome men whose names had been given in did not respond or were not found, compelled the consuls to make the rounds of the villages and there investigate and conduct trials. Those who had merely been initiated and had made their prayers in accordance with the ritual formula, the priest dictating the words, in which the wicked conspiracy to all vice and lust was contained, but had committed none of the acts to which they were bound by the oath against either themselves or others, they left in chains; upon those who had permitted themselves to be defiled by debauchery or murder, who had polluted themselves by false testimony, forged seals, substitution of wills or other frauds, they inflicted capital punishment. More were killed than were thrown into prison. There was a large number of men and women in both classes. Convicted women were turned over to their relatives or to those who had authority over them, that they might be punished in private: if there was no suitable person to exact it, the penalty was inflicted by the State.

Then the task was entrusted to the consuls of destroying all forms of Bacchic worship, first at Rome and then throughout Italy, except in cases where an ancient altar or image had been consecrated. For the future it was then provided by decree of the Senate that there should be no Bacchanalia in Rome or Italy. If any person considered such worship to be ordained by tradition or to be necessary, and believed that he could not omit it without sin and atonement, he was to make a declaration before the city praetor, and the latter would consult the Senate. If permission were granted to him, at a meeting where not fewer than one hundred were in attendance, he should offer the sacrifice, provided that not more than five people should take part in the rite, and that there should be no common purse or master of sacrifices or priest.

Chapter Four

ON SLAVES

Slaves

After the murder, ancient custom required that every slave residing under the same roof must be executed. But a crowd gathered, eager to save so many innocent lives; and rioting began. The senate house was besieged. Inside, there was a feeling against excessive severity, but the majority opposed any change ... Those favouring execution prevailed. However, great crowds ready with stones and torches prevented the order from being carried out. Nero rebuked the population by edict and lined with troops the whole route along which those condemned were taken for execution.

This passage from Tacitus tells us of when, in 61AD, the senate voted to put to death all the slaves belonging to the city prefect Lucius Pedanius Secundus, all 400 of them, because he had been killed by one of their number. The outcry among the plebs at this intolerably harsh reaction goes some way to inform us of the relationship between themselves and un-manumitted slaves. It's impossible not to think of some of the protesters as newly freed slaves themselves who are looking out for their brothers and sisters or as simply plebs who see more in common with the slaves than with the senatorial class that has condemned them. The problem is, like most of ancient history, that the voices of these people are never recorded. The rarity of these instances of empathy between the bottom rungs of society could be attributed to a degree of insouciance. But as always, absence of evidence is not evidence of absence and, if anything, the incredible injustice alone has riled the plebs. It must be noted that the public outcry is not enough to save them. So the risk of widespread disorder enough to cause serious damage to the city, or to the reputation of the Emperor, is not strong enough to save them.

The slave population of Rome was huge and very visible. In law, they were the property of their owners, but they were still recognised as human beings, even if only because their value as property required them to be seen as such. As such, they could have certain 'rights', especially in circumstances that were confined to relationships between them, such as disputes or, of course, physical relationships. There was a state of marriage between slaves called *contubernium* which allowed them to live as man and wife, but without any of the normal benefits of doing so. Any property they owned still belonged to the master and neither could inherit. Any children the marriage produced belonged to the owner as well. The same owner could annul the marriage at will. Far from being something that an owner would disapprove of, these relationships were seen as easy ways of generating more slaves and such marriages were sometimes encouraged more than discouraged for precisely that outcome. Women slaves who produced enough children could be 'rewarded' with reduced duties or even a form of retirement from work entirely.

The brutality of slavery was always there and attempts at 'sweetening' the relationship seem, through a modern prism, to be just another form of cruelty. But attempts at offering a slave something other than brutality followed by death resulted in attempts to make life for them better, if only because slaves would sometimes move into managerial positions in the household which held great responsibility.

Slaves might be rewarded for their work by a *peculium*, money given by the master. This money, which gained legal status in the late Republican period, came in a wide variety of forms, from a weekly stipend to regular bonuses to lavish gifts. Slaves with enough freedom could go out and spend it on what they wanted. There are instances of slaves drinking in bars in Pompeii, for example. Some of them might expect to save their *peculium* for long enough to buy their own freedom. We often say that anything has its price and as a slave was, at the end of the day, a commodity with a financial value. Once that value was met, it didn't really matter who it was met by. If it was met by the slave themselves, then so be it.

Although Augustus instigated new buildings, a new order, fire brigades and even a rudimentary police force, and even though under this new system, freed slaves could soar up the social ranks, nothing stopped poverty, and crime or stopped the city from burning to the ground in 64AD under Nero. It was still a city and a society in which only the elite could lead comfortable lives and, crucially, a city that they could afford to leave when it became too hot or dangerous to their health. The wealthy could afford to treat Rome as a playground.

The Abuse of Slaves

Despite the ubiquity of slaves in Roman society, there were some who campaigned for better conditions, particularly among the Stoics. The following examples are of legislation against the abuse of slaves. They come from various sources, including the *Historia Augusta*, *Digest*, Suetonius and Gaius' *Institutes*.

Since the passage of the Petronian Law [which must pre-date 79AD] and the decrees of the Senate relating thereto, masters have been deprived of the power of turning over slaves at their own discretion to fight with wild beasts. If, however, a slave has been brought before a judge and the complaint of the master should prove to be valid, then such penalty may be imposed.

When certain men were abandoning their sick and worn-out slaves on the Island of Aesculapius because of the trouble of treating them, Claudius decreed that all slaves thus abandoned, if they recovered, would be free and would not revert to the power of their masters. And if anyone chose to kill such a slave instead of abandoning him, he would be liable to the charge of homicide.

The island in question is Isola Tiberina in the middle of the Tiber in Rome, where there was a sanctuary of Aesculapius, the god of healing. Slaves who were freed under this law were granted 'Latin' status.

The deified Vespasian decreed that a female slave would become free if she were made a prostitute after being sold on condition that she should not be made a prostitute; and that if she were later sold to someone else by the purchaser without such stipulation, she would become free by virtue of such sale and would become the freedwoman of the former seller.

Hadrian forbade masters to kill their slaves, ordering that any who deserved such punishment must be sentenced by the courts. He forbade anyone to sell a slave or slave girl to a procurer or trainer of gladiators without furnishing a reason ... He abolished private prisons for slaves and free ... He ordained that if a slave owner were murdered in his home not all the slaves should be subjected to questioning but only those who could have been near enough to notice anything.

A rescript of the deified Hadrian to Sennius Sabinus ... reads as follows: "Recourse to torturing of slaves should be had only when there is a suspect under indictment and other evidence brings the proof so close that only the confession of slaves appears necessary [to complete it]

At the present time neither Roman citizens nor any other persons who are under the rule of the Roman people are permitted to treat their slaves with excessive and baseless cruelty. For, by enactment of the Emperor Antoninus, a man who kills his own slave without cause is ordered to be held just as liable as one who kills another's slave. And even excessive severity of masters is restrained by enactment of the same Emperor. For, when consulted by certain governors of provinces about those slaves who seek asylum in temples of the gods or at statues of the Emperors, he ordained that if the cruelty of the masters is found to be intolerable they are to be compelled to sell their slaves. A rescript of the deified [Antoninus] Pius to Aelius Marcianus, proconsul of Baetica ... follows: "The power of masters over their slaves ought to remain unimpaired, nor should any man be deprived of his lawful rights, but it is to the masters' interest that relief against cruelty, hunger, or intolerable wrong should not be denied those who seek it without cause. Investigate, therefore, the complaints of those of Julius Sabinus' slave household who have fled for protection to [my] statue and if you find that they have been treated more harshly than is just, or subjected to indecent acts, order them to be sold with the stipulation that they may not revert to Sabinus' power. And if the said Sabinus seeks to evade my ordinance, he will learn that I will deal more severely with his offences."

Torture, Torture, Torture

The writer Juvenal once remarked, rather sourly, on how the credibility of a witness in a trial depended on their wealth and the testimony of a gentleman was by degrees more valuable than that of a slave. To the extent that the testimony of a slave might only be admissible if it had been extracted under torture, the idea being that such a person is so unworthy that anything they say can only be believed if it has first been tested under the lash.

The incongruous nature of a slave saying anything that their abuser wants to hear simply to get the torture to stop cannot have been lost on the Romans, which gives one pause for thought as to why they actually insisted on it. Ultimately, like slavery itself, there were plenty of people in Roman society, even at the elite level, who found such behaviour abhorrent. Rules of evidence are discussed often:

> The Julian Claudian Law Concerning Violence [enacted under Augustus] provides that the following are not permitted to give testimony under this statute against a defendant; a person who has obtained freedom from him or his father, or persons who are under age, or anyone who has been condemned in a public trail and has not been completely reinstated, or who is in chains or in a public prison, or who has hired himself out to fight with wild beasts, or any woman who is or has been a prostitute [of course], or anyone who has been sentenced or convicted for having taken money for giving or withholding of testimony. For some persons should no be admitted to credibility of testimony because of deference to persons, others because of the unreliability of their judgement, and still others because of the stigma and public disgrace of their lives.

Here, we begin to see how Roman social attitudes towards those deemed unworthy affect how reliable such individuals are. A prostitute is deemed an unreliable witness simply by association with her profession, not by the merits of her character. Similarly, then, it's maybe not such a leap to see that if society can dismiss persons simply by association with certain lifestyles, it can also deem that they are treated in horrendous ways. You might be able to get a more truthful testimony by plying a Senator with the finest wines and a plate of stuffed dormice but give those to a slave, and all you will have is a slightly fatter, drunk slave. The finer aspects of bribery don't work on people who don't appreciate them. In a similar fashion, beat the living crap out of a Senator, and all you have is a terrified Senator with a black eye. It's still an incongruous way of approaching the problem, but Rome didn't always function in the most sensible ways.

> Witnesses should not be summoned rashly from great distances, and much less should soldiers be called away from their units or duties for the purpose of presenting testimony, as the deified Hadrian rules in a rescript....

> The deposition of a slave is to be believed when there is no other proof for getting at the truth.

This last part is interesting. Ostensibly, it is suggesting that the testimony of a slave can have equal value, but what it actually says is that if you have no other choice, you can believe what the slave is telling you. That also suggests that if you do have other options, you should not believe the slave, even if they are telling you the truth and even if that truth is evident. Say you have a man who is clearly lying and a slave who is clearly telling the truth then, in theory at least and as long as you can determine that you will arrive at the truth of the matter, you can ignore the truth and judge the matter according to the lie. That doesn't then mean you will arrive at the incorrect decision. As I said, Rome doesn't always work in sensible ways.

A father is not a competent witness for a son, nor a son for a father.

It is understood that no one is a competent witness in his own case.

If the circumstances of a case are such that we are compelled to admit a gladiator or similar person [so a slave] as a witness, his testimony is not to be believed unless taken under torture.

Manumission

There were several ways of manumitting slaves and none of them were particularly complicated or required much effort. Roman Law could, in some cases, be surprisingly straightforward - as long as you had enough witnesses, you could just get on with it. The most common forms of manumission were via a will or via a ceremony 'of the rod' known as *vindicta*. Manumission (lit. 'from the hand' - de manu missio) is the same principle by which a father releases a son into adulthood; by physically 'letting go' of them. Incidentally, the release of a son by a father was called 'emancipatio', from which we get the word 'emancipation'. *Vindicta* was a letting go ceremony performed before a magistrate in which another citizen, often one who was buying the slave's freedom, would request their release and after an exchange of some kind, usually money and sometimes money paid by the slave themselves from gifts accrued during service. The former owner would then say some sort of oath, touch the slave with a rod - the *vindicta* - and that would be that. As you can probably guess from the name, the *vindicta* was a rod normally used for more violent means, and this touching can be seen as one last symbolic beating by the master.

Under the [Aelian-Sentian] Law a master under twenty years of age is not permitted to manumit a slave in any other manner except by the rod after proof of adequate cause for manumission before a council.

When the Emperor manumits a slave he does not apply the rod, but at his pleasure a person becomes free who is manumitted in accordance with the law of Augustus. The Law provides that a slave under thirty years who has been manumitted by the rod shall not become a Roman citizen unless cause has been proved before a council... but it stipulates that a person manumitted by will us in the same status as if he were free with the consent of the master, and therefore he become a Latin.

In accordance with the Aelian-Sentian Law, anyone under thirty who has been manumitted and has become a Latin, if he marries either a Roman citizen or a Latin colonist or a woman of the same status as himself and so attests with not less than seven adult Roman citizens as witnesses, and begets a child, when this child reaches the age of one the right is granted him by this law to come before a praetor, or in the provinces before the provincial governor and prove that, in accordance with the Law, he has married and has a one-year-old child from this marriage and if the one before whom the case is proved finds that this is so, then the Latin himself and his wife, if she also is of the same status, and the child, is it is also of the same status are ordained to be Roman citizens.

Replenishing the Army

For during the Second Punic War the Roman youth of military age having been drained by several unfavourable battles, the senate, on motion of the consul Tiberius Gracchus, decreed that slaves should be bought up out of public moneys for use in repulsing the enemy. After a plebiscite was passed on this matter by the people through the intervention of the tribunes of the plebs, a commission of three men was chosen to purchase 24,000 slaves* and, having administered an oath to them that they would give zealous and courageous service and that they would bear arms as long as the Carthaginians were in Italy, they sent them to the camp. From Apulia and the Paediculi were also bought 270 slaves for replacements in the cavalry ... The city, which up to this time had disdained to have as soldiers even free men without property added to its army as almost its chief support persons were taken from slave lodgings and slaves gathered from shepherd huts.

*The above account, from *Memorable Deeds and Sayings* by Valerius Maximus, probably exaggerates this number. Livy states it was 8,000, and it's a bit daft to think he understated it.

A Large Estate

The life of an urban slave might be very different to that of those on the larger agricultural estates. Let's not kid ourselves that the life of a slave was ever anything other than horrendous, but an urban slave might, in comparison to their rural cousins, be relatively comfortable. It is these urban slaves that are more valuable, better educated and more likely to be set free and then live pleasant lives as freedmen.

The life of an estate slave was more comparable to how we view slavery with our modern eyes, namely through the terrible experiences of African slavery. The following comes from Columella's *On Agriculture,* written in the first century AD, and serves as something of an instruction booklet for the wealthy estate owner. It outlines the treatment of the slaves on such an estate.

The next point is with regard to slaves - over what duty it is proper to place each, and to what sort of tasks to assign them. So my advice at the start is not to appoint an overseer from the sort of slaves who are physically attractive, and certainly not from that class which has been engaged in the voluptuous occupations of the city. This lazy and sleepy headed class of slaves, accustomed to idling, to the Field of Mars [the bohemian downtown area of Rome], the circus and the theatres, to gambling, to taverns, to bawdy houses, never ceases to dream of these follies; and when they carry them over into their farming, the master suffers not so much loss in the slave himself as in his whole estate.

Clearly, Columella warns against appointing as a foreman the type of urban slave he sees as lazy and feckless. It also highlights how the life of the urban slave can involve something of a life outside that lived in the master's house. We might have a view of slaves as living lives entirely 'locked up' in the house and not allowed any form of social life outside that house. But here we see urban slaves visiting taverns, prostitutes and theatres, and for that, of course, they needed money. Conversely, he is suggesting that the life of the estate slave is much more brutal and for that, the urban slave is incapable. What is clear is that urban slaves might not always remain in their relatively comfortable lives in the city and that such movement from the city to the estate must have happened frequently enough for Columella to warn against it.

A man should be chosen who has been hardened by farm work from his infancy, on who has been tested by experience ... He should be of middle age and of strong physique, skilled in farm operations or at least very painstaking, so that he may learn the more readily; for it is not in keeping with his business of ours for one man to give orders and another to give instruction, nor can a man properly exact work when he is being tutored by an underling as to what is to be done and in what way. Even an illiterate person, if only he have a retentive mind, can manage affairs well enough. Cornelius

Celsus says that an overseer of this sort brings money to his master oftener than he does his book, because being illiterate, he is either less able to falsify accounts or is afraid to do so through a second party, because that would make another aware of the deception.

But be the overseer what he may, he should be given a woman companion to keep him within bounds and moreover in certain matters be a help to him ... He must be urged to take care of the equipment and the iron tools, and to keep in repair and stored away twice as many as the number of slaves requires, so that there will be no need of borrowing from a neighbour; for the loss in slave labour exceeds the cost of articles of this sort. in the care and clothing of the slave household he should have an eye to the usefulness rather than appearance, taking care to keep them fortified against wind, cold and rain, all of which are warded off with long-sleeved tunics, garments of patchwork, or hooded cloaks. If this be done, no weather is unbearable but that some work may be done in the open. He should be not only skilled in the tasks of husbandry but should also be endowed, as far as the servile disposition allows, with such qualities of mind that he may exercise authority without laxness and without cruelty, and always humour some of the better hands, at the same time being forbearing even with those of lesser worth, so that they may rather fear his sternness than detest his cruelty ...

In the case of the other slaves, the following are, in general, the precepts to be observed, and I do not regret having held to them myself: to talk rather familiarly with the country slaves, provided only that they have not conducted themselves unbecomingly, more frequently than I would with town slaves; and when I perceived that their unending toil was lightened by such friendliness on the part of the master, I would even jest with them at times and allow them also to jest more freely. Nowadays I make it a practice to call them into consultation on any new work, as if they were more experienced, and to discover by this means what sort of ability is possessed by each of them and how intelligent he is. Furthermore, I observe that they are more willing to set about a piece of work on which they think that their opinions have been asked and their advice followed. Again, it is the established custom of all men of caution to inspect the slaves in the prison, to find out whether they are carefully chained, whether the places of confinement are quite safe and properly guarded, whether they overseer has put anyone in fetters or removed his shackles without the master's knowledge.

... And the investigation of the householder should be the more painstaking in the interest of the salves of this sort, that they may not be treated unjustly in the matter of clothing or other allowances, inasmuch as, being subject to a greater number of people, such as overseers, taskmasters, and jailers, they are the more liable to unjust punishment, and again, when smarting under cruelty and greed, they are more to be feared. Accordingly, a careful master inquiries not only of them, but also of those who are not in bonds, as being more worthy of belief, whether they are receiving what is due to them under his instructions. He also tests the quality of their food and drink by tasting it himself and examines their clothing, mittens, and foot covering. In addition, he should give them frequent opportunities for making complaints against those persons who treat them cruelly or dishonestly. In fact, I now and then avenge those who have just cause for grievance, as well as punish whose who incite the slaves to revolt or who slander their taskmasters; and, on the other hand, I reward those who conduct themselves with energy and diligence. Also, to women who are unusually prolific, and who ought to be rewarded for the bearing of a certain number of offspring. I have granted exemption from work and sometimes even freedom after they have reared many children; a mother of three children received exemption from work, a mother of more, her freedom as well. Such justice and consideration on the part of the master contributes greatly to the increase of his estate.

This last bit is terrifying. Whilst Columella is claiming to be generous and kind to his female slaves by granting them exemption from work (and by this, he means a form of retirement) and even freedom, he is doing so because they are bearing children. What he is not mentioning, clearly, by what he calls 'justice and consideration' is that he is keeping their children as new slaves. The mother may be given freedom, but they are not free to take their own children with them. Those kids remain the property of Columella. When he says 'the increase of his estate', he means an increase in slave numbers.

In the Imperial period, slave owners turned more often to breeding and rearing their own slaves than to replenishing slave stock as they did in the days of conquest when huge numbers of captured slaves - the booty of war - were dumped on a market that struggled to deal with so many.

What we also have to remember from Columella's advice that masters try treating their salves with some fairness, is that the only reason he is proposing this is to maximise productivity rather than to maximise kindness. It's also worth considering that by having to point out that being nice might result in more profit, that overseers and masters did not regularly treat their slaves with any kindness in the first place. There's also nothing here to suggest that any of them took his advice.

Piracy and Slaves

Piracy, which had always been rife throughout the Mediterranean, became a massive problem in the latter years of the
Republic. When Rome destroyed the sea power of Rhodes
in the second century BC, it removed the force that had
effectively policed the eastern end of the Mediterranean for
centuries. As Rome maintained no standing navy of its own
at the time, the floodgates to piracy opened, and from their
headquarters in Cilicia, on the south coast of Asia Minor, the
pirates swarmed all over the seas, creating mayhem. Initially, Rome met the pirate problem with some indifference
because the chaos the pirates caused could be offset by the
economic function they served. The pirates kidnapped thousands and, by doing so, supplied large numbers of slaves
which the Roman ruling classes snapped up for their estates
and urban homes.

As the number of kidnap victims soared in the first century BC, the market for slaves became saturated to the extent
that Rome no longer needed the pirates to supply them with
new stock. With their economic benefit waning, the pirates
simply became an annoyance, and Rome finally moved to
suppress them.

The Price of Slaves

The price of a slave in ancient Rome varied depending on the
gender, age, and skilfulness of the individual. The average
price for an unskilled or moderately skilled slave in the first
three centuries AD was roughly 2,000 sesterces. For reference, in the first century AD, a legionary received a salary of
about 1,000 sesterces per year – less following deductions
for rations, boots, and various other things. A centurion was
paid about 15 times more, so they only needed to save wages
for a few months to afford a slave.

Skilled slaves could cost considerably more. Elsewhere
Columella tells us that a vinedresser might set you back

between 6,000 and 8,000 sesterces. No problem for a wealthy landowner.

Roman households could have hundreds, if not thousands, of slaves, some of them highly trained and specialised, and fortunes were invested in buying servants as well as maintaining them. Some slaves were owned by the public purse and, therefore, paid at public expense. In first-century Rome, some 700 slaves worked on the maintenance of aqueducts.

The Mines

Some of the worst conditions were found in the mines. Slaves were forced to work with little rest in appalling conditions. The work was demanding and dangerous, with the constant risk of collapse. Diodorus Siculus, writing in the 1st century BC, described the horror:

> ... the slaves who are engaged in the working of [the mines] produce for their masters' revenues in sums defying belief, but they themselves wear out their bodies both by day and by night in the diggings under the earth, dying in large numbers because of the exceptional hardships they endure. For no respite or pause is granted them in their labours, but compelled beneath blows of the overseers to endure the severity of their plight, they throw away their lives in this wretched manner ... indeed death in their eyes is more to be desired than life, because of the magnitude of the hardships they must bear.

Being Kind

Contrary to Columella's advice that slaves be treated nicely to maximise profit, some people advised that slaves be treated kindly because they were people. This viewpoint was common among the Stoics, such as Seneca here, writing in *de Clementia*, but again, remember that Seneca still owned slaves and even if he considered them people, he considered them people who were 'below' him.

It is creditable to a man to keep within reasonable bounds in his treatment of his slaves. Even in the case of a human chattel one ought to consider, not how much one can torture him with impunity, but how far such treatment is permitted by natural goodness and justice, which prompts us to act kindly towards even prisoners of war and slaves bought for a price (how much more towards free-born, respectable gentlemen?), and not to treat them with scornful brutality as human chattels, but as persons somewhat below ourselves in station, who have been placed under our protection rather than assigned to us as servants.

It smacks a little of Seneca trying to persuade himself that he is doing no wrong by owning slaves rather than trying to convince the reader. He can call them 'servants under his protection' all he wants. They're still slaves.

Banquets

Whilst household slaves mostly enjoyed a better quality of life than those working in mines or estates, they too could be victims of physical, mental and sexual abuse. In general, they were required to perform tasks unseen unless, for example, when serving a banquet, where they would be required to not only provide perfect service but to play a series of roles and even be available for use by the guests. Here Seneca describes the abuse slaves were subject to in elite houses.

When we recline at a banquet, one slave mops up the disgorged food, another crouches beneath the table and gathers up the left-overs of the tipsy guests.

Another carves the priceless game birds ... Hapless fellow, to live only for the purpose of cutting fat capons correctly ... Another, who serves the wine, must dress like a woman and wrestle with his advancing years; he cannot get away from his boyhood; he is dragged back to it; and though he has already acquired a soldier's figure, he is kept beardless by having his hair smoothed away or plucked out by the roots, and he must remain awake throughout the night, dividing his time between his master's drunkenness and his lust; in the chamber he must be a man, at the feast a boy.

Chapter Five

OF GODS AND MEN

The Census

The Bible contains two accounts of Jesus's birth. One, Matthew 2, dates it to the reign of Herod the Great, who, by common acceptance, died in 4BC. The second, Luke 2, dates it to the time of the census held in Judea by Quirinius, governor of Syria, in 6AD.

> And it came to pass in those days, that there went out a decree from Caesar Augustus that all the world should be taxed. (And this taxing was first made when Cyrenius was governor of Syria). And all went to be taxed, every one into his own city. And Joseph also went up from Galilee, out of the city of Nazareth, into Judaea, unto the city of David, which is called Bethlehem; (because he was of the house and lineage of David:) (Luke 2.1-4)

The census is often a source of contention, with some claiming it never happened. However, a tombstone dedicated to a soldier named Quintus Aemilius Secundus, found in Beirut and dated to around 20AD contains the following line:

iussu Quirini censum egi Apamenae civitatis millium homin(um) civium CXVII

"On the orders of Quirinius, I took the census in Apamea, a city of 117,000 people."

Apamea is now in modern-day Syria but in the first century AD, was in Judea. In 6AD, Quirinius removed the ethnarch and son of Herod, Archelaus, from his position as a Roman client ruler in Judea when he became governor of Syria. He then ordered the census in the neighbouring province as a precursor to fully integrating it into the Empire. Although the two accounts of the birth of Jesus are contradictory in many respects, not least the ten-year gap between them, it is absolutely demonstrable that the census occurred.

Curses

One of the ways people could interact with the gods, who for most of the time couldn't give two shits what humans were up to, was to entreat them to perform some horrible curse on or cast some weird spell at someone you didn't like, for whatever reason. The pagan gods weren't arbiters of human morality, so if you asked them to do something really shitty, and they did it for you, the moral repercussions of what they did was your problem, not theirs. The curse, or magic spell, could be written on a papyrus or a lead tablet and then deposited at a shrine, and some of them have been preserved, including this absolutely batshit example from the home of all things batshit, Egypt.

[To be wrought by the help] of a boy, with a lamp, a bowl, and a stand. I invoke thee, O Zeus, Helius, Mithra, Sarapis, unconquerable, possessor of honey, Melicertes, father of honey, abraalbabachambechi, baibeizoth, ebaibeboth, seriabeboth, amelchipsithiouthipithoio, pnoutenin, thereterou, iueueoo, aieia, eeoia, eeai, eueie, ooooo, eueoiao, ai, bakaxichuch, bosepsteth, phobe, biboth, the great, great Sarapis, samasphreth, odargazas, odarmagas, odaphar, ykiaboth, aphia, zelearthar, methomeo, lamarmera, potebi, ptebi, marianou, appear and give heed to him who has manifested before fire and snow, terrible-eyed-thundering-and-lightning-swift-footed-one, pintouche, etomthoout, opsianaeak, arourongoa, paphtha, enosade, iae, iaoai, aoiao, oeu…. Tell what I inquire of thee. Say as follows; Let the throne of the god enter, zatera, kyma, kyma, Iuageu, apsitardus, ge moliandron, bonblilon, peuchre. Let the throne be brought in. Then if it be borne by four men, inquire what they are crowned with and what precedes the throne. If he says "They are crowned with olive, and a censer precedes," the boy speaks true. The dismissal: Depart, lord, to thine own world, and to thine own thrones, to thine own orbits, and guard me and this boy, unhurt, in the name of the most high god Samasphreth. Perform [this divination] when the moon is in a firm sign of the zodiac in conjunction with beneficent stars, or when she is in favourable limits, not when she is at the full, for thus it is better, and thus is the divination performed in orderly fashion. But in other versions it has been recorded that it should be performed when the moon is full.

None of that is incorrect, or the result of my falling asleep on the keyboard, nor do any of those words make more sense than what you see here. That is verbatim what this magic ceremony requires be repeated.

Or, if you had a few coins riding on a horse in tomorrow's big race, you could always ask the gods to make sure the bloke you wanted to lose fell off.

I conjure you up, holy beings and holy names; join in aiding this spell, and bind, enchant, thwart, strike, overturn, conspire against, destroy, kill break Eucherius, the charioteer, and all his horses tomorrow in the Circus at Rome. May he not leave the barriers well; may he not be quick in the contest; may he not outstrip anyone; may he not make the turns well; may he not win any prizes. and if he has pressed someone hard, may he not come off the victor; and if he follows someone from behind, may he not overtake him; but may he meet with an accident; may he be bound; may he be broken; may he be dragged along by your power in the morning and afternoon races. Now! Now! Quickly! Quickly!

The Gods

In Roman and Greek polytheism, the gods were not all necessarily omnipotent, universe creating mega-beings, able to bend the forces of existence to their will at the snap of the fingers. Which is why there was so many of them. In the Abrahamic model, you only need one God because He can do whatever he wants, but Romans made do with more specialist divine beings with explicit powers to match.

The major difference between humans and the gods was that they had what might be best described as superpowers not available to humans, although some gods had more powers than others and the fact that they were immortal. Fans of the Marvel Universe will immediately recognize these superhumans in characters like Thor, whose fingers don't crackle with the omnipotence of the Christian God, but he'll live forever, and he can smash people through skyscrapers with a mallet.

It was not such a stretch of the imagination, therefore, to believe that a human could become a god, especially when such a person had either been given powers that most normal people don't have - superpowers, one might say - or had displayed such in life, either by daring deed on the battlefield or by the performance of some kind of 'miracle'.

Coins were minted in the same year of Caesar's murder bearing the motto DIVVS IVLIVS or Divine Julius and in 42BC, the senate and the people agreed and recognized him as a god. Accordingly, a temple to Divus Julius was constructed in the forum at Rome and was dedicated in 29.

Octavian, Caesar's adopted son, recognized the opportunity and seized upon it, naming himself *divi filius* - Son of a God.

In life, Caesar had been a man of unique power, far beyond that afforded to any other Roman, both politically and in terms of his prowess in war. A 'superman' if you like. That's halfway to being a god without even dying.

Worshipping living people had always been possible in the Roman world. More specifically, what was worshipped was specific elements of the individual's *genius* or guardian angel. A person's *genius*, which by its nature is divine or 'holy', watched over them from birth and imbued that person with their characteristics. It's the origin of the word genie. If someone of note was engaged in an activity where they needed the support of the people or just a little extra luck, then sacrifices, normally in the form of libations, could be offered to their *genius* to urge them onwards to their goal.

Imagine England football fans all fervently beseeching the genius of Harry Kane to help slot home the winning penalty in the World Cup by offering up a can of terrible, cheap lager over a hastily cobbled-together voodoo doll around the back of the stadium.

If one could then imagine that after death, such a person became non-corporeally immortal - a ghost if you will - then all the component parts of divinity were in place. Therefore, there was no reason why anyone would treat the idea of the Emperor becoming divine with anything but absolute conviction.

And there could be signs from the gods that helped that conviction stick. When Julius Caesar died in 44BC, a great comet appeared in the sky, the *Caesaris Astrum*, Star of Caesar, interpreted by Romans as the soul of the departed Caesar ascending to the heavens.

"When beggars die there are no comets seen." As Calpurnia puts it in Shakespeare's Julius Caesar. "The heavens themselves blaze forth the death of princes."

'Paganism' isn't a word you'll find used anywhere in either the Republic or the Early Empire period of Rome and was only ever used by later Christians to describe the polytheistic practices of people who were neither Christian nor Jewish.

The word 'pagan' comes from the word 'pagus' (Late Latin - 'paganus'), meaning a villager or a country dweller. It's the opposite of 'urban' and implies someone who is unsophisticated and simple. A country bumpkin, if you like.

By contrast, for the Roman polytheist, there was no word used to describe their common set of shared beliefs. For them, apart from the odd Jew or Christian or those who liked to tie themselves in philosophical knots, what they believed was as self-evident and as unassailable as understanding that the Sun came up and the Sun went down. There simply wasn't any need for a word to define what they were because they just were.

Although it's possible to go online and find a list of Roman (or Greek) gods and goddesses, their true number was unknown and unknowable. Especially when one began to factor in all the gods of other nations that they didn't even know about yet. The concept of a 'jealous' god who wanted no other to exist wasn't a credible option. All the gods existed, including the ones you'd never heard of yet, and if you weren't sure, you could just assume that one existed and start worshipping it. Consequently, the relationship between all these gods was also unknown, just like the relationship between all humans was unknown. It seemed unlikely, again like all humans, that all the gods even knew each other existed.

However, there were attempts to explain the relationship of some of the gods, particularly those who were worshipped in certain circumstances, such as the gods of Egypt or in cities where the worship of certain gods was traditional. To help with this, myths were formed about divine collaborations in which heroes, nymphs, gods, and minor gods could be said to be working together. Gods with similar attributes could be said to be different aspects of the same divine being. Minor gods of the wind, for example, could be lumped together as different faces of the same overall wind god.

But what if you didn't worship the gods? What would the gods do about it? The first theological hurdle to clear was, as discussed earlier that there were some gods that as yet they didn't even know about. It was, therefore, theoretically possible that there were gods that no humans knew about, and the consequences of not worshipping them were either nothing at all or manifesting in a way that wasn't particularly obvious. Perhaps all sorts of events could be ascribed to the 'revenge' of gods that humans were simply ignoring or didn't even know existed. But as humans seemed to be largely flourishing without them, did it even matter? Tragedy and misfortune could always be attributed to an angry god, but it was generally considered that gods had other things to do than to be constantly mad at humans. Humans were neither the perpetual playthings of the gods nor did they treat them as errant children who needed scolding and correcting in their ways.

However, to ignore a god that had openly demanded worship by appearing in a vision, delivering an omen or sending a message via an oracle was fraught with danger. When the god wanted your attention, you'd better give it. Rather than the gods treating humans like demanding children, it could be seen as being the other way around, with humans believing that the gods were always demanding something if only attention. Fail to maintain this supply of fawning and timely ritual and the gods might get annoyed. But if the god had no previous interaction with you, then you could rest easy that they would leave you alone, at least until they sent a sign that you'd better start grovelling, or else.

Miracles

Jesus wasn't the only person who healed the sick with miracles. Our old friend Vespasian, who didn't want to become a god, was pretty good at healing people, too. Here's what Tacitus has to say about one episode:

> One of the common people of Alexandria, well known for his blindness, threw himself at the Emperor's knees and implored him with groans to heal his infirmity. This he did by the advice of the god Serapis, whom this nation, devoted as it is to many superstitions, worships more than any other. He begged Vespasian that he would deign to moisten his cheeks and eyeballs with his spittle. Another with a diseased hand, at the counsel of the same god, prayed that the limb might feel the print of a Caesar's foot. At first Vespasian ridiculed and repulsed them. They persisted and he, though on one hand he feared the scandal of a fruitless attempt, yet on the other, was induced by the entreaties of the men and by the language of his flatterers to hope for success. At last he ordered that the opinion of physicians should be taken, as to whether such blindness and infirmity were within the reach of human skill. They discussed the matter from different points of view. "In the one case", they said, "the faculty of sight was not wholly destroyed and might return, if the obstacles are removed; in the other case, the limb, which had fallen into a diseased condition, might be restored if a healing influence were applied; such, perhaps, might be the pleasure of the gods, and the Emperor might be chosen to be the minister of the divine will; at any rate, all the glory of a successful remedy would be Caesar's, while the ridicule of

failure would fall on the sufferers". And so Vespasian, supposing that all things were possible to his good fortune, and that nothing was any longer past belief, with a joyful countenance, amid the intense expectation of the multitude of bystanders, accomplished what was required. The hand was instantly restored, and the light of the day shone again upon the blind.

The Graeco-Roman god of medicine, Aesculapius, performed his 'medicine' via the medium of miraculous cures. Of course. What were you expecting him to do? Hand out Aspirin?

> In these very days [Aesculapius] gave a response to a certain Gaius, a blind person, to go to the sacred platform and make obeisance, then to go from right to left and place his five fingers on the platform and lift up his hand and place it on his own eyes; and he recovered his sight, in the presence of the populace, who rejoiced that the active divine powers manifested themselves during the reign of our Augustus, Antoninus [Caracalla].

> [Aesculapius] gave a response to Lucius who was suffering from pleurisy and was given up in despair by everyone, to go and lift up the ashes from the altar and mix well with wine and apply it to his side; and he was saved, and he gave thanks to the god publicly, and the populace rejoiced with him.

> [Aesculapius] gave a response to Julianus, who was spitting up blood and had been given up in despair by everyone, to go and lift up from the altar pine-cone seed and eat them with honey for three days; and he was cured, and he came and gave thanks publicly before the populace.

> The god gave response to the blind soldier Valerius Aper that he should go and take blood from a white

cock and mix an eye salve with honey, and smear it on his eyes for three days; and he recovered his sight, and he came and gave thanks publicly to the god.

Christians

To those superintending the sacrifices of the village of Theadelphia, from Aurelia Bellias, daughter of Peteres and her daughter Capinus. We have sacrificed to the gods all along, and now in your presence according to orders I poured a libation and sacrificed and tasted of the sacred offerings, and I request you to subscribe this for us. Farewell [signatures] We, Aurelius Serenus and Aurelius Hermas, saw you sacrificing. Signed by me, Hermas

So what? Some people made a sacrifice. Big deal. Well, this papyrus is an example of a 'loyalty certificate' issued by the Emperor Decius whereby everyone was required to demonstrate that they were loyal to the pagan gods and the cult of the Emperor. The point was to weed out Christians, and although there's no evidence that the people in this example were Christians, many of them managed to obtain such certificates either by bribery, influence, or by openly performing pagan sacrifice whilst mentally keeping their fingers crossed. The question of readmitting such certificate holders after the persecutions were over caused some excitable discussion among Church authorities.

Funerals

Whilst the funerals of the elite were major events, with all the pomp you'd expect, the funerals of the lower classes were much simpler affairs. Most of them happened at night or before dawn, partly because some people thought that the gods might get angry about all the dead people being hauled into the temple and at night they couldn't see it happening, and partly because carrying a stinky, potentially disease-ridden corpse through the streets in the middle of the day wasn't a good idea for several reasons. The risk of infection from a body was well known, and for that reason, it was forbidden to bury a corpse within the city walls. Any cemeteries that are now within city walls started life outside of them and were subsumed into the city as it grew.

The pallbearers would be made up of male relatives or slaves, particularly those who stood to gain their freedom from their master's death. Any eulogy would be read at the graveside, but it wouldn't be required that any sort of priest attend the service.

One of the most popular ways of guaranteeing a good send-off was to hire professional funeral musicians who would turn up and play something suitably sad for you. This became a bit of an issue when people paid small fortunes for whole orchestras of flute-tooting misery merchants to swan about behind the byre, jamming up the streets and making a racket. Sumptuary laws limited the number of flute players, depending on certain criteria, and there could be trumpet and horn players, too, making a fearful din.

Jesus Christ

The Roman writer Josephus mentions 'Jesus' twice. Not some random Jesus, but *the* Jesus. The water-into-wine, walk-across-my-swimming-pool one. He also mentions a few other people called Jesus, but who cares about them? One passage from his works is widely known to have been altered somewhat by the hands of nefarious monks, probably sometime after the 11th Century. The other, however, which mentions 'James, brother of Jesus', is believed to be entirely the work of Josephus himself. In *Antiquities of the Jews*, (XX.ix.i), he writes:

When, therefore, Ananus was of this disposition, he thought he had now a proper opportunity. Festus was now dead, and Albinus was upon the road; so he assembled the Sanhedrin of judges, and brought before them the brother of Jesus, who was called Messiah, whose name was James, and some others. And, when he had formed an accusation against them as breakers of the law, he delivered them to be stoned. But as for those who seemed the most equitable of the citizens, and such as were the most uneasy at the breach of the laws, they disliked what was done; they also sent to the king, desiring him to send to Ananus that he should act so no more, for that what he had already done was not to be justified; nay, some of them went also to meet Albinus, as he was upon his journey from Alexandria, and informed him that it was not lawful for Ananus to assemble a Sanhedrin without his consent. Whereupon Albinus complied with what they said, and wrote in anger to Ananus, and threatened that he would bring him to punishment for what he had done; on which king Agrippa took the high priesthood from him when he had ruled but three months, and made Jesus, the son of Damneus, high priest.

James, brother of Jesus, is not to be confused with a bunch of other people called James (including me!) Especially James, one of the 12 disciples. The brothers of Jesus are normally considered to be the *adelphoi*, James, Simon, Jude and Joses. Whether these are actually brothers of Jesus is a controversial talking point. They might have been cousins or stepbrothers from a previous relationship by Joseph. There are two sisters, too, but they aren't named because women don't matter much in the ancient world, even sisters of gods. So, when Josephus uses the term 'brother of Jesus', he is not suggesting that he was a colleague of his, or a camp follower of his, or an attendee to a sect that followed Jesus; he is definitively calling him his brother.

This James is the one mentioned in *Acts* 21. He is the one the Apostle Paul visits in Jerusalem to deliver funds raised for the Christians there. James is one of the people the Risen Christ appears to in *I Corinthians* 15. He's one of the Three Pillars of the Church from *Galatians* 2, alongside Peter and John the Apostle. James is the one who performs the circumcision of Gentiles who wish to become Christian. It is James who demands Paul ritually cleanse himself at the Temple to demonstrate his faith.

This James is a big player in Jerusalem's early Christian history. It's not some other James who just happened to have a brother called Jesus, because the Sanhedrin, the legislative and judicial body of Jewish elders, is specifically assembled to try him, against the direct orders of the Roman governor Albinus. Such meetings aren't called for when dealing with some bloke called James who has stolen a gourd. The Sanhedrin, for example, was assembled for the trial of Jesus Christ.

And the crucial thing is that during the year 65AD, both James and Josephus, who was still called Yosef ben Matityahu at that point, but important enough to become, at some point, the rebel leader of an army of 60,000 men, lived in Jerusalem. They were both important men in the city. Josephus almost certainly *knew* the brother of Jesus.

The Abyss

Seneca the Younger, ever the Stoic, sums up the march of time in this doom-laden prophecy. The Stoics were big fans of the cyclical nature of history first espoused by Greek historians.

The entire human race, both present and future, is condemned to death. All the cities that have ever held dominion or have been the splendid jewels of Empires belonging to others - some day men will ask where they were. And they will be swept away by various kinds of destruction: some will be ruined by wars, others will be destroyed by idleness and a peace that ends in sloth, or by luxury, the bane of those of great wealth. All these fertile plains will be blotted out of sight by a sudden overflowing of the sea, or the subsiding of the land will sweep them suddenly into the abyss.

More Christians

When Pliny the Younger was governor of Bythinia-Pontus from 111-113AD (it's on the north coast of Turkey, to save you the bother), he wrote a series of letters back to the Emperor Trajan asking for advice on all matter of legal questions, which go some way towards showing us what Emperors got up to all day - answering letters from fucking Pliny - and how the minutiae of legal flimflam was administered in the provinces.

In one very famous example, Pliny has made some new friends he calls 'Christians' and he knows they're a rotten bunch, but he's not sure what to do about them legally. he writes to Trajan for advice:

It is my preference, my lord, to refer to you all matters concerning which I am in doubt. For who can better give guidance to my hesitation or inform my igno-rance? I have never participated in trials of Christians. I therefore do not know what offences it is the practice to punish or investigate and to what extent. And I have been not a little hesitant as to whether there should be nay distinction on account of age or no difference between the very young and the more mature; whether pardon is to be granted for repentance, or, if a man has once been a Christian, it does him no good to have ceased to be one; whether the name itself, even without offences, or only the offences associated with the name are to be punished.

Meanwhile, in the case of those who were denounced to me as Christians, I have observed the following procedure: I interrogated these as to whether they were Christians; those who confessed I interrogated a second and a third time, threatening them with punishment; those who persisted I ordered executed. For I had no doubt that, whatever the nature of their creed, stubbornness and inflexible obstinacy surely deserve to be punished. There were others possessed of the same folly; but because they were Roman citizens, I signed an order for them to be transferred to Rome.

Pliny then goes on to describe the customs of Christians, sounding aghast that they "sing responsively a hymn to Christ as to a god.." and how they meet up on a fixed day to -get this - eat ordinary food. He postpones his investigations, noting that although the superstition is spreading, the temples are still full and people might be reformed if an opportunity for repentance is given.
Trajan writes back:

You observed proper procedure, my dear Pliny, in sifting the cases of those who had been denounced to you as Christians. For it is not possible to lay down and general rule to serve as a kind of fixed standard. They are not to be sought out; if they are denounced and proved guilty, they are to be punished, with this reservation, that whoever denies that he is a Christian and really proves it - that is, by worshipping our gods - even though he was under suspicion in the past, shall obtain pardon through repentance. But anonymously posted accusations ought to have no place in any prosecution. For this is both a dangerous kind of precedent and out of keeping with [the spirit of] our age.

Chapter Six

THE
ROMAN PEOPLE

The Races of Man

Here, Vitruvius, in his work *on Architecture*, starts trying to explain the difference between those who live in the 'south', so the southern Mediterranean area, and those who live in the 'north', so swarthy German barbarians and so forth. He puts Rome right in the middle. How this has anything to do with architecture, I don't know, but off he goes!

Southern peoples, owing to the rarity of the atmosphere, with their minds rendered acute by the heat, are more readily and swiftly inclined to resourcefulness in planning; but northern peoples, steeped in a thick climate amid reluctant air, are chilled by the damp and have sluggish minds. We can observe this in the case of snakes: they move quickest when the heat has drawn away the damp with its chilling effect; but in the cold and wintry seasons they are chilled by the change of climate, and are sluggish and motionless. Hence we need not wonder if warm air renders the human mind more acute, and a cool air impedes.

Now, while the southern peoples are of acute intelligence and infinite resource in planning, they give way when courage is demanded, because their strength is drained away by the sun; but those who are born in colder regions, by their fearless courage are better equipped for the clash of arms, yet by their slowness of mind they rush on without reflection, and through lack of tactics are balked of their purpose. Since, therefore the disposition of the world is such by nature, and all other peoples differ by their unbalanced temperament, it is in the true mean within the space of all the world and the regions of the earth that the Roman people hold its territories. For in Italy the inhabitants are exactly tempered in either direction, both in the structure of the body and by strength of mind corresponding to their courage. For just as the planet Jupiter is tempered by running in the middle between the heat of Mars and the cold of Saturn, in the same manner Italy presents laudable qualities which are tempered by admixture from either side both north and south, and are consequently unsurpassed. And so by its policy it shatters the courage of the barbarians and by its strong hand the plans of the southerners. Thus the divine mind placed the state of the Roman people in an excellent and temperate region in order that it might obtain dominion over the whole world.

Women

It might come as a surprise to find women in a class of their own. After all, there are rich women poor women and slave women. They could be wives of Senators, Emperors, plebs or, as we saw, slaves. So why have I chosen to put them in a class of their own? The answer is quite straightforward; Roman society treated them as a class apart. In legal terms, women had very few, if any rights that extended beyond those of their husbands or guardians, even if this distinction became less obvious in the Empire, where everyone lived under the rule of one man. The Imperial period also allowed women to take more prominent positions, as wives and mothers of Emperors, than they ever had under the Republic, but that greater exposure didn't manifest itself in greater rights. Again it's impossible to paint a full picture of the lives of women because history ignores both their narrative and their actual voices. It's very much a man's world and the history of it is written from a man's viewpoint. Women are incidental to their own narratives and when they do appear in the story, it's as a bitch, a witch or a whore. Women don't get their own metanarratives in history unless they are snake-haired monsters, snake-hipped enchantresses or Machiavellian schemers out to ruin the greater plans of men.

What we see is a world in which their rights are severely curtailed and their absence from the wider narrative says volumes about how the patriarchal society treated them. They were controlled and corralled from birth until death and they were expected to act in ways in public that adhered to extremely restrictive codes.

The social status of a woman relied entirely on that of her husband or her nearest male relations. Even though in the late Republican and early Imperial periods, women had begun to gain a measure of financial freedom, the law offered them very little in terms of practical freedom, certainly within the family. Widows could gain more freedom than most, but even then they were expected to be restricted by a male guardian.

Women who were emancipated (the legal process of being released by your father, as opposed to the modern use of freeing slaves) or unmarried when their father died, had their control handed over to a tutor, a male guardian who was the nearest male relative on their father's side (if possible), which might, of course, mean their own son. A measure of financial freedom, or at least the ability to control family finances, might come with marriage.

Marriage itself was essentially just a private agreement between two people to live together in union. There was no such thing as a marriage certificate or any form of required ceremony. A public wedding ceremony was just an excuse for a party. There was a tradition of formally handing over control of the bride from her father to her new husband, but by the Imperial period, this was as informal as the father of the bride 'handing over' his daughter is today. On the other hand, a new custom of the gift of dowry had become common and this could be demanded back, from the husband, if there was a divorce. Divorce itself was as simple as marriage was. Two people who agreed to get married could simply agree to be unmarried again and either side had the same right to initiate it, with some exceptions. The only financial obligations in a divorce revolved around the dowry. This also meant, however, that a divorced woman had no claim over her ex-husband's wealth outside of that dowry whilst he, if she owned anything at all, could keep it. She could inherit his wealth if she was named an heir, but not simply by dint of being his wife. If he died without naming her in his will, any money would go to the children (with the sons, of course, getting the lion's share) and she might only get what they decided she deserved, if anything at all. Daughters could also be named as heirs by their fathers.

Widows might then be expected to have a good degree of financial independence, especially if they could persuade a magistrate to free them from their guardians. Even without that freedom, a formidable woman with a lot of money could be too much for a young guardian male to 'handle'.

Pliny the Younger tells a tale (Letters, 7.24) of an extraordinary widow named Ummidia Quadratilla who lived to be 80 and was not only drippingly rich but lived her life exactly how she wanted, much to the evident embarrassment of Pliny and his 'friend' (conspiratorial wink), her grandson Ummidius Quadratus, whom Pliny described as 'extremely beautiful'.

He lived in the family of his grandmother, who was exceedingly devoted to the pleasures of the town, with great severity of conduct, yet at the same time with the utmost compliance. She retained a set of pantomimes, whom she encouraged more than becomes a lady of quality. But Quadratus never witnessed their performances, either when she exhibited them in the theatre, or in her own house; nor did she exact his attendance. I once heard her say, when she was commending her grandson's oratorical studies to my care, that it was her habit, being a woman and as such debarred from active life, to amuse herself with playing at chess or backgammon, and to look on at the mimicry of her pantomimes; but that before engaging in either diversion, she constantly sent away her grandson to his studies: a custom, I imagine, which she observed as much out of a certain reverence, as affection, to the youth.

I was a good deal surprised, as I am persuaded you will be, at what he told me the last time the Sacerdotal Games were exhibited. As we were coming out of the theatre together, where we had been entertained with a contest of these pantomimes, "Do you know," said he, "this is the first time I ever saw one of my grandmother's freedmen dance?" Such was the conduct of the grandson; while a set of men of a far different stamp, in order to do honour to Quadratilla (I am ashamed to employ that word to what, in truth, was but the lowest and grossest flattery) used to flock to the theatre, where they would rise up and clap in an excess of admiration at the performances of those pantomimes, slavishly copying all the while, with shrieks of applause, every sign of approbation given by the lady patroness of this company. But now all that these claqueurs have got in pay is only a few trifling legacies, which they have the mortification to receive from an heir who was never so much as present at Quadratilla's shows.

Retaining 'a set of pantomimes' is a shockingly brazen display for a wealthy lady about town, especially one of her advanced age (she died at the age of 80), especially as she has them dancing in her own house. Actors, pantomimes and gladiators are all people who, by profession, sell their bodies for public consumption and as such are on the same social level as prostitutes. Pantomimes were troops of dancers and actors made up entirely of young men. Young men who would dance for her whilst not wearing very much. Quadratilla is not employing them for their dancing skills, let's put it that way. She is having the time of her life, good on her.

Quadratus is at pains to say that he has never seen any of this shameful nonsense going on and has nothing to do with it. He's also admitting, by extension, that he cannot stop her from doing it, even if he wants to. And he clearly wants to because her lewd conduct with these scantily clad dancers is a potential barrier to his own career in public life. The whole point of this letter and account is for him to try and distance himself from his grandmother's actions because he is supposed to be able to control her and he very clearly can't.

Considering how little we know about Roman women and how narrow the window is on their lives, Quadratilla is still one of the coolest people in ancient Roman history. She was absolutely badass and she didn't give a fuck who knew it.

Other literary sources and funerary inscriptions give a good idea of what qualities were deemed desirable in a woman. Women were expected to be proud of having known only one husband; there was even a word for it - *univira*. No such label for a man, of course. In the same way, the fidelity of wives was extolled as a virtue on tombstones, as much as a badge of honour for him as for her. Adultery, one of the moral degeneracies that Augustus tried to clamp down on, could be punished by the wronged husband who could retain the dowry, or part of it, and sue and even kill the wife's lover. There were no corresponding tariffs against a philandering husband. Monogamy was the norm, even if some level of infidelity might be excused as long as the sanctity of the marriage agreements were stuck to. Nobody expected widows or widowers to remain faithful to dead spouses.

Plebs

The plebeian class in the city of Rome itself, was comprised of the common people who were not part of the aristocracy or patrician class. They formed the majority of the urban population and were essential to the functioning of the city. The plebeians in Rome were primarily comprised of small landowners, artisans, labourers, merchants, and freed slaves. They lived in crowded apartment buildings known as *insulae*, and often faced economic hardship and social inequality.

The provision of free corn to the plebs had been instigated by Clodius Pulcher in 58BC as a means of increasing popularity at a time when it was considered that the people's vote actually had some power. As such, appealing to this class specifically became the focus of later Emperors, even if the democratic power was all but gone. Augustus, who made a point of letting everyone know his generosity to the plebs, redefining them as no longer 'everyone else' but as distinct set of people entitled to the free corn dole by the provision of a special ticket. Incongruously, the dole of free corn was given not to the destitute or poor, who might have benefited most from it, but to the more respectable plebs of middle class means whose support the Emperor could more rely on. These were the people who would take such pride in their status as citizens and in their city that the maintaining of the status quo was in their own, and hence the Emperor's, best interests. The actual poor people could fend for themselves. Nobody cared about them.

The living conditions of the plebeians in ancient Rome were often challenging. Many lived in cramped and poorly constructed multi-story apartment buildings, where they faced the constant threat of fire, collapse, and unsanitary conditions. The majority of plebeians worked as labourers, artisans, and merchants, and struggled to make ends meet in a highly competitive and stratified society.

Despite their economic challenges, the plebeians played a vital role in the daily life of ancient Rome. They formed the backbone of the urban workforce, contributing to the construction, trade, and commerce of the city. Many plebeians were also involved in the production of goods and services that sustained the urban population.

The plebeians in Rome also had their own political and social institutions. They were represented in the Roman government by tribunes, who advocated for their interests and had the power to veto the decisions of the patrician magistrates. The plebeians also had their own assembly, the Plebeian Council, where they could voice their concerns and pass resolutions that directly affected their lives.

Over time, the plebeians in Rome gained greater rights and opportunities. They were eventually allowed to hold public office, and some rose to prominence as successful businessmen, artisans, and even military leaders. Interactions between the plebeian and patrician classes became more common, contributing to a more integrated and cohesive society within the city of Rome.

Know Your Place, Women!

Women aren't very clever. Look. Don't blame me, alright? That's not the point of view of this writer. But it's certainly true that whilst some Roman women were educated, even the lower class ones, they were crushed by arguably the most patriarchal system ever devised. As a result, women weren't deemed capable of looking after themselves and needed a guardian at all times. Here's Cicero's view on the matter:

> Our ancestors established the rule that all women, because of their weakness of intellect, should be under the power of guardians.

Guardians are appointed for males as well as females: for males only when under age, on account of their tender age; but for females when under and of age; on account of the weakness of their sex and their ignorance of business matters.

The Atilian Law orders that, for women and for wards who have none, guardians be granted by the praetor and a majority of the tribune of the plebs, and these we call Atilian guardians. But, because the Atilian Law is in force only at Rome, it is provided by the Julian-Titian Law that guardians of such persons be similarly granted in the provinces also by the governors.

The guardians of male and female wards transact their business and give their authorisation; the guardians of women merely give their authorisation.
The authority of a guardian is necessary for women in the following transactions; if they take legal action in accordance with statute or judgement, if they undertake an obligation, if they transact and civil business, if they permit a freedwoman of theirs to cohabit with the slave of another, if they alienate saleable property.

Freedom?

Good news, ladies, you lucky things! You don't have to spend your whole life under the guardianship of some asshole. Oh no! You could be set free. One way of being set free was to do your job and breed. Women who had three children could apply to have their guardianship lifted under what was called the 'three-children privilege'.

......[laws have been made], Most Eminent Prefect, which empower women who are honoured with the right of three children to be independent and act without a guardian in whatever business they transact, especially those who know how to write. Accordingly, as I have been fortunate in being blessed with goodly offspring and am literate and able to write with a high degree of ease, it is with complete assurance that I address Your highness through this petition of mine with the object of being empowered to accomplish without hindrance whatever business I henceforth transact. I beg you to place it without prejudice to my rights in Your Eminence's file, in order that I may obtain your aid and acknowledge my eternal appropriate gratitude. Farewell.

There are then two signatures. One from the petitioner:

[Signed] I, Aurelia Thaisous, also called Lolliana, transmitted this for submission, Year 10, Epeiph 21 [263AD]

And one, rather dismissive, response from the official:

Your petition shall be kept on file.

Literacy wasn't needed for the petition, Lolliana has added that detail to give further evidence of her capability to conduct her own affairs. The official doesn't seem overly keen to grant her request.

This time, the official, faced with an illiterate woman who is being cajoled into something by two blokes, seems a little keener to do his job:

To Valerius Firmus, prefect of Egypt, from Aurelia Arsinoe. I beg, my lord, that you assign Aurelius Herminus to me as guardian in accordance with the Julian and Titian Laws. Submitted on May 21 in the consulship of Emperor Philip Augustus and Titianus. [245AD]. I, Aurelia Arsinoe, daughter of Sarapio, have submitted the petition requesting that Aurelius Herminus be appointed my guardian. I, Aurelius Timagenes, son of..... wrote for her since she is illiterate.

Unless you are under the control of another guardian, I grant you the guardian you request.

The City of Rome

When according to Suetonius, Augustus claimed that he found Rome a city made of brick and turned it into one made from marble; it's hard not to disagree. He spent hugely on building new temples and renovating old ones; a whole new forum alongside, but more glorious than, Julius Caesar's old one; enormous and spectacular aqueducts to fix the city's antiquated water supply, public baths for it to go somewhere, and new sewers to get rid of it again. He paved streets, and previously privately luxurious gardens were turned over for public recreation. Other Emperors were to keep the building going in their own style and erect buildings of equal dominance, such as Trajan with his baths and forum or Nero with the Domus Aurea, but nobody had a lasting effect on the city of Rome than Augustus.

The changes weren't confined to outward appearances, either. Augustus began to change the way the city was governed as a place where people lived and worked. The city was divided into fourteen *regiones*, each consisting of a set number of *vici*. Each *vicus* would have its own magistrate, who would oversee construction codes laid down by Augustus himself. In addition, each one would have its own municipal fire-fighting service to keep it safe. The walls and gates of the city were repaired, as much for the symbolic message of safety it sent as for protection from any lurking enemy.

Augustus was bringing order and structure - civic pride if you like - to the previous urban chaos of the city. Laws were introduced dictating who could sit where in the theatre. Everyone must know their place and be proud to take it. Even the plebs were allocated places not because they were 'lower' than anyone else but because that is where they could best express their own place in the city's hierarchy. Also, they smelled a bit, so getting them out of the way was nice. Rome might have been the biggest city in the known world when Augustus came to power and one of the most spectacular, but it was far from the most impressive. Augustus wanted the citizens of his new city to feel they were part of an ordered, civilized, and structured new regime and that this system would apply across the Empire. How could the city of Roma civilize the world if it couldn't first civilize itself? Within fifty years, he had transformed the city into one to rival any in the east and despite the trouble and decay of the third century, Rome was to remain one of the most glorious cities of the world well into the medieval period.

The Rome of Julius Caesar was another matter.

The city had expanded rapidly during the second century BC, becoming a sprawling mess of a metropolis as conquest and wealth attracted people from far and wide, across Italy and beyond. Slavery swelled the population and, on manumission, increased the ranks of skilled and unskilled citizens. By the middle of the second century BC, a good chunk of the population was probably descended from freed slaves and this number would only get bigger over time. The Plebian population of the city that became reliant on slavery later in the Republican and Imperial periods was largely made up of people descended from it. The ethnic background of this population was, accordingly, incredibly varied, ranging from North Africa to Germany to Syria, but the intermingling of these people went on without comment. Rome was many things, and an awful lot of those things were, in modern eyes, at least, terrible. It was always a dreadful place to be a woman, for example, or, obviously, a slave. However, the total absence of any form of racism is notable and likely explained by the diverse ethnic background on which the whole of Roman society was founded. Racism is something that later societies invented, sadly.

Despite what modern media might tell us, Rome had a wide and diverse range of people from all sorts of ethnic backgrounds. Exactly in what proportion is hard to say because nobody ever thought it worthy of mentioning. Iconography from the time shows people of all sorts of backgrounds, and Rome could certainly be snobbish to other societies, particularly to 'barbarians' who were seen as socially inferior. Certain communities were 'apart' from the norm because of their religious practices, such as Jews, who might be eyed with some suspicion, but skin colour never came into it. Compare this with the White Might fantasy world of the modern interpretation of the Roman demographic, and it's hard not to conclude that this is one area where the modern view of Rome gets it terribly wrong. Rome was a city as diverse, or even more so, than New York or London is today. When a movie like *Gladiator* has a sum total of two black people in it (one a slave and one a slave trader, naturally), you know that they have somewhat misunderstood the demographic of the Roman population. This way of depicting people of colour in an 'old-fashioned' setting is heavily influenced by our own Western views of where black people fit into what white people believe is uniquely their own history. In white history, black people were slaves, and because we consider Roman history to be white history, that's where they fit into it, too. If Hollywood puts a black person into a Roman movie, the only place it can find for them is in the same context as the history it understands - as a slave. In second century BC Roma, and beyond, people of all skin colours held the same positions as anyone else. Roman history is the history of the entire population of the European, North African and Middle-Eastern world. It's not just white people's history.

But what was the city actually like? Grotty is probably the best description. Huge and sprawling and diverse, certainly, but architecturally and in terms of aesthetics, not much. Hunkered around the forum were a few unimpressive public buildings. On the Capitoline Hill, some rather run-down old temples. When Augustus gained power, the new forum begun by Julius Caesar had yet to be completed but was set to be larger and grander than the previous one, with a new senate house and a temple to Venus underway. Next to that was a suburban area of great townhouses of the rich and elite, complete with landscaped gardens. Around them was a ring of cheaply built mud brick, wood and thatch apartment blocks. The very poorest lived in the streets, sleeping in the labyrinth of narrow passageways and alleys at night. The more well-off would have workshops or retail spaces at the front of the building from where they would hawk their wares directly into the crowded and teeming streets.

The streets themselves ran in seemingly random directions, reflecting the way Rome had grown naturally over the centuries, swelling like a tumour without, seemingly, any guided direction. In this way, it resembled more the urban, meandering sprawl of Victorian London than the carefully planned street and block system of a city laid out with purpose like New York. Augustus changed all that, charging those who ran the new *vici* with laying out regulated streets and replacing teetering slums with codified structures.

But as much as physical change, the changes brought about by Augustus were as much as changing the fabric of society. Augustus was not just trying to sweep away the detritus and mess of the streets but also trying to clean up what he saw as late Republican immorality and societal imprudence. He was not only trying to give Romans a city to be proud of but a society of which they could feel proud, too. For Augustus, the regeneration of the city was simply one part of an agenda of strengthening the morality of its people, fighting what he saw as sexual degeneracy, profligacy and sloth.

Roman society was dominated by a strict pyramid structure, with the Emperor at the top and slaves and plebs at the bottom and in between were the equites and the senatorial class, who together might be called the 'nobles'. Movement between these strata was almost impossible, with two exceptions. One could move up from the equites to the Emperor by force. Anyone could do anything by force, of course, but one of the best ways of moving yourself from the rank of general to the Emperor was to simply bash enough people over the head when they complained about you getting too big for your boots. Vespasian was a great example. The other was the possible movement from, incongruously, slaves who, on manumission, could move from the absolute bottom of society to the very shoulder of ultimate power, like Claudius' freedman, Narcissus, who not only became stupendously wealthy but powerful enough to dictate imperial policy. They could almost move outside of this pyramid system in ways that others simply couldn't. On manumission, a freed slave might be simply able to move wholesale into the same societal strata as his former master.

The Graffiti of Pompeii

The walls of the houses and shops facing the streets of Pompeii were prime canvasses for the graffiti of the day. Painted normally in red, they contain all sorts of messages from election campaigns to reviews of bars, from notices of entertainment and market days to the scrawling of drunks, shoppers and the lovelorn hopeless. In places, the walls are thick with them, painting a vivid kaleidoscopic picture of a vibrant street-life that was captured at a moment in time by the Vesuvian eruption.

The first set is all election notices dating from around 80BC

Lucius Aquitius, a fine man; settlers, I appeal to you to elect him duovir.

Numerius Barcha, a fine man, I appeal to you to elect him duovir. So may Venus of Pompeii, holy, hallowed goddess, be kind to you.

Your best friend - Marcus Marius. Elect him aedile!

Marcus Marius, a fine man; I appeal to you, settlers.

Marcus Marius; I appeal to you to elect him aedile.

Quintus Caecilius, a generous man; to be quaestor - I appeal to you.

Publius Carpinius, a fine man, I appeal to you to elect him duovir.

Publius Furius, a fine man, I appeal to you to elect him.

Lucius Niraemius, a fine man, to be duovir.

Marcus Sepumius, a fine man, I appeal to you, settlers - duovir

All very pleasant and well-behaved, so it seems. But not everyone is in such a positive and forgiving mood.

Numerius Veius Barcha, MAY YOU ROT!

Quinticus, let anyone who votes against him take a seat by an ass!

The following examples of graffiti are all contemporary with the Vesuvian eruption.

Twenty pairs of gladiators of Decimus Lucretius Satrius Valens, lifetime flamen of Nero son of Caesar Augustus, and ten pairs of gladiators of Decimus Lucretius Valens, his son, will fight at Pompeii on April 8, 9, 10, 11, 12. There will be a full card of wild beast combats and awnings [for the spectators], Aemilius Celer [painted this sign], all alone in the moonlight.

Market days: Saturday in Pompeii, Sunday in Nuceria, Monday in Atella, Tuesday in Nola, Wednesday in Cumae, Thursday in Puteoli, and Friday in Rome.

In Latin, the days of the week are named after Saturn, Sun, Moon, Mars, Mercury, Jupiter and Venus like they are in the Romance languages.

One of the most popular things to scribble on the walls of Pompeii were expressions of love, either because the author simply couldn't hold back any longer, or in the hope that the target of their affection would notice and fall hopelessly in love. Whether or not this worked isn't known, but it's a tactic people have been trying for millennia. The next one is a very famous example in which two people, rather strangely, have an argument about a girl via graffiti.

> The weaver Successus loves the innkeeper's slave girl, Iris by name. She doesn't care for him, but he begs her to take pity on him. Written by his rival. So long!

Successus isn't taking this shit lying down. He replies:

> Just because you're bursting with envy, don't pick on a handsomer man, a lady-killer and a gallant!

The first chap has the last word:

> There's nothing more to say or write. You love Iris, who doesn't care for you.

Some of the expressions of love are quite beautiful:

> I write at Love's dictation and Cupid's instruction:
> But damn it! I don't want to be a god without you.

As always, some people in love are having a hard time of it.

> Anybody in love, come here. I want to break Venus' ribs with a club and cripple the goddess' loins. if she can pierce my tender breast, why can't I break her head with a club?

Elsewhere, love can be celebrated:

Methe, a slave of Cominia, from the town of Atella,
loves Chrestus. May Pompeian Venus be propitious
in her heart to them both and may they always
live harmoniously.

Lovers, like bees, lead a honeyed life.
I wish!

The second line (velle!) appears to have been written in
another hand.

Sabinus, handsome guy -- Hermeros loves you

If you could feel the fires of love, (mule-)driver, you
would hurry faster, so that you could see Venus.

I love a charming young man. I'm asking you, spur on
(the mule), let's go! You've had a drink. Let's get going!
Take the reins and move it! Head toward Pompeii
where love is sweet. You are my...

Fortunatus loves Amplianda. Ianuarius loves Veneria.
We ask mistress Venus that you keep us in mind (and
also) that which we now ask of you.

Greetings to Primigenia from Nuceria. I wish I were a
gem-stone for no more than an hour so that I could give
you pressed kisses as you sign your letters.

But be careful, though. All that love in the air might get you
into trouble!

Take your lewd looks and flirting eyes off another
man's wife, and show some decency on your face!

Some graffiti had a more serious purpose. The graffiti below is part of a series of messages written at strategic points around the town during the Social War of the first century BC when Pompeii was at war with Rome. The graffiti details instructions for citizens in times of attack. They also tell us the original names for parts of the city. The Salt Gate was the original name for the Herculaneum Gate, for instance.

> Go by this route between the twelfth tower and the salt gate, where Marcus Atrius, son of Vibius, gives instructions.

With there being no Google Review available in ancient Rome, if you wanted to leave your opinion of an establishment you had just eaten, drunk or stayed at, you could simply go outside and scribble it on the wall for everyone to see. Maybe go around the corner a bit if you were unhappy though.

> We pissed the bed. I admit it, host, we messed up.
> If you'll ask me, 'why?' There was no chamberpot.

> Traveler, at Pompeii you eat bread (but) at Nuceria you will drink! At Nuceria, you will drink.

> May he who has given me payment for teaching have whatever he asks from the gods.

> Wine was received by the master on the 7th day before the Ides of April.

> Nuts, drinks(?) - 14 (coins)
> Pork rinds - 3
> Three (Loaves of) bread - 51
> Three cutlets - 12
> Four sausages - 8
> At Pompeii(?) 3 1/2 (coins)
> 1 pound of lard - 3 coins

Wine - 1 1/2 coins
Cheese - 1 1/2 coins
Olive oil - 1 coin
Bread - 2 1/2 coins
Pork - 4 coins

6th: Cheese 1, bread 8, oil 3, wine 3
7th: Bread 8, oil 5, onions 5, bowl 1, bread for the slave 2, wine 2
8th: Bread 8, bread for the slave 4, grits 1
9th: Wine for the winner 1 denarius, bread 8, wine 2, cheese 2
10th: ... 1 denarius, bread 2, for women 8, wheat 1 denarius, cucumber 1, dates 1, incense 1, cheese 1, sausage 1, soft cheese 4, oil 7

Apollinaris, doctor, slave of the Emperor Titus, had a good shit here.

Two friends were here, and they had a servant named Epaphroditus who was terrible at everything for the whole time, so they finally kicked him out. (Then?) they spent 105 1/2 sestertii most delightfully when they had sex.

These two are regular customers:

Apelles, the bedroom attendant, with Dexter, (slave) of Caesar, ate lunch here most agreeably and also had sex.

Apelles Mus (was here) with his brother Dexter. We had a great time (literally, lovingly had intercourse), twice with two girls.

Here, 'Bombycion' and 'Rufa' are not being judged at their ability to do the job. If you get the drift.

Bombycion sucks

The men of the third legion were here. Farewell, Rufa because you suck well.

Pleasure says: "You can get a drink here for an as, a better drink for two, Falerian for four"

Falerian was a fine wine from the Campania region. The poet Horace wrote odes to it, so it must have been good. Or strong. Elsewhere, a criminal is on the loose:

A copper pot is missing from this shop, 65 sesterces reward if anybody brings it back, 20 sesterces if he reveals the thief so we can get our property back.

People from one profession would just say hello to each other. Like Crescens.

Crescens gives greetings to the dry-cleaners (clothes launderers) here and everywhere.

The dry-cleaner Crescens says hi to the innkeeper!

Some of the graffiti are in the form of fun word games:

If someone by chance has noticed the games of the serpent, which the young man Sepumius cleverly made, if you are an audience member at the theatre or a fan of race horses, may you always and everywhere have the gods on your side.

The last one is written in the shape of a snake.

SVNIBAS OIVRVC SAL
(Sabinus to Curvius: hi!)

The names are written backwards.

Perhaps the most moving piece of graffiti from Pompeii is the following, very simple prostitute sign. For reference, an 'as' is the smallest coin available. It's the equivalent of a penny.

I am yours for 2 asses, cash.

One of the most famous example of Pompeiian wall doodling is where some wag, on the bottom of a wall covered in political graffiti, has written the following:

Admiror o pariens te non cecidisse ruinis qui tot scriptorum taedia sustineas

I'm amazed, oh wall, that you haven't fallen into ruins since you hold the boring scribbles of so many writers.

Seating Capacity

The following passage is taken from an anonymous document known as *Curiosum Urbis Romae*, written sometime in the middle of the 4th Century but based on earlier information. It lists the contents of each of Rome's fourteen districts—buildings, temples, shrines, and so on. It's a long and mostly not very exciting list, but out of interest, here's the entry for one well known district:

District III, 'Isis and Serapis', contains:

Mint; amphitheatre, which has 87,000 loca; great training school for gladiators, house of Buttius Praesens; central theatrical storehouse; Shepherd's Fountain; ... Baths of Titus and Trajan; Portico of Livia; camp of the sailors of the Misenum fleet; wards - 12; crossroad shrines - 12; block captains - 48; commissioners - 2; blocks of tenements - 2,757; private houses - 60; storehouses - 18; baths - 80; fountains - 65; bakeries - 16; area - 12.350 feet.

The amphitheatre, which has 87,000 *loca*, is, of course, The Colosseum. The term *loca* means running feet of seating space, and from this, we can calculate the seating capacity of The Colosseum at a little over 45,000.

Colossus

The following passage, from the *Historia Augusta*, records some of the works performed under the patronage of Hadrian, including the restoration of the Pantheon and the moving of a colossal bronze statue of Nero. It is also claimed here that The Colossus of Nero was redecorated and rededicated under Hadrian, but this is a mistake as that work was done under Vespasian. The Colossus once stood in the middle of, or on the side of, the boating lake that Nero had built outside his great Domus Aurea, the 'Golden House' he had constructed in the centre of Rome following the Great Fire of 64AD. Vespasian began the construction of the Flavian Arena partly on the site of the Domus Aurea and when Hadrian moved the Colossus to a site northwest of the Flavian Arena, one leant its name to the other, becoming the Colosseum.

He built public works in all places and without number, but he inscribed his own name on none of them except the temple of his father Trajan. At Rome he restored the Pantheon, the voting enclosure, the Basilica of Neptune, many temples, the Forum of Augustus, the Baths of Agrippa, and dedicated all of them in the names of their original builders. Also he constructed the bridge named after himself, a tomb on the bank of the Tiber*, and the temple of the Bona Dea. With the aid of the architect Decrianus he lifted the Colossus and, keeping it in an upright position, moved it away from the place in which the Temple of Rome now stands, though its weight was so vast that he had to furnish for the work as many as twenty-four elephants. This statue he then consecrated to the Sun after removing the features of Nero to whom it had been previously dedicated, and he also planned with the assistance of the architect Apollodorus to make a similar one for the Moon.

The Colossus is last mentioned as standing in the *Chronology of 354* after which its fate isn't known. It probably fell in an earthquake. The remains of the brick-faced masonry pedestal, once covered with marble, on which it stood were removed in 1936 on the orders of Benito Mussolini. The foundations were excavated in the 1980s and can be seen to this day.

Engineering Problems

Most large-scale infrastructure projects, particularly in the provinces, were carried out by the army. Senior officers might be qualified engineers or architects, and as such, certain legions became known for their capabilities in the construction of certain types of buildings. Such specialists could be called up from around the Empire to help out in other regions. While moving the entire legion simply to help build an aqueduct, say, might be impractical, the temporary secondment of one or more engineers from one legion to another is well known.

Such an example comes from North Africa and dates to about 153AD. A retired surveyor of the 3rd Augusta called Nonius Datus was called up to correct something that had gone disastrously wrong with the construction of an aqueduct to supply the city of Saldae (near Béjaïa, Algeria). Nonius Datus had carried out the original survey and then left. But when the work goes wrong, he is sent for to lend a hand. In the following inscription, he takes up the story:

I set out and on the way endured an attack by bandits. Although stripped and wounded, I got away with my team and reached Saldae. I met Varius Clemens [the procurator]. He took me to the mountain where they were crying over a tunnel of doubtful workmanship, which they thought had to be abandoned because the penetration of the digging of the tunnel had been carried further than the width of the mountain. It was apparent that the digging had strayed from the line, so much so that the upper tunnel turned right, to the south, and likewise the lower tunnel turned north, to its right. So the two ends were out of line and had gone astray ... When I assigned the work, so they knew who had what quote of digging, I set up a work competition between the marines and the auxiliary troop. And so they lined up where the mountain was pierced ... When the water flowed.

The reference to bandits shows that even at the height of the Antonine period, law and order out in the sticks was still sporadic. It also serves to remind us that the Empire didn't work entirely smoothly at all times.

The Humble Roman Soldier

The following account from Livy's *History of Rome* is a detailed account of the life of a humble soldier. It gives an idea of the career path of a citizen-soldier and an insight into their ordinary life.

Spurius Ligustinus ... requested the consul and the tribunes to permit him to say a few words to the people. With the permission of all he is reported to have spoken as follows: "Quirites, I Spurius Ligustinus of the Crustuminian trib, am of Sabine origin. My father left me a *iugerum* [about 0.623 of an acre] of land and a small cottage in which I was born and bred, and I am living there today.

As soon as I came of age, my father gave me to wife his brother's daughter, who brought nothing with her by her free birth and her chastity, and together with these a fruitfulness which would be enough even for a wealthy house. We have six sons and two daughters, both of them already married. Four of our sons wear the *toga virilis*, two the *praetexta**. I became a soldier in the consulship of Publius Sulpicius and Gaius Aurelius [200BC]. For two years I served as a common soldier in the army which was taken over to Macedonia, fighting against Philip; in the third year Titus Quinctius Flaminus made me, for my bravery, centurion of the tenth maniple of the infantry.

After Philip and the Macedonians were defeated and we were brought back to Italy and discharged, I at once volunteered to go with the consul Marcus Porcius to Spain [in 195BC] Those who during long service had experience of him and of other generals know that of all living commanders no one was a keener observer and judge of bravery. It was this commander who thought me worthy of being appointed centurion of the first century of the infantry. Again I served, for the third time, as a volunteer in the army which was sent against the Aetolians and King Antiochus.

I was made first centurion of the heavy infantry by Manius Acilius Glabrio [consul in 191]. After Antiochus was driven out and the Aetolians subjugated, we were brought back to Italy, and after that I was in campaigns in which the legions served for a year. Then I served in Spain twice, once under the praetor Quintus Fulvius

Flaccus [181BC], and again under the praetor Tiberius Sempronius Gracchus [180BC]. I was brought home by Flaccus among those whom, as a reward for their bravery, he was bringing home for his triumph.

I joined Tiberius Gracchus in the province at his request. Four times, within a few years, I held the rank of chief centurion; thirty-four times have I been rewarded for bravery by my commanders; I have received six civic crowns**. I have served for twenty-two years in the army and I am more than fifty years old. But even if I had not served my full time and my age did not yet give me exemption, still, Publius Licinius, as I was able to give you four soldiers to replace me, it would have been right that I should be discharged.

But I want you to take what I have said simply as a statement of my case. For my part, as long as anyone who is enrolling troops judges me fit for service, I will never plead excuses. What rank the military tribunes think that I deserve is for them to decide; I will see to it that no man in the army surpasses me in bravery; and that I always have done so my commanders and those who have served with me are witnesses. And as for you, fellow soldiers, though you are within your rights making this appeal, it is proper that, as in your youth you never did anything against the authority of the magistrates and the senate, so now, too, you should place yourselves at the disposal of the consuls and the senate, and consider any position in which you will be defending your country as an honourable one."

*The *toga virilis* was worn by Roman boys at the age of 16 or 17. Before that, the *toga praetexta*, which was distinguished by a stripe was worn.
**The civic crown was awarded for saving the life of a fellow citizen.

Chapter Seven

KINGS OF THE WORLD

Equites

Before the emergence of the equites as a distinct social class of their own, Roman society was divided into pretty much two sections. Senators and everyone else. Originally, as the name might suggest, the equites were wealthy individuals who could afford to serve in the Roman cavalry, where providing your own horse and equipment was required of you. By the end of the second century BC, this was redundant as the cavalry was provided by allied auxiliaries instead. They only became prominent as a social class when a law was introduced that judges in jury trials should be drawn from their number and their organisation as a distinct order, like that of the senate, can probably be assigned to the same time period.

The number of equites available was strictly defined at first as the first eighteen centuries of the centuriate assembly. Still, their number may have been more significant, particularly after their introduction to jury cases. There were financial requirements of a minimum of 400,000 sesterces per man, so broadly speaking, anyone who was more prosperous than that was, as long as the census confirmed their wealth, able to be called an *eques*. This financial tide mark was the same level of property value that was required of a man to enter the senate. As you can see, moving from the equite class to the senatorial one was relatively smooth in financial terms. All that was required, once you had demonstrated that you had enough money, was to be of the right age (25 or older) and ambitious enough to dedicate oneself to the pursuit of public office. Those who lacked the ambition or were too protective of their neck to enter the cut-throat world of public office were perfectly welcome to stay at equite rank, and it wasn't unknown for members of the same family to move up to senatorial rank and others to remain as equites. These two classes shared common interests, being the preserve of the landed gentry classes. However, they might also find themselves occasionally at odds, such as when contract disputes arose involving laws made by the senate or when a senator was on trial for something that he might expect his peers to do him a 'favour' in respect of.

Equites themselves had no political power or voice. They didn't need to. If that's what you wanted, you could move into public life. One could look at them as somewhat disinterested rich playboys. Gentlemen about town who spent their days at the club and whose broad interests were also those of the state. If one needed a political favour or two brought in, all one had to do was give a nudge or a wink in the right direction and then slip back to the couch with a glass of something red.

An annual parade of selected equites (5,000 of them, apparently) would be held by the younger members of the senate house, and roughly the same number held the office of juror under Augustus. Under Tiberius, all these and more came to be honoured under the broad title of 'the public horse' and were given the right to wear a unique gold ring and sit in the theatre's front row, as did the Senators. This official window-dressing might have given the equites some sort of public-facing role. A lot of them were the sons or nephews of Senators who not only didn't want to move into public life but, if they chose to, might have dislodged a father or uncle on the way up. It kept them happy and gave them a sheen of respectability that they otherwise might not merit.

Newly minted citizens could proudly boast of their new equestrian rank, even if they held no official or unofficial position, and were *eques* only because they had a lot of money. Add to that the title of procurator, which was often appointed directly by the Emperor from the equestrian ranks, and soon enough, there was an underclass of political ambition under the senatorial level to rival the clamour of that for public office.

Augustus's promotion of the equites was a pivotal moment in the social structure of ancient Rome. While he professed to be restoring the old ways of Roman tradition, his changes were far-reaching and innovative. He broadened the class by introducing a diverse range of Italian municipal families and wealthy provincials, some with no prior connection to Rome. This inclusivity extended to the Senate as well. By elevating the equestrian rank, he effectively bolstered the power and prestige of the senatorial classes, thereby enhancing their influence and status. Under Augustus, for the first time, the financial requirements for those in the senatorial class were higher than those for the equestrian. With the new prestige a senator could expect to enjoy, he was expected to be able to prove he had a cool 1 million sesterces.

Senators

The entire social fabric of Rome was intricately woven with the influences of the Imperial Court. From the most mundane aspects like haircuts to the more sophisticated elements like literary trends and theatre preferences, the court's decisions reverberated across the city. A new haircut for the Emperor meant a new trend for Rome. This interplay of power and influence is a fascinating way to date iconography.

At the centre of court life were the Senators who saw themselves as the natural heirs of the grand attitudes of the Republic and the values they at least aspired to follow were the noble aims of freedom of speech, military might, the dignity of office and the right to glory and honour. Nominally, at least, the Emperor saw himself as one of their number and the other Senators as equals. In practice, the Emperor was always superior, if only because he had his legion of Praetorians camped outside the city which held the threat of strangling people and throwing them in the Tiber just to remind everyone who the actual boss was.

Emperors would always weed from the Senate those they found unsuitable, openly antagonistic, or just plain annoying, and Augustus was no different, trimming those he found morally unworthy of the position until he had found what he considered to be a balanced body of the elite.

The irony of all this mildly competitive mutual appreciation was some incredibly pointless and rather banal self-importance. Of the Senators we know well, men like Tacitus and Pliny, most of them owed their position to nothing more than the patronage of consuls or Emperors. Nothing they did other than greasing the right palm, coming from the right family, or being obsequiously fawning at the right moment qualified them for their jobs. It wasn't a meritocracy. Most of what they actually did was tediously banal, so it seems. Anything of any importance was handled further up the food chain than themselves. Yet, they had convinced themselves that they were of such importance that minor tiffs and irrelevant squabbles over arcane laws and petty court cases became the grand affairs of state for men who considered themselves in such high regard. The actual day-to-day running of the Empire was done in the Imperial Palace, not the Senate House, and it was being done by advisers to the Emperor who were not only not Senators but not even politicians at all.

So what did they even do all day? How could these grand men of state have fooled themselves into thinking that their positions as Senators were in any way valuable?

There's always the element in such things as the 'Emperor's new clothes', where everyone can see what's wrong, but nobody dares mention it. This applied to many aspects of the machinery of the Roman state where people who were always one or two steps away from being hurled in the Tiber thought it wiser to remain silent than to put a head above the parapet and point out that things are, well, a bit shit. Nobody ever dared point out, for instance, that the total lack of any legal or constitutional framework surrounding the appointment of, or even the need for, a new Emperor was a really stupid way of running the state, mostly because Augustus had come up with it and he was a god. If Augustus had come up with the system, then who were they to point out that it was a stupid system? It is better to pretend the system was divinely inspired, and hence perfect than to change it. This is how, of course, one ended up with buffoons like Nero in charge. Rather than blame the system or Augustus, blame Nero. That's how many of the Emperors, even the bad ones, had their reputations posthumously ruined.

If Senators didn't have other jobs, like a magistracy, then they apparently didn't do very much apart from sitting around and convincing themselves they were busy. Pliny was an advocate in courts where wills were discussed and became a well-known expert on such legal matters. Either that or he sat about attending literary symposiums and chatting. Tacitus, when he wasn't writing, practiced the art of oratory - public speaking - thinking that this supposedly noble art was a pursuit as worthy as any great office of state.

The Senate only met twice a month, but even then not everyone attended. Prolonged absence might provoke murmuring in the corridors and require one to show one's face every once in a while, but the number of Senators necessary for a quorum was lowered several times to the extent that most of them could quite easily skip meetings altogether with little repercussion. The only Senators who might show up consistently were not those interested in executing the official business of the Empire because other people were doing that elsewhere, but rather the people who were most ruthlessly ambitious in public life. Doddery old Senators who just wanted the free wine and the front-row seats in the theatre could skip proceedings altogether.

There was a period between 18BC and 14AD when matters in the Senate House were effectively pointless. All the discussion occurred prior to the Senators being asked to vote on things. They simply became a body of electors. Tiberius made them feel more important by bringing them things to do, like judge cases of treason or adultery among high-ranking citizens and giving them essential roles in the election of magistrates, but it must have felt like a total betrayal when he slipped off to Capri in 26AD, into a semi-retirement and took all the important people of court with him.

It seems then that the only tangible benefit for a Senator, outside of the admittedly quite tempting honour and prestige, was the position of magistrate, for which they became uniquely eligible.

The position of proconsul, particularly in esteemed regions like Africa or Asia, was the pinnacle of Senatorial achievement. It was a role traditionally reserved for the most senior Senators, often ex-consuls. Reaching the top of the senatorial cursus and not being considered for such a position was viewed as a significant oversight. Tacitus even records the extreme reaction of one Senator who was passed over for nomination, a testament to the prestige of the role:

> Gaius Galba, meanwhile, and the Blaesi perished by a voluntary death.; Galba because a harsh letter from the Emperor forbade him to have a province allotted to him ...

Surprisingly, these prestigious positions held less power than one might assume. By the time of Caligula, proconsuls were not in direct control of a legion, a responsibility that had been transferred to the imperial legate. If it was military might the Senators desired, there were other paths to pursue, and they would have been more likely to achieve it earlier in their careers. The proconsulship was not a retirement position, as they didn't do much to warrant retirement, but it also didn't entail much more work. The opportunity to enhance one's status in the public eye at the end of life was seen as a great honour, despite the limited power it held.

Even with all these supposedly high positions, including priesthoods and the election of what were, in effect, substitute consuls, these were more window-dressing than any sincerely effective body of government. The Senators simply convinced themselves that all these whistles and bells were important and that by carrying out these otherwise tedious rubber-stamping exercises, they were somehow at the beating heart of the Roman state. Some effective power could be wielded if one was given control of one of the urban prefectures, but in reality, the greatest benefit of being a Senator was bathing in the reflective glow of being in the Emperor's extended milieu. As always in Rome, it was better to be seen pretending to be doing something in the right place than actually doing something in the right place. It was for this reason that all manner of Senators found themselves at theatre shows they had no interest in or enthusiastically attending gladiatorial contests they otherwise professed to find appalling. Be seen or be nowhere.

By the time of Tiberius, the Senatorial class was filled with people who aspired to but had no direct links to the grand old Republican families of two centuries before. This nouveau-riche class was partly because of the new wealth regulations. Rich old families tended to have many descendants, and their wealth spread among many heirs. Augustus had also granted the right to wear the *latus clavus*, the broad purple stripe on the tunic, to descendants of Senators down to the third generation, which meant the visual social cachet of being a Senator, or descended from one, was now pretty widely available to whole generations of people. Let's not forget that being seen was more important than actually doing anything. Thus, the actual Senatorial ranks tended to fill up with people yet to get aboard this particularly succulent gravy train. One didn't need to actually be a Senator if

Grandpa had been one, and you got to wear all the official badges of state because he did.

Augustus intended to make the Senatorial class the preserve of the elite but instead made it an Old Boys Club to which family members could be invited. Within a few decades, the practice of the *latus clavus* became meaningless as Emperors granted the right to wear it to anyone they fancied, even if they didn't qualify in any respect.

The origins of new Senators, as the old families wandered off into the distance, became as much about patronage as ability, with a whole rash of Senators coming from whatever regions the more senior Senators had an allegiance towards. Spanish Senators such as Seneca would promote Spanish-born nobles behind them. For a while, Gaulish Senators were all the rage, then Greek, then African. Poor old Britain never got a single one.

As new ideas became popular among the senior members or even with the Emperors, so did the number of new Senators who suddenly found themselves ostentatiously interested in the works of the Stoics, just like, say, Marcus Aurelius, who totally incidentally happened to also be the Emperor. What a happy coincidence. These new fellows could also take their responsibilities a little too seriously. The grand old moral stances of the Republican families were fine to espouse in theory, but rocking the boat by deciding to die on a particularly small hill might result in one dying on an actual hill, or at least at the bottom of the Tiber.

One chap, Thrasea Paetus, was so enthused with his right to speak freely in the Senate, which technically he was, that his loud protestations of his inability to do so implied that Nero was being autocratic by denying him the ability to speak freely. Which was fine, but this was Nero he was rubbing up against. Thrasea very publicly refused to attend the Senate in protest at Nero's supposed tyranny. Nero tried to refute the charge of tyranny by, because he was Nero, ordering Thrasea to kill himself. It got worse because Thrasea's son-in-law, Helvidius Priscus, tried the same trick under Vespasian, who wasn't taking any of his shit, either. Obviously, nobody in this family learned a lesson because his son, among others, was slaughtered by Domitian for the same thing. One can only assume they then learned to shut the hell up.

These seemingly heroic stands against oppression were utterly futile but also served to make all the other Senators look like fawning yes-men, which impugned the dignity of their office, if not their actual pride. They were supposed to be equals. Not only that, but some of the condemned were given trials by, you guessed it, the Senate. So not only did they appear cowards, but they were implicit in the tyranny they were apparently terrified of.

Most Senators preferred to see themselves not as timid lickspittles but as great men with a natural born tendency to aristocracy whose high status was the result of centuries of breeding and privilege, and their position was the result of patronage of the Emperor who was a peer, if an important one. They had convinced themselves that not only was the system infallible because Augustus had come up with it, so that they also agreed wholeheartedly with everything the Emperor said and did, because they were, nominally at least, part of the decision-making process. They agreed with him because otherwise they'd end up in the Tiber, but they would rather fool themselves than openly admit it.

For the Emperors, encouraging this self-delusion was beneficial. It not only served to give the Senators a sense of worth and reinforced the idea that they were actually doing something, but it also kept them from actually trying to do something and then interfering in the actual business of bashing people over the head and wrestling with barbarians. Augustus seemingly introduced laws that he thought the Senators might approve of or that looked as if he was further defining their role when in reality, their role and the laws introduced to govern it were rather meaningless. He introduced a law against bribing people to vote for them, suggesting that competition for places was so tight that Senators needed to hand out money in order to secure positions and then simply appointed everyone who was nominated to the Praetorian positions without a vote anyway.

Above all, Emperors needed compliant and contented Senators and any that weren't could just be drowned. So be contented or else. To help with their contentment, provincial governors were paid substantial amounts of money for their time, alongside the opportunity to boost their own coffers in ways legal and illegal. He also invented prestigious-sounding new positions, some of which were actually even vaguely useful, like city prefectures, and, above all, maybe, increased the visibility and public prestige of the office of Senator to glorious new levels. He stoked their pockets and stroked their egos.

In the late Republican period, the two things that seemed to drive the Senatorial lifestyle were sex and money. The rather boisterous lifestyles of excessive banqueting, bribery, and sexual freedom (homosexual as well as heterosexual) were used to cement ties between nobles. Augustus, ever the prude, introduced laws to restrict all this fun, designed to restrict spending on things like houses, jewellery and banquets. If there had been an expense account, he would have got rid of it. Tiberius tried to encourage the general population to settle down and start families, and he included the Senators in that moral crusade. The idea was to try and change the Senatorial lifestyle from one of society playboy to that of serious family man. Augustus promoted laws to restrict adultery and fornication under which, hilariously, he was eventually to accuse his own daughter and granddaughter. Augustus had been caught in a trap of his own making, forgetting that telling other people to behave in certain ways also requires one to act in the same way. Despite all this, the Senatorial lifestyle remained one of hedonistic debauchery. That the Senators themselves were the arbiters of their own behaviour, as long as the Emperor didn't watch too closely, only encouraged them. It took the rather more pragmatic and bourgeois values of Vespasian to finally put their shenanigans to an end.

State Bureaucracy

With the Senators safely engaged in their own policies of lolling about drinking and having sex whilst believing themselves to be some aristocratic elite, the Emperor was ultimately the sole power in the Empire. But, as we saw earlier, even the Emperors didn't operate in isolation, and the imperial household operated as its own bureaucratic system of secretaries, advisers, whisperers, freedmen, wives and children. In trying to maintain the illusion that the Emperor was simply the first among equals, it would never do to openly flaunt the possibility that one's wife held more political sway than any Senator or consul, but at the same time, whilst the public image of the happy Imperial Family did wonders for the Emperor's public image, there was nothing unconstitutional about it either. Mostly because there was nothing constitutional about any of this.

The Republic managed to conquer huge swathes of territory without ever having a centralised state bureaucratic system, something that some people find a little surprising, especially for a civilisation that was famous for the way it ran things with a brutal efficiency. That's not to say that there wasn't brutal efficiency; it was just that it wasn't state-wide. Magistrates relied on their own initiative and resources to run the affairs for which they were responsible, and at times, as we've seen earlier, this might mean that they were also financially responsible for it. This resourcing out of responsibility was convenient at times and inconvenient at other times. The slaves of magistrates could act as secretaries when required, taking dictation, doing the accounts and so forth. If more resources were needed, they could be drawn from the wider family or even from a circle of experienced and financially independent friends. It might also serve as an experience for those family members before moving into public life. Wives always gave advice, as would adult children, but ultimately, the decision was that of the magistrate himself.

The imperial family was no different. By the end of the Julio-Claudian period, the Emperor's extended family and hangers-on had become known as the *aula* (court), which began to take on some of the characteristics of the great Medieval courts of Europe with a king surrounded by dozens of whispering advisers and plotters. This entourage grew so big, as a family after family interbred with the only people they were societally and legally allowed to marry - each other - that by the time of Nero, the chattering classes of the Imperial Court could number in the hundreds and, by extension, into the thousands outside the throne room. Nero eventually began to realise that all of these wagging tongues belonged to people who were not only as equally removed from Augustus as he was, but they were as rich as he was and were also in charge of bodies of potentially quite angry men. In effect, if he could be Emperor, so could they be, and as there was no constitutional barrier to anyone being Emperor, and he had no heir, there was nothing to stop them from becoming Emperor either. Well, apart from his head still being attached to his neck, that is. No wonder he went a little barmy.

The Emperor would receive guests and friends in a particular semi-public outer throne room known as a *salutatio*, just like an Edwardian gentleman receiving visitors in one of his reception rooms, but admission to the deeper chambers, where the patronage of the Emperor was really given, was fiercely guarded. Even getting into the *salutatio* could be devilishly difficult, and one would have to run a gambit of stone-faced freedmen, some of whom took particular delight in denying access to the Emperor for no other reason than they recognised a former master among the petitioners. It must have been very publicly and painfully galling to appeal to the Emperor, only to be turned away at the door by someone who used to be your slave.

That most of these extended friends consisted of people from the elite classes of society was more than just a product of the Emperor moving in such circles. Although one might reasonably expect him only to have friends who were his peers, there was a constant wave of nobles from all over the place - Rome, the provinces, sons of client kings, foreign dignitaries - vying with the Emperor's nearest and dearest to be granted admission to the inner circle, even to the extent of people jostling for position to be introduced as potential lovers and future wives. There was no formal way to approach an Emperor to suggest a wife; you had to get her under the wing of an influential freedman and hope he could jostle her into a position where the Emperor might notice her. After Claudius' wife, Messlina, was murdered at the behest of his freedman Narcissus (see earlier), the other freedmen engaged in a fierce battle to see who could get their own candidate next in line, with Claudius constantly changing his mind as they were nudged before him. In the end, famously, his freedman Pallas got his pick, Agrippina, to the head of the queue, and she brought with her a little snotty kid called Nero.

Naturally, the whole court was filled with cabals, cliques, plots and rumours. At the centre of all this was the whim of the Emperor which, as one can imagine, might be some-what terrifying, even when the Emperor wasn't a deranged man-child like Caligula. Even dour old sour-puss Tiberius was known to challenge courtiers to drinking games and promote those who won. These same seemingly irrational whims could suddenly set the whole of society on a new course, from launching an invasion against some unsus-pecting barbarians to everyone suddenly wearing a new fashion in shoes. Access to this inner circle could be both invigorating and terrifying. A wiser man would keep his head down and stay out of it entirely, but to do so would keep them away from any promise of serious advancement in political life. It was a scary place to be close to and a scary place to be too far away from. Clever men could play the game per-fectly, genuflecting entirely when the focus turned on them and staring nonchalantly out of the window when things happened that you knew you shouldn't be seeing. Playing the game sometimes involved not playing the game at all.

Playing the patronage game wasn't the only thing the court was for, however, and when the important business of state came up, the Emperor's inner circle would shrink accordingly to only a few close advisers. Key decisions didn't tend to be made by chattering masses. It might be in his most intimate moments that the Emperor was best influenced, and, as such, only those extremely close to him could be said to have any consistent degree of influence over him. Augustus' wife, Livia, for example, was probably his closest confidant and adviser, to the extent that she could have been called the co-ruler, at least unofficially. His sons entered into more official positions within his retinue, but these are symbolic moves more than anything else. By the time of his death in 14AD, he directed the people of Rome to ask his slaves and freedmen if they should wish to discover the true financial state of the Empire. The number of slaves and freedmen had, over forty years, reached a huge number, and almost all of the imperial slaves could expect to be freed at some point in their servitude.

As a result, there were an enormous amount of freedmen knocking about with intimate knowledge of the inner workings of the state, and their names cropped up all over the records. By the end of Nero's reign, there must have been thousands upon thousands of them, all with knowledge of where the bodies were buried and with the ears of all the correct people in all the correct places. This super-sect of highly influential freedmen, who, in theory at least, had no allegiance to any particular social class or, particularly after the death of a certain Emperor, any allegiance to anyone apart from themselves, was a terrifyingly powerful prospect. And they knew it. The trouble is, the Senators knew it, too, and they didn't take too kindly to seeing the emergence of this large number of what were former slaves who held the same amount of power as they did.

Augustus managed to avoid any direct comparison by studiously avoiding treating his freedmen as social equals. He refused to dine with them nor permit them to flaunt their power in public. Claudius and Nero weren't so careful, and the humiliation Senators felt at seeing freedmen treated with the same respect as they were entitled to was cutting. Seneca recounts one example when the former master of the freedman Callistus was forced to wait outside his door while other Senators were ushered inside.

Under Nero, things got even more complicated. Senators had freedmen, too, and promoting them to positions of power in their own households was a wise thing to do. The problem was that by doing so, they risked being seen as copying the Emperor and whilst copying the Emperor might be seen as a good idea when it came to haircuts, copying him when it came to how one administered one's own power might be seen as an attempt at preparing to take that power. If you went around promoting your own freedmen with titles that were equal to those of the Emperor's freedmen, it began to look as though you were building your own imperial court that you could simply parachute into place once you'd poisoned the correct plate of mushrooms.

Emperors had freedmen *ab epistulis* (in charge of letters), another *a libellis* (in charge of petitions), another *a rationibus* (in charge of accounts) and so on. These, unlike Senators, were real jobs with real importance. Letters and requests flooded in from all over the Empire, not least from our old chum Pliny the Younger, and the Emperor couldn't possibly be expected to answer them all personally. The majority of them could be intercepted by secretaries and dealt with accordingly. Those the Emperor replied to personally were dictated to secretaries who then organised the reply, which might be checked and have a subscript added by the Emperor himself before being sent. Such an addition might only be a personal greeting, or it might be a more substantial reply to the petition.

By the time of Hadrian, many of these administrative duties had been given to free Romans who eagerly took the positions for the power they came with. If it was prestige you were after, then the public cursus was still the way. Slinking about in the corridors of power might be cool, but if you wanted the adoration of your peers and the front-row seats at the bullfighting, you still had to take up public office. Into this new strata were invited the equites, and over time, the majority of the secretarial duties of the imperial freedmen were taken over by eager young men of equestrian rank. Suetonius was a secretary to Hadrian, which gave him great insight into the internal workings of the Imperial Family and, hence, the Roman state. He passed over a potentially lucrative and more prestigious military career to stay at the heart of government.

The whole administrative *aula* was peripatetic and went where the Emperor went, which, as we saw earlier, could annoy the Senate when the entire shooting match simply pissed off somewhere else for a while and left them hanging. But when he was on campaign, for example, the whole household moved with him, family and all. While taking the entire government and royal family to war might sound mad, the working administration demanded it. The Emperor was still expected, even vicariously through his administrative staff, to run the Empire, and he wasn't about to leave it in the incapable hands of the Senate, nor risk leaving his closest advisers behind and allow new and potentially more sinister sparrows to whisper in his ear.

This wholesale moving of the entire system of government created absolute chaos, not least in the sheer magnitude of records that had to be firstly moved with them, secondly generated whilst on the go and then, thirdly, safely returned to the archives when they got back. If they got back. Things became lost on the campaign or disappeared into poorly archived black holes. Laws written down decades before were never seen again, causing frantic searching through building after building stacked full of dusty old scrolls.

And those buildings themselves became ever grander. The Imperial Palace spread over all of the Palatine Hill, dominating the view over the forum and the Circus Maximus. Numerous private residences, temples and libraries all became one great interconnected complex of buildings. The staff, both slave and free citizens, was enormous. All of this grandiosity and wealth was nominally the private possession of the Emperor himself, but in practice, it just passed down the line to whoever came next, a mix between private and public property. He could have sold it all had he wished, but who to? Who would afford it, and who would dare to buy it and risk seeming as if they wanted to be Emperor instead? The Emperor was technically a magistrate with his own fisc (from *fiscus*, a basket) into which all the revenues of his province flowed. In theory, the surplus from this fisc was the state's property, but the Emperor virtually was the state, so they could count it as their own money. Augustus was unbelievably rich, richer than any man alive today, and as the fisc and his patronage were inevitably linked, he could legitimately claim to be running the entire Empire from his own pockets. This incredible excess - literally more money than anyone could ever spend - was what enabled each Emperor to simply step into the boots of the old in ways that modern governments could only dream of.

If complicated decisions needed to be made, the Emperor might call a council called a *consilium*, which could include a select number of magistrates and Senators. However, the point of this was largely to flatter those who were invited. These were separate from the ordinary councils called to attend to normal courtly matters and were not public affairs, and either way, the Emperor was not bound to abide by their decisions. Because they were private affairs, people who would not normally be allowed anywhere near such an important cabal were invited, including women, such as Augutus' wife, Livia or Caligula's sisters. But not his horse. That was a myth,

The important thing to emphasise is that whilst the Senate rambled on with its rather silly pointlessness in full view of the public - very deliberately - the real business of running the Empire happened behind closed doors. Any advice that was given to the Emperor in public, and sometimes it might beholden the Emperor to be seen to be listening, would be restricted to something quite mundane or not really advice at all.

"I'd like to advise my lord that he is doing a magnificent job and would he like to declare a holiday next month to celebrate?" That sort of thing.

But since the Emperor was supposed to be the smartest and wisest man around, publicly giving him really sound advice that the Emperor already hadn't thought of would mean a rather early and somewhat permanent dip in the Tiber.

Satyricon

Rome wouldn't be Rome without living up to its image of gaudy excess now, would it? What could be more Roman than lounging around at some horrendous banquet, stuffing one's face like a fucking pig and treating slaves like shit? Immediately, one thinks of the famous Roman novel '*Satyricon*' by Petronius.

Very little of the work exists, but one of the most famous passages covers a dinner given by an extravagantly rich freedman called Trimalchio. His lowly birth (as a slave from Asia) betrays his gaudy excess and uncouth ways but also shows how slaves could become fantastically wealthy (and forget their origins and behave towards their former peers appallingly).

The scorn of the 'nouveau-riche' is evident in the work, and it must also be understood that there is exaggeration for comic effect here (it was called the '*Satyricon*', after all). Petronius is making the characters of the story, and their actions, grotesque not only for laughs, but to make a point about how ridiculous the whole situation is. But it can also give a suggestion of just how absolutely bonkers it might have been like to have been at a Roman feast.

The narrator, Encolpius, arrives at Trimalchio's lavish villa for a feast with his companions:

"At length we took our places and Egyptian slaves poured iced water on our hands and other attendants for the feet came in and pared our toenails carefully. Even during this unpleasant duty, they sang the whole time"

Intrigued, Encolpius calls for a drink and a slave supplied it

'at once, singing every bit as shrilly...that you would have thought it a theatrical performance rather than a dining room.."

Soon the appetizers are served, and everyone takes their places at the table, with Trimalchio still absent but his seat reserved "as is the custom".

They are served a tray of relishes on which stands an ass (a donkey, of course - stop sniggering at the back) made of Corinthian bronze, with two panniers containing white and black olives. It's flanked by two large sliver dishes that, brazenly, have the hallmark of the weight of silver broadly displayed on the side alongside the name of Trimalchio himself. On the dishes are two silver bridges laden with dormice 'sprinkled with honey and poppyseed'. There are also smoked sausages served on a silver gridiron with damsons and pomegranates.

Soon, Trimalchio himself is borne into the dining room on a litter by his slaves 'plumped up on tiny pillows' to the extent that people snort with laughter at the ridiculous sight. He is wearing a scarlet mantle through which he

"..has poked his shaven pate..and wrapped his neck, already well covered with clothes, in a napkin with a broad purple stripe and fringes all around."

On the little finger of his left hand, he has a 'gilded' ring and on the next finger he has an iron ring "picked out with star-like designs to suggest gold" but is iron. Here, Trimalchio is trying to suggest he is of 'equestrian' rank as they wore such rings made of pure gold, but as a freedman he can never achieve such ranks.

Picking his teeth with a silver dagger, he announces that he is sorry for being late and asks his guests if they would allow him to finish the game of draughts that had delayed him. A slave brings in a draught board made of crystal and juniper wood with the pieces made of gold and silver coins. As he plays, he uses, literally 'weaver's talk'; coarse words that betray his lowly birth.

As he plays, the next course is served. A silver tray weaved like a basket containing a wooden hen nesting on her eggs. A band plays a loud fanfare, and the guests are invited to rummage for the eggs. Once everyone has an egg, they are given silver spoons "weighing at least half a pound each" to break the eggs which are actually made of pastry.

Encolpius is horrified to find what he thinks is a chick foetus inside and nearly throws it away only to be told that it is a baked '*beccafico*' [a European Garden Warbler] served with pepper inside a yolk.

Suddenly Trimalchio finishes his game, orders more mead and in a flurry of trumpets and activity, a slave drops a tray. Trimalchio orders the slave punished. In rush two 'hairy Ethiopian slaves' carrying wineskins "like those used to sprinkle the sand in the arena" [saffron was sprinkled in arenas to perfume the air] and they poured wine over the hands of the diners "for nobody offered so much as water."

A Fire Brigade

Pliny, in a letter to Trajan, tells of a disaster he witnessed during a trip to Nicomedia, an ancient Greek city in what is now Turkey, and proposes to do something about it.

While I was making a tour of another part of the province, an enormous fire at Nicomedia destroyed many private dwellings and two public structures - the old men's shelter and the temple of Isis - though they stood

on opposite sides of the street. It spread so far firstly
owing to the force of the wind, and secondly to the
inactivity of the people, who, it is clear, stood idle and
motionless spectators of such a terrible calamity, and
in any case the city possessed not a single pump of fire
bucket or any equipment at all for fighting fires. These
will, however, be procured, as I have already ordered.
Do you, my lord, consider whether you think it well
to organise an association of firemen, not to exceed
150 members. I will see to it that none but firemen are
admitted into it, and that the privileges granted shall
not be abused for any other granted shall not be abused
for any other purpose; and they would be so few, it
would not be difficult to keep them under surveillance.

Trajan replies:

You are of course thinking of the examples of a number
of other places in suggesting that an association of
firemen might be organised in Nicomedia. But we must
remember that the peace of your province [Bythinia],
and particularly of those cities, has been repeatedly
disturbed by organisations of this kind. Whatever
name we give them, and for whatever purpose, men
who have been gathered together will all the same
become a political association before long. It is therefore better to provide equipment which can be helpful
for controlling fires, advise property owners to use
these themselves, and, if the situation warrants it, call
on the populace for assistance.

So no fire brigade, Nicomedia. Learn to use the
pumps yourselves.

Vulgar Professions

The upper-class Roman gentleman would never have been seen dead metaphorically getting their hands dirty in the 'trades'. There were some professions for which a gentleman was suited and others for which they were not. The problem was that the 'trades' were also a jolly good way of making a lot of money. Slaves, or more accurately freedmen, were, however, under no such social rules and were free to engage in any trade they liked without offending the sensitive mores of the Roman elite. A rich slave owner could then train slaves in the mercantile art, free them, set them up in business and take a cut of the profits. Both the freedman and the former master could then reap the benefits without the master being seen to have stooped so low as to peddle grain.

Cicero, who was a tremendous snob, in *On Duties* gives his summary of who he sees as engaging in worthy occupations or not. His disdain for merchants and tax collectors is a great example of the snobbery levelled at freedmen in these professions. When he refers to 'agriculture' as 'becoming' to a gentleman as a profession, he doesn't mean 'farmer'. Instead he means being a landowner whose land is farmed, so a villa owner or similar.

Now in regard to trade and other means of livelihood, which ones are to be considered becoming to a gentleman and which ones are vulgar, we have been taught, in general, as follows. First those means of livelihood are to be rejected as undesirable which incur people's ill will, as those customs collectors and usurers. Unbecoming to a gentleman too, and vulgar are the means of livelihood of all hire workmen whom we pay for mere manual labour, not for artistic skill; for in their case the very wages they receive is a pledge of their slavery. Vulgar we must consider those who buy from wholesale merchants to retail immediately; for they would get no profits without a great deal of downright lying; and indeed, there is no action meaner than misrepresentation. And all mechanics are engaged in vulgar trades, for no workshop can have anything liberal about it. Least respectable of all are those trades that cater to sensual pleasures. Fishmongers, butchers, cooks and poulterers. And fishermen. Add to these, if you please, the perfumers, dancers and the whole corps de ballet.

But the profession in which either a higher degree of intelligence is required or from which no small benefit to society is derived - medicine and architecture, for example, and teaching - these are proper for those whose social position they become. Trade, if it is on a small scale, it is to be considered vulgar; but if wholesale and on a large scale, without misrepresentation, it is not to be greatly disparaged. Nay, it even seems to deserve the highest respect, if those who are engaged in it satiated, or rather, I should say, satisfied with the fortunes they have made, make their way from the port to farmlands and country estates, as they have often made it from the sea into port. But of all the occupations by which gain is secured, none is better than agriculture, none more profitable, none more delightful, none more becoming to a freeman ...

As for property, it is a duty to make money, but only by honorable means; it is a duty also to save it and increase it by care and thrift. These principles Xenophon, a pupil of Scorates, has set forth most happily in his book entitled Oeconomicus. When I was about your present age, I translated it from Greek into Latin*

But this whole subject of acquiring money, investing money (I wish I could include also spending money) is more profitably discussed by certain worthy gentlemen on the Exchange than could be done by any philosophers of any school. We must, nevertheless, take cognisance of these matters, for they come fitly under the head of expediency, and that is the subject of the present book.

But it is often necessary to weigh one expediency against another ... Outward advantages may also be weighed against one another: glory, for example, may be preferred to riches, an income derived from city property to one derived from the farm. To this class of comparison belongs that famous saying of old Cato's; when he was asked what was the most profitable feature of an estate, he replied, "Raising cattle successfully." What next to that? "Raising cattle with fair success." And next? "Raising cattle with but slight success." And fourth? "Raising crops." And when the questioner said, "How about moneylending?" Cato replied, "How about murder?"

*Cicero wrote his treatise in 44BC for his son who was then twenty-one years old.

The Six Year Old Councillor

Surprisingly little is known about the background of one of Rome's most famous historians, Tacitus, including what his full name was, where he was born and when. However, we can estimate that he was born in either 56 or 57AD because he tells us that he entered political life as a quaestor in 81 or 82, under Titus, at 'the earliest opportunity'. Men could not enter public office until they reached the age of 25 and so he could not have been born before 56. In Pompeii, there is a dedication on the front of the Temple of Isis that tells us something very interesting about this age rule. The temple was being rebuilt with, as is usual, the benefaction of a rich private individual, probably after the damage it suffered in the earthquakes of 62, which were a prelude to the massive eruption that destroyed the city some 15 years later. It reads like this:

Numerius Popidius Ampliatus, son of Numerius, at his own expense restored from its foundations the Temple of Isis, which had collapsed in the earthquake. Because of his generosity, although he was six years old, the councillors enrolled him into their number without fee.

The first thing to consider is 'without fee'. There wasn't a charge for joining the town council (ordo), but individuals had to prove they had a certain level of wealth. They have waived this condition.

The second, more obvious, issue is the fact that not only is this a child, he is only six years old. How can a six-year-old child fund the rebuilding of a temple, and how can he sit on the town council? He can't, of course. The key to this is his father, 'Numerius'.

The son, and hence the father, both have the name 'Popidius' and the Popidii were a famous and very rich old family from Pompeii. Numerius son and father are not members of that family, but they carry the name because the father is one of their freedmen. Freed slaves would very often adopt the name of their former master.

As a freedman, Numerius Senior is ineligible to serve on the town council, although he is very obviously a rich and successful person in his post-servile life. He has enough money to spend on rebuilding a temple and enough social influence and standing that the other members of the town council want him among their number. The only way they can think of letting him sit on the council is to accept his six-year-old son, who is a freeborn Roman citizen, on the council in his place, allowing the father to sit on the council vicariously.

Private Wealth

Elsewhere in *Natural History*, Pliny recounts a story about seeing a woman called Lollia Paulina at a wedding. It demonstrates the staggering extent of private wealth in the Empire. Lollia Paulina was Caligula's third wife and the granddaughter of Marcus Lollius, an ally of Octavian and the first governor of Galatia. His trading with the 'Eastern Kings', that Pliny finds so distasteful, is how Lollia got her money. It's worth noting that the wedding in question is not even her own wedding and that one sesterii is worth about $1, so you can work out the value of her dress.

> I have seen Lollia Paulina ... at an ordinary betrothal banquet covered with emeralds and pearls interlaced with each other and shining all over her head, hair, ears, neck and fingers, their total value amounting to 40,000,000 sesterces, and she herself ready at a moment's notice to show the bills of sale in proof of ownership; they were not gifts from an extravagant Emperor but heirlooms acquired actually with the spoils of provinces. This is the outcome of plunder, it was for this that Marcus Lollius disgraced himself by taking gifts from kings throughout the East ... that his granddaughter might glitter in the lamplight covered with 40,000,000 sesterces!

Elsewhere, he tells a story about some really expensive furniture:

> There still exists a table that belonged to Marcus Cicero for which with his slender resources and, what is more surprising, at that date, he paid half a million sesterces, and also one is recorded as belonging to Asinius Gallus that cost a million. Also two hanging tables were sold at auction by King Juba [of Numidia] of which one fetched 1,200,000 sesterces and the other a little less. A table

that was lately destroyed in a fire came down from the Cethegi [an old Roman family] and had changed hands at 1,300,000 sesterces - the price of a large estate, supposing somebody preferred to devote so large a sum to the purchase of landed property.

Riders

Roman governors weren't particularly gregarious sorts, but convention and the need to do something apart from lolling about on cushions, getting rich and eating olives, meant that they would occasionally venture out of the villa into the countryside that they purported to run. But they didn't just wander around at random, they had organised itineraries, like this one from Egypt:

> ....the prefect on his journey will stop first at Pelusium, where he will hold the assizes for the Tanite, Sethroite, Arabian and Avian nomes; then at Memphis similarly for the Thebaid, the Heptanomia, and the Arsinoite nome; and for the remaining nomes of the Lower Country..... in Alexandria....

But they weren't going out among the plebs to listen to their whiny bullshit without something to tempt them from the luxuries of the villa. They needed riders.

> From the village scribes. In accordance with your request for a list of persons to provide the necessities being made ready for the beneficent visit of Valerius Proculus [governor of Egypt from 144-147AD], most glorious prefect, we submit, omitting those excused in accordance with official memoranda, [a list of persons] in place of those transferred to other public services and of those deceased [since the last time he visited and whose absence with goodies and trinkets this time can thus be excused on account of being dead]

There then follows a long, *long* list of names of individuals who will be responsible for all the things Proculus is going to eat, or look at and then not eat, or ignore, or use or just needs to be available should he want. Among the list are [pure] bread, lamb, wine, vinegar, hay, chaff, barley, wood, charcoal [for the fire, duh! He's not eating wood], torches, lamps, geese, oil, relishes, cheeses, vegetables, fish and a whole bunch of pack asses to carry it all home should he want to keep it.

The Roman Treasury

Writing in *Natural History* (xxiii.xvii), Pliny the Elder tells us about what is in the coffers of the Roman state:

In the consulship of Sextus Julius and Lucius Aurelius [157BC] seven years before the beginning of the Third Punic War, there were in the treasury of the Roman people 17,410 pounds weight of uncoined gold, 22,070 pounds weight of silver, and in specie 6,133,400 sesterces. In the consulship Sextus Julius and Lucius Marcius [91BC], i.e at the beginning of the Social War, there were 1,620,831 sesterces in the public treasury. Gaius Caesar, at his first entry into Rome during the Civil War which bears his name [49BC], withdrew from the treasury 15,000 pounds of gold bullion, 30,000 pounds in uncoined silver and 30,000,000 sesterces: indeed, at no point was the Republic more wealthy. Aemilius Paullus, too, after the defeat of King Perseus, paid into the public treasury from the spoils obtained in Macedonia 300,000,000 sesterces, and from that time the Roman people ceased to pay the *tributum.*

This *tributum* was a tax issued to pay war costs first abolished in 167BC and then reimposed in 43 to pay for the war between Octavian and Mark Antony.

Abject Terror

Despite outward appearances, there was no legal, constitutional or political need for an 'Emperor'. None of them had any legal 'right' to rule and only did so at the behest of the Senate. Unless the Senate endorsed the rule of the Emperor, then there was no reason for one to exist.

It also followed then that when one died, there was no legal reason to have another. Rome could simply have reverted to a Republic at any point.

In practice Rome was run by a combination of abject terror, implied terror and applied terror and the only Legion allowed within strangling reach of the Senate House were the Praetorians who were, nominally at least, under the direct personal command of whoever the Emperor was.

In theory the Empire was run by the elected consuls, with the 'Emperor' forming one corner of a legislative triangle. Under this theory, the consuls had as much legal power as he did, but what they didn't have is a camp full of slightly drunk, rather bored, and eminently bloodthirsty swordsmen on hand, should anyone need persuading who the actual boss was.

That many Emperors are seen to have been at open conflict with the Senate, with whom, you would have thought, it would make more sense to work closely to consolidate the future of Rome, was largely down to the fact that because there were no rules about who could be Emperor, anyone could be Emperor.

Particularly when, after a few generations, the elite of Roman society was fairly brimming with rich, ambitious young men who commanded their own legions and could draw some sort of lineage from Augustus.

With so many potential pretenders to the throne knocking about and the only thing stopping them from being Emperor being the metaphorical wink from the Senate, it was hardly surprising then to see so many of those same pretenders and those that might do the winking, bobbing up and down in a sack in the Tiber.

As a result, the law sometimes has to be adapted to give the Emperor some sort of specific legal power, if only to keep his strangling urges in check. The overall concept of law was still sacrosanct to Roman legal minds and, as such, simply tossing it all aside and, legally, allowing the Emperor to do what he wanted was unthinkable. But certain elements of the law could be adapted to account for his specific urges, if only to add a sheen of legitimacy to his wilder decrees. None of this meant jack shit once the stabbing started, mind.

Imperial Constitutions

What the Emperor has determined has the force of a statute; seeing that by a royal law which was passed concerning his authority the people transfers to him and upon him the whole of its own authority and power. Accordingly, whatever the Emperor has laid down by letter with his signature, or has decreed upon judicial investigation, or has pronounced extrajudicially, or ordained by edict, amounts beyond question to a statute. Clearly, some of these are individual application and are not extended into a precedent; for whatever an Emperor grants to anyone for his merits, or if he imposes and penalty or provides someone with unprecedented aid, it applies only to the individual. (Ulpian, Institutes, I)

Conscription

The conscription of manual labour for public works, particularly in the Greek city-states, was a tradition seen as part of one's civic duty. The compulsory assignment of public offices, called liturgies, to people who could afford them, both in terms of time and money was also a well-developed tradition. The Romans, being the Romans, had to, of course, take what was a pretty simple system and add all manner of whistles and bells and turn it into a complicated system of provincial and local administration. The province where East and West clashed most gloriously, Egypt, is where this system became the most grandiose.

In order to maintain a steady supply of people willing to do the administrative jobs of the Empire, the Empire first relied on a salaried class and on the competition for those jobs and any expenses were covered by the incumbents. By the end of the 1st Century, this pen-pusher class was such a lucrative gig, despite the expenses having to be defrayed by the bureaucrat, that they could use it to line their own nests with spectacular results. It was also remarkably expensive to the state which forced the Empire to begin to abandon it. That doesn't mean everyone was sacked overnight but with the Emperors and governors having to then intervene personally on so many petty matters, it became necessary to draft in unwilling candidates to fill those roles as part of a compulsory system.

By the middle of the 2nd Century, the liturgical system had been expanded to fill almost all administrative roles and the system had become a well-established part of the well-to-do citizen's life, as long as they had certain minimum standards of property ownership, age and, of course, financial clout. This also applied to the assignment of imperial and public land for compulsory farming when no private lessees were interested. The Empire was growing and Emperors liked to give away free bread. It had to be grown somewhere.

Magistrates, councillors, and all other liturgists were collectively responsible for the finances of their offices. They were expected to pay the state a certain amount of money and the collection of enough money to cover that, and their own expenses, were their responsibility. This collective responsibility means that if one of them didn't bring in enough to cover his share, then the others would have to.

For some of the liturgists, this was an annoying burden on their time and finances, for others it was a chance to grift the system and benefit from it and for others, the financial burden was huge and ruined them. The main idea was to get public work done at private expense and in effect, it was a heavy tax on the rich, some of whom it brought to ruin. Oh dear. What a pity. Never mind. Sometimes those people under the greatest burden would simply run away from their responsibilities, so you had a situation in which the poor were running one way from the tax farmers and some of the tax farmers were running in the other.

There were certain people who were exempt from liturgical service, such as those performing certain state administrative tasks, or the army. Among them were soldiers, both serving and veteran, priests, professional athletes, those over sixty-five and members of learned professions, but even then some of these could be 'persuaded' into service.

The tax farmers in the following papyrus have a monthly quota which they must pay to the government, regardless of the amount they actually collect. Perhaps not surprisingly, they employ an armed guard (another expense, of course), which serves the purpose of making sure nobody steals their takings and also proves quite handy for clouting people over the head should they prove to be reluctant to pay up.

We, Heracles, Athenodorus, Hero and Zoilus, all four collectors of the poll tax of the village of Tebtynis, agree voluntarily and all of our own free will that we have made a division [of our duties], from the 15th of the month Hathyr, the receipts of which are credited to Phaophi, of the third year of the lord TRAJAN Caesar for the current third year only of the Emperor Caesar Nerva TRAJAN Augustus Germanicus [100AD]; and that Athenodorus and Heracles have been allowed the inhabitants of and settlers in the village, while Hero and Zoilus have for their part been allowed all the inhabitants and settlers [of Tebtynis] at other villages or in the metropolis, with the stipulation that those who have been allotted the external district shall pay each month 1,100 silver drachmas, while those who have been allotted the village shall make up the balance of the monthly quota for the poll tax, the wages of the armed guard being chargeable to those who have been allotted the village. If any one of us four violates any of the aforesaid provisions, he shall pay to the party abiding by them 500 drachmas and to the public treasury an equal sum. This bond shall be valid as if it had been publicly registered. The coming extra levy of the current third year shall be collected by each of them from the persons allotted to him. Year 3 of the Emperor Caesar Nerva TRAJAN Augustus Germanicus, Hathyr ....

Year 15 of the deified Trajan, Phamenoth 25, Naucratis. Dioscorus son of Dionysius appeared and said, "We are two brothers in compulsory public services, and I request that one of us be released in order to have the time to attend to our farming." SulpiciusSimilis [prefect of Egypt 107-12AD, the date of this hearing is 112] asked, "Have you a father [living]?" When he replied, "No," Sulpicius Similis ordered, "One is to be released."

From the orders of Mettius Rufus [Prefect of Egypt 89-91AD] sent to the strategi. If any persons discharging compulsory public services appear to you to be unsuitable either because they do not have the requisite wealth or because of physical disability or because they seem unworthy for any other reason, you will send me three names in place of each one, after investigating that all are suitable not only in property but also in age and in the conduct of life which those who are performing the Emperor's business ought to have. Accordingly, you will add their wealth, their ages, whether they are literate, and what public offices they previously held. And be careful that the three are not from one household or from the same locality, that they have not improper conduct in other offices, and that the officials for the same locality are not relatives.

Copy of announcement. Serenus, royal secretary of the Arsinoite nome, division of Heraclides, and acting strategus. To be assessors of unsold [state] lands - in place of Gaius Julius Ptollis, Amarantus, son of Hestiaeus, Hero surnamed Eudaemo, and Diodorus son of Theogito, who have all four completed the prescribed period, and of Anubio son of Hero and Demetrius son of Suchammo, both stated to be deceased - the persons named below have been nominated by the city secretaries as well-to-do and suitable for compulsory public services. They are ordered to take up the task entrusted to them honestly and faithfully, so as not to incur blame in any respect. Signed. Year 9 of the lord [MARCUS] AURELIUS Antoninus Caesar Armeniacus Medicus Parthicus Maximus*, Mesore 17.

They are.
Gaius Julius Apollinaris, owning land at Caranis, having property worth 4,000 drachmas; Mysthes son of Cornemlius, owning land at New Ptolemais, having property worth one talent; Antonius Herclianus, owning land at the hamlet of Nestus, likewise 4,000 drachmas; Gaius Julius Saturnilus, owning land at Tanis, having property worth 4,000 drachmas; Prolemaeus or however he is styled, public secretary of Pharbaetha worth 4,000 drachmas; Pasio son of Petermuthis (son of Petermuthis) of the Hellenium quarter [of Arsinoe], having property worth 4,000 drachmas. Registered by me, Hero, special assistant, Mesore 20.

*This is Marcus Aurelius with his then full 'victory titles'. Armeniacus for victory in Armenia, 164AD; Medicus for victory in Media, 166 and Parthicus Maximus for 'great victory in Parthia', 166.
He goes on to add 'Germanicus' for victory in Germania in 172 and 'Samarticus' for victory in Sarmatia in 175. As it's 'year 9', this letter thereby dates to 169. Isn't history cool?

Chapter Eight

LAW AND JUSTICE

Traitor

It's safe to say that, by any measure, Augustus was very good at being a Roman Emperor and being a good Roman Emperor meant that he was a power-mad demagogue, one wrong look away from sending the Praetorians on a murderous rampage through the streets, stabbing people in the throat and throwing their children in the Tiber. A good Roman Emperor was kind when it suited him, a tyrant when that suited him, and a murderous lunatic who ruled with no constitutional power whatsoever and someone who needed to keep people terrified of him. As a result, most Emperors were knuckle-chewing, paranoid train wrecks of human beings.

This paranoia peaked with the introduction of rewards for those who informed on potentially treasonable action, normally a quarter of the condemned man's property. This meant that if you could inform on someone who was rich as fuck, you stood to make a tidy sum. You couldn't just make shit up and then inform the authorities, but if you were an inventive sort of asshole, you could see some sort of slight against the Emperor in the smallest actions of your peers, foam that particularly salty latte of nothingness into the makings of a plot, report it, and then watch the poor bastard get thrown off a tower into a gorse thicket from the comfort of his former dining room.

This led to the inevitable rise of professional spies and informers and a terror that gripped Roman society lest the most minor infraction be reported to the authorities. This terror peaks under the reign of Tiberius.

Seneca tells a tale of how one man is trapped by an informer only to have his slave come to his rescue.

Under Tiberius Caesar there was such a common and almost universal frenzy for bringing charges of treason that it decimated the citizenry more severely than did the whole civil war. It seized upon the talk of drunks, upon innocent words spoken in jest. Nothing was safe. Anything served as an excuse for venting this rage and the fate of the accused was never in doubt, for there was but one outcome.

Paulus, a man of praetorian rank, was dining with company once, wearing a ring with a conspicuous stone engraved with a likeness of Tiberius Caesar. It would be very silly for me to try at this point to find a polite way of saying – he took a chamberpot in his hands. This action was noticed simultaneously by Maro, one of the notorious spies of that time and by a slave of Paulus. While the trap was being set, the slave drew off the ring from the finger of his drunken master. And when Maro called the company to witness that the Emperor's image had been brought into contact with filth and begin to affix his signature to the accusation, the slave showed the ring on his own hand.

It doesn't say what happened to the slave, but a quarter of fuck-all is fuck-all, so probably nothing. Elsewhere, Cassius Dio is flabbergasted by one story:

> Tiberius put to death a man of consular rank on the charge of having carried in his bosom a coin bearing the Emperor's likeness when he retired to a latrine!

Yup. Taking a coin with the Emperor's face on into the toilet with you was enough to get you killed, as long as some sneaky little bastard was ready enough to turn you in to the authorities. Augustus changed the law on treason to include 'affronts to the majesty of the Emperor' but that's such a loose term that it could include just about anything. Tiberius seems to have encouraged the practice especially, but most of that evidence comes from Tacitus who is very adept at projecting the terror of Domitian (under who he lived) back onto the time of Tiberius (who he hates), so it may be exaggerated.

Capital

The term 'Capital Punishment' comes from the Latin term 'caput', which means 'head'. A citizen's caput was either, literally, his head, which under capital punishment he could lose or, politically speaking, his civic status. The loss of status could come from confiscation of property, demotion to working in the mines, or even something as simple sounding as deportation. Terms such as 'interdiction from fire and water' mean exile, usually to an island. Now I don't know about you, but being sent to live on a remote Mediterranean island sounds positively divine, but to an urban elite Roman this was a mortifying fate. They might literally have preferred death. If you weren't hanging around the corridors of the Imperial complexes, chattering about whatever important nonsense was the secret-du-jour and eating pickled ostrich tongues or some shit, then you were a nobody. And being a nobody was worse than being dead. Either way, any penalty which impaired the caput in one sense or another was a form of 'capital' punishment.

> Public trials are so called because generally any citizen at all has the right to institute their own prosecution. Of public prosecutions some are capital, some are not capital. We call those capital which inflict the supreme penalty, or interdiction from fire and water, or deportation, or condemnation to the mines, the others, if they impose public disgrace and money fine, are public but not capital.
> (Justinian, Institutes iv xviii 1-2)

The 'supreme penalty' means, of course, death.

Extenuating Circumstances

The legal systems of Western countries didn't just pop into existence in the 17th and 18th Centuries. Most of them are based on systems developed in ancient times. As such, don't be surprised to find in what might otherwise seem a wildly unreasonable world in which men could be tossed in a river for carrying a coin to the toilet with them, that there are other legal constructs that seem forward thinking and even quite modern. Like extenuating circumstances:

> In inflicting penalties, the age and inexperience of the guilty party must be taken into account.

> In penal cases the most benevolent construction should be adopted.

> (Justinian, Digest L. xvii 108 and 155)

Digest

The *Digest*, or the *Pandects*, if you prefer, is a compendium of laws assembled by order of the Byzantine Emperor Justinian in around 530AD. The 50 or so books of *Digest* cover all the known Roman laws and in assembling them, Justinian ordered that all the contradictory stuff be sorted out. They cover laws going back hundreds of years before Justinian's time. Here's some examples and I'm not going to put the little reference after each one, because nobody got time for all that. Well, I do, but you don't.

Again, you'll see that some while some Roman laws could be utterly bonkers, others formed the basis of legal standards we still hold today:

That which is faulty in the beginning cannot become valid with the passage of time.

Not cohabitation but consent makes a marriage.

No one who has the power to condemn lacks the power to acquit.

Anything not permitted the defendant ought not to be allowed the plaintiff

He who has knowledge [of a crime] but is unable to prevent it is free of blame

In cases of doubt, the more liberal interpretations should always be preferred

Whenever the principle of natural desire or doubt as to the law blocks enquiry, the matter should be tempered by just decisions.

In all matters certainly, but especially in the case of law, equity should be given due regard

If a copyist commits an error in transcribing the text of a stipulation, it in no way impairs the liability of the debtor and the surety.

In ambiguous language the intention of the party who produced it should be given chief consideration

When a statute makes mention of two months, a party who appears on the sixty-first day should be heard; for thus the Emperor Antoninus together with his deified father ruled in a rescript

No one may be forcibly removed from his own home Liberty is a possession on which no evaluation can be placed.

In cases of obscurity it is customary to consider what is more likely or what the general practice is

No one suffers a penalty for what he thinks

Seditious Persons

The following famous passage from Paulus shows exactly how punishment according to rank works. To you and me, some of these punishments look far, far worse than others, but they are designed to punish equally. If someone of equestrian rank is bashed over the head with something heavy and thrown down the stairs into the Tiber, then that's the end of that. His family can happily - for a family in mourning - carry on without him, as long as they too get to dodge the slaughter, which is far from guaranteed. But the loss of social status is far more difficult for a family, and vitally its name, to bounce back from. Deportation might not be for ever, especially if you can wait out an Emperor's reign.

> Concerning Seditious Persons. Instigators of sedition and riot or rousers of the people are, according to the nature of their rank, either crucified, thrown to wild beasts, or deported to an island. As for those who dig up or plough up boundary stones or destroy boundary trees, if slaves do it of their own volition, they are condemned to the mines; if humble persons, to [labour on] public works; if of superior rank, they are deprived of one third of their property and relegated to an island or driven into exile. Roman citizens who permit themselves or their slaves to be circumcised under the Jewish rite are deprived of their property and relegated to an island for life; the physicians [who perform the operation] suffer capital punishment....
> (Paulus, Opinions v. xxii-xxiv)

The original part of this law is exactly the sort of thing Roman authorities might charge annoying, itinerant Jewish carpenters with, should they go around somewhere like Judea making trouble. And such a character, as a lowly non-citizen, would qualify perfectly for the punishment of crucifixion. If you could think of anyone knocking around in the Roman Empire in the 1st Century AD who might fit such a description.

Taxes

The following inscription was found at the town of Zaraï, the modern day Aïn Oulmene in Algeria. It dates from 202AD and contains the regulations of an interior tax station in the province of Africa.

As with other interior stations, as opposed to tax stations that regulated the importation of goods, such as ports, the taxes are not raised 'ad valorem', that is to say, not as a percentage of the value of the goods and are hence lower than the taxes levied at frontiers.

That doesn't mean, of course, that these items couldn't be taxed at both ends. Which, as you may imagine, sometimes caused some unhappiness among the people.

The date is given using the standard Roman procedure of 'consular dating' rather than giving the year a number and the two Emperors mentioned, as consuls, are Septimius Severus and his son, Marcus Aurelius Antoninus, better known as 'Caracalla'.

The inscription has been posted to revise taxation after the removal of an unnamed Cohort, but the reason for their removal isn't known. The military was exempt from custom duties on items purchased for their personal needs, but their departure rendered the previous tax regime obsolete.

There is no evidence that the military was ever used for the collection of taxes. Instead that duty was the responsibility of collectors that the Romans described as 'tax farmers.' If it was ever necessary for them to use strong-arm tactics to enforce tax collection, the tax farmers would have a unit of 'bodyguards' who could be employed to persuade people, with the aid of something sharp if necessary, that paying up was in their best interest.

In turn these tax farmers got their legal power from local magistrates who could, when needed, lend the support of their own bodyguards, known as 'lictors'. As a sign of their authority, each lictor carried a 'fasces', a bundle of rods and an Etruscan axe, tightly bound together. The fasces not only served as a symbol of power, but it could also be used to clonk reluctant peasants over the head with should they not be willing to shut the hell up and pay their dues. The 'fasces' is also the origin of the word 'fascism'.

In the consulship of the Emperor Caesar Lucius Septimius Severus Augustus Pius, for the third time, and of the Emperor Caesar Marcus Aurelius Antoninus Augustus Pius. Customs regulations instituted after the departure of the cohort:

Regulation for tax per head
Slaves, each - 1 ½ denarii
Horse; mare - 1 ½ denarii
Mule; she-mule - 1 ½ denarii
Ass; cow - ½ denarius
Pig - 1 sesterce
Suckling pig - ½ sesterce
Sheep, goat - 1 sesterce
Kid, lamb - ½ sesterce
Cattle for market, duty free
Regulation for imported clothing
Dinner mantle - 1 ½ denarii
Tunic costing 300 sesterces - 1 ½ denarii
Blanket - ½ denarius
Purple cloak - 1 denarius
Other African clothing, per garment - ½ denarius
Regulation on hides
Hide, dressed - ½ denarius
Hide, with hair - ½ sesterce
Sheepskin; goatskin - ½ sesterce
Supple saddle hides, per 100lbs - ......
Coarse hides, per 100lbs - ½ denarius
Glue, per 10lbs - ½ sesterce
Sponges, per 10lbs - ½ sesterce
Miscellaneous customs regulations
Cattle, beasts of burden, duty free; other items as above
Wine, per amphora; garum* per amphora - 1 sesterce
Dates, per 100lbs - ½ denarius
Figs, per 100lbs - ....
Green peas, in the pod, per 10 modi** - ....
Nuts, per 10 modi - ....
Resin, pitch, alum, per 100lbs - ....
[The rest of the inscription is lost.]

*Garum was a sauce made from fermented fish, similar
to the fish sauce used in oriental cookery today

** A modius was a unit of volumetric measurement roughly equivalent to about 8.7 litres or 3.5 gallons.

Benevolence

During the time of the Empire, benevolent societies gained official recognition. The most prevalent among these were "burial societies," each named after a patron deity. These groups convened monthly and during holidays to collect dues, perform religious ceremonies, and share festival meals.

Unlike modern guilds or unions, these societies didn't actively advocate for better working conditions. Instead, they functioned as social clubs. People from diverse backgrounds—shipwrights, bakers, weavers, traders, and even slaves—gathered for subsidised or free food, companionship, and the promise of a decent burial.

While benevolent societies focused on caring for the poor, public benefaction became a duty for wealthier citizens. Funding for public projects often came from affluent individuals who not only built temples, baths, and forums but also sought to elevate their social standing and advance within society through such altruism.

Additionally, some expressed benevolence by establishing assistance funds, primarily aimed at impoverished children (known as "alimenta"). These acts of philanthropy are documented in inscriptions across the southern part of the Empire, frequently found in wills . An example of which is the grant offered by Helvius Basila to his hometown of Atina in Latium:

To Titus Helvius Basila, son of Titus, aedile, praetor, proconsul, imperial legate, who bequeathed to the people of Atina 400,000 sesterces. Out of the income from this bequest their children are to be given grain until they reach maturity, and thereafter 1,000 sesterces each. Procula, his daughter, set this up.

As a rough comparison, a sesterce is the equivalent of a dollar. Elsewhere, we find other examples:

> Caelia Macrina, daughter of Gaius, left 300,000 sesterces in her will for the construction of this monument and….. thousand sesterces for its decoration and upkeep. She also left 1,000,000 sesterces to the town of Tarracina in memory of her son, Macer, so that out of the income from this money child assistance subsidies might be paid to one hundred boys and one hundred girls. To each boy, 5 denarii each month, to each girl 3 denarii each month, the boys up to sixteen years, the girls up to fourteen years - in such a way that the payments should always be received by groups of a hundred boys and a hundred girls

One denarius is roughly 4 sesterces. In Numidia, too, there are examples.

> To Publius Licinius Papirianus, son of Marcus, of the Quirine tribe, imperial procurator of revenues of the Emperors Caesar Marcus Aurelius Antoninus Augustus [Marcus Aurelius] and the deified [Lucius] Verus, to whom the most illustrious senate of Sicca, because of his services….
> To my fellow townsmen of Cirta Sicca, most dear to me, I desire to give 1,300,000 sesterces. I commit this to your trust, my dearest fellow townsmen, so that out of the five percent interest on this sum, three hundred boys and two hundred girls may be supported each year. The boys from the age of three to the age of fifteen, the girls from the age of three to the age of thirteen. Each boy to receive 2.5 denarii per month, each girl to receive 2 denarii per month. Moreover residents as well as townspeople are to be chosen, provided they are residents who remain domiciled within the confines of our colony. It will be best, if you approve, for them to be chosen by the duovirs of each year and

care should be taken to fill the place of each grown-up or deceased child promptly, so that the full number will always be supported.

The Mines

Being sent to the mines was a punishment dependant on social rank. No senator would ever be sent to the mines, unless a particularly mischievous Emperor personally ordered it and then who is going to say no? Working the mines was also a profession and Romans had work contracts to, at the very least, guarantee payment terms.

In the consulship of Macrinus and Celsus, May 20 [164AD]. I, Flavius Secundinus [probably an office clerk] at the request of Memmius son of Asclepius (because he declared he was illiterate) [but he has signed his name, incidentally, he was probably just a bit lazy and couldn't be bothered to write all this out] have recorded here the fact that he declared that he had let,and he did in fact let, his labour in the gold mine to Aurelius Adjutor from this day to November 13 next for seventy denarii and board. He shall be entitled to receive his wages in instalments. He shall be required to render healthy and vigorous labour to the above-mentioned employer. If he wants to quit or stop working against the employer's wishes, he shall have to pay five sesterces for each day, deducted from his total wages. If a flood hinders operations, he shall be required to prorate accordingly. If the employer delays payment of the wages when the time is up, he shall be subject to the same penalty after three days of grace. Done at Immenosum Maius [the gold mining district of Dacia]
[signed] Titus, son of Beusans, also known as Bradua; Socratio, son of Socratio; Memmius, son of Asclepius.

As I said, the last signature is the 'illiterate' worker, suggesting the first two are those of agents working for the employer and mine owner.

More Taxes

Oh boy did the Romans love taxes. Not only was it a way of making huge amounts of money, the Empire increasingly needed it, too, if only so Emperors could continue to exploit public affection with tons of free shit. It also had the benefit of enfranchising people in the Roman 'dream'. What better way to demonstrate one's allegiance to the Roman project than by paying taxes? This ultimately meant that people racked up terrifying amounts of tax arrears and issuing a remission of, or moratorium on, the payment of taxes was a great way for Emperors to curry public favour whilst also writing off debt that they were never going to see anyway. If you're never going to get the money, wiping away the debt can seem more like a magnanimous gesture than a practical solution.

In the 2nd Century, Hadrian's public tax remissions were celebrated with the issue of coinage bearing the legend "Nine hundred million sesterces in old arrears cancelled" An inscription went up in Rome:

[Dedicated by] the Roman senate and people to the Emperor Caesar Trajan Hadrian Augustus, son of the deified Trajan Parthicus, grandson of the deified Nerva, pontifex maximus, holder of the tribunician power for the second year [so 118AD], twice consul, the first and only one of all the Emperors to cancel 900,100,000 sesterces owed to the fisc and by this liberality to render not only the citizens now living but also their descendants free from worry.

The *Historia Augusta*, records the same event

Hadrian cancelled a countless sum of money owed to the fisc by private debtors in Rome and Italy ,and also vast sums of arrears in the provinces, and he burned the records of indebtedness on the Forum of the deified Trajan in order to strengthen the general sense of security.

He wasn't the only Emperor to be so 'generous'. Here's Cassius Dio talking about Marcus Aurelius.

Marcus Aurelius remitted all debts by anyone to the imperial fisc or to the state treasury over a period of forty-five years in addition to the fifteen years of Hadrian and he ordered all the records relating to these debts to be burned in the Forum.

Hadrian's remissions of 118AD extended until 133 and Marcus Aurelius then forgave the same from 133 to 178.

The Wrongs of Rights

Augustus and Tiberius issued all sorts of legislation that, on the face of it, appeared to restrict the ability of owners to manumit slaves and limiting the freedoms of those who had been freed. Writers like Suetonius claimed that Augustus was trying to protect the 'purity' of the Roman bloodline by keeping the servile classes at bay, but in practical terms it can be seen as the other way around. By ring-fencing the right to citizenship via manumission, Augustus is instead formally legitimising the transition.

Slaves who had been manumitted in the late Republican period existed in a form of legal no-man's-land and their former owners could reassert their rights over them at any time, take their property of even claim their children into servitude. He introduced the *lex Junia* sometime around 17BC which granted slaves the status of 'Junian Latins' allowing them a clear pathway to full citizenship. The *lex*

Aelia Sentia of 4AD cleared up the relationship between freedmen and their former owners. Later legislation offered all sorts of temptations for Junians to become full citizens via public service.

> No-one in the town of the Municipium Flavium Irni-
> tanum [in Spain] or where buildings are continuous
> with that town, is to unroof or destroy or see to the
> demolition of a building, except by resolution of the
> decuriones or conscripti, when the majority of them
> is present, unless he is going to replace it within the
> next year. Whoever acts against these rules, is to be
> condemned to pay to the municipes of the Municip-
> ium Flavium Irnitanum as much money as the case is
> worth, and the rights of action, suit and claim of that
> money and concerning that money is to belong to any
> municipes of that municipium who wishes and who is
> entitled under this statute.

> The Julio-Claudian Law on Curbing Adultery pun-
> ishes not only defilers of the marriages of others... but
> also the crime of debauchery when anyone without
> the use of force violates either a virgin or a widow of
> respectable character.
> By the second section [of the law] a father, if he catches
> an adulterer of his daughter... in his own home or that
> of his son-in-law, or if the latter summons him in such
> an affair, is permitted to kill that adulterer with impu-
> nity, just as he may forthwith kill his daughter.

> A husband also is permitted to kill an adulterer of his
> wife, but not anyone at all as is the father's right. For
> this law provides that a husband is permitted to kill
> [a procurer, actor, gladiator, criminal, freedman or
> slave] caught in the act of adultery with his wife in his
> own home (but not in that of his father-in-law). And
> it directs a husband who has killed any one of these
> to divorce his wife without delay. Moreover, he must

make a report to the official who has jurisdiction in the place where the killing has occurred and he must divorce his wife; if he does not do this, he does not slay with impunity.

The law punishes as a procurer a husband who retains his wife after she has been caught in adultery and lets the adulterer go (for he ought to be enraged at his wife, who violated the marriage). In such a case the husband should be punished since he cannot claim the excuse of ignorance or feign patience on the pretext of not believing it.

He by whose aid or advice with malice aforethought it is made possible for a man or woman caught in adultery to evade punishment through bribe or any other collusion is condemned to the same penalty as is fixed for those who are convicted of the crime of procuring.

He who makes a profit from the adultery of his wife is scourged... If a wife receives any profit from the adultery of her husband she is liable under the Julian Law as if she were an adulteress.... anyone who marries a woman convicted of adultery is liable under this law. The law prescribes that when notice of divorce has been sent on suspicion of the crime of adultery, the emancipation of slaves who belong to the wife or husband or their parents is to be delayed for a space of two months, reckoned from the date of the divorce, to allow for employing examination under torture if the need arises.

It was enacted that women convicted of adultery be punished by confiscation of half of their dowry and a third of their property and by relegation to an island, and that the male adulterers be punished by like relegation to an island and by confiscation of half of their property, with the proviso that they be relegated to different islands.

You'll note that wives who catch their husbands cheating are not allowed to murder them with impunity. Surprise, surprise.

Marrying a Prostitute

In Roman society, you can happily fall in love with just about whoever you like, of any sex or any gender. You could live with them as a form of concubine and even have them as a lover. As long as you respected the 'sanctity' of marriage and fulfilled your obligations in that respect, you could go nuts. What you couldn't do is just marry whoever you liked, particularly if it was to someone below one's social standing. Even the Emperor Vespasian was forbidden from marrying his long-term concubine, Caenis, due to her lowly birth.

> The Julian Law provides as follows: No one who is or shall be a senator, or a son, grandson born of a son, or great-grandson born of a son's son of any one of these, shall knowingly and with malice aforethought have as betrothed or wife a freedwoman or any woman who herself or whose father or mother is or has been an actor. And no daughter of a senator or granddaughter born of a son or great-granddaughter born of a grandson (a son's son) shall knowingly and with malice aforethought be betrothed or married to a freedman or to a man who himself or whose father or mother is or has been an actor, and no such man shall be knowingly or with malice aforethought have her as betrothed or wife.

Actors, as you can see, were considered to be of the same social standing as prostitutes and gladiators.

Freeborn men are forbidden to marry a prostitute, a procuress, a woman manumitted by a procurer or procuress, on caught in adultery, one convicted in a public action or one who has been an actress.

A freedwoman who is married to her patron shall not have the right of divorce.. as long as the patron wants her to be his wife.

The Right of Inheritance

Inheritance laws show a little more balance between the rights of a husband and a wife. For a change.

A man or a wife can, by virtue of marriage, inherit a tenth of the other's estate. But if they have living children from a previous marriage, in addition to the tenth which they take by virtue of marriage they receive as many tenths as the number of children. Likewise a common son or daughter lost after the day of naming adds one tenth and two lost after the ninth day ad two tenths. Besides the tenth they can receive also the usufruct [a temporary right to use] of a third part of the estate, and whenever they have children, the ownership of the same part.

Sometimes a man or wife can inherit the other's entire estate, for example, if both or either are not yet of the age at which the law requires children - that is, if the husband is under twenty-five and the wife under twenty; or if they both have while married passed the age prescribed by the Papian Law - that is, the man sixty, the woman fifty.... They enjoy testamentary freedom in each other's favour if they have obtained the 'right of children' from the Emperor, if they have a common son or daughter, or if they have lost a fourteen-year-old son or twelve-year old daughter or two three-year-olds or three after the day of naming... Likewise if the wife has a child by her husband within ten months after his death she takes the whole of his estate.

Sometimes they inherit nothing from each other, that is, if they contract a marriage contrary to the Julian and Papian-Poppaean Law (for example if anyone marries a woman of ill repute or a senator marries a freedwoman)

Bachelors are also forbidden by the Julian Law to receive inheritances or legacies... Likewise by the Papian Law childless persons, precisely because they have no children, lose one half of inheritances and legacies...

The Julian Law exempts women from marriage for one year after the death of a husband and six months after a divorce; the Papian law [raised it to] two years after the death of a husband and a year and six months after a divorce.

No such exemption applies to a man whose wife dies or who obtains a divorce. They can get married whenever they like.

In keeping with the thirty-fifth section of the Julian Law, those who without just cause prevent any children in their power from marrying or refuse to give a dowry... are compelled to give them in marriage and bestow a dowry.

If there is no one entitled to the possession of an estate, or if there is someone but he has failed to exercise his right, the estate passes to the public treasury.

Egypt

Egypt was at once the jewel in the Roman crown and the special cousin they had locked in the attic. As such, it required its own set of regulations that steered the administration of the *idiologus*, a high ranking official with nominally the same equestrian rank as a provincial governor who had charge of the special account - *idios logos* - under which revenues of the imperial machine other than taxes were collected - fines, confiscations, sale of property and so on. It highlights the way that Egypt was both treated as a special case when it comes to respecting the traditions and customs of the ancient kingdom and how it was ruthlessly oppressed by the Roman state. They venerated it on one hand and milked it dry on the other.

This is one of the most famous documents from Roman Egypt, Berlin Papyrus No. 1210, dated to between 150 and 161 AD. It contains 115 clauses, including the following:

> 5. Property bequeathed by Alexandrians to persons not qualified is given to those who can legally inherit from them, if such there be and if they claim it at law.
>
> 8. If to a Roman will is added a clause saying "Whatever bequests I make in Greek codicils shall be valid", it is not admissible, for a Roman is not permitted to write a Greek will.
>
> 19. Bequests made to freedmen who have not yet acquired legal emancipation are confiscated. It is legal emancipation if the person freed is over thirty years of age. [this emancipation is referring to parental emancipation, not manumission of a slave]
>
> 20. Bequests made to one who as a slave was put in chains and afterwards freed or who was freed when not yet thirty years old are confiscated.
>
> 22. The property of deceased Latins [Junian Latins, as mentioned before] is given to their patron and to the sons and daughters and heirs of these; and bequests

made by those who have not yet acquired legal Roman freedom are confiscated.

23. Romans are not permitted to marry their sisters or their aunts, but marriage with their brothers' daughters has been conceded. Pardalas [an idiologus] indeed, when a brother married a sister, confiscated the property.

Note how this last one specifically refers to 'Romans', i.e. the non Egyptian or 'Greek' population. Those fuckers can marry their sister of they want.

29. A freeborn Roman woman having a property of 20,000 sesterces pays 1 percent annually as long as she is unmarried, and a freedwoman possessing 20,000 sesterces pays the same until she marries.

30. Inheritances left to Roman women possessing 50,000 sesterces are confiscated if they are unmarried and childless

31. A Roman woman is permitted to leave her husband the tenth part of what she possesses, anything more is confiscated.

32. Romans possessing more than 100,000 sesterces if unmarried and childless do not inherit, but those who have less inherit.

These might seem like punitive measures towards the 'Roman' population, but they can also be seen as temptations for the Romans to marry and breed. Ethnic cleansing if you like.

35. Children and kinsmen of soldiers in active service who die intestate are permitted to inherit from them, if the claimants are of the same nationality.

37. Those who acted in any way contrary to edicts of the kings or prefects were fined, some a fourth of their estates, some a half, and others their entire estates.

41. If an Egyptian rears a child exposed on a dung heap and adopts him, a fourth of his estate is confiscated on death.

42. Those who style themselves improperly [this refers to how one describes oneself - Egyptian, Greek, Roman, etc. on documents] and those who knowingly concur therein are fined a fourth of their estates.

43. A fourth of the estate has been confiscated in the case of any Egyptian who after the death of his father has declared himself as a Roman.

60. Those who fail to register slaves suffer confiscation of the slaves only

66. Persons permitted to depart by sea who sail without a pass are fined a third of their property and if they export slaves of their own without a pass they suffer confiscation of the whole.

70. Persons engaged in public services and members of their families are not permitted to engage in buying or moneylending in the districts in which they function, nor [acquire] land registered as unproductive or sold at public auction in the entire nome. Dummies put up for them are equally accountable, and such purchases were sometimes confiscated. The penalties are as follows; if a purchase from a private citizen, an amount equal to the purchase price; if a loan, an amount equal to the principal, if a sale, the bona fide price received; and dummies the same, at the risk of their principals.

76. A priest wearing a woollen garment and long hair suffers a penalty of 1,000 drachmas

92. A child who has been exposed on a dung heap cannot become a priest.

106. It is not permitted to exchange money at more than the value fixed by law.

111. Soldiers on active duty are forbidden to acquire property in the province in which they were stationed.

A Report of a Crime

Whilst there was no police force in the sense we might understand it, there were still local officials charged with investigating crime, apprehending bad guys and issuing fines for window tint violations and other vital stuff. I made that last bit up, obviously. Crime reports are quite common.

To Serapio, chief of police, from Orsenuphis son of Harpaesis, notable of the village of Euthemeria in the division of Themistes. In the month of Mesore of the past fourteenth year of Tiberius Caesar Augustus [28AD], I was having some old walls on my premises demolished by the builder Petesuchus son of Petesuchus, and while I was absent from home to gain my living, Petesuchus in the process of demolition discovered a hoard which had been secreted by my mother in a little box as long ago as the sixteenth year of [Augustus] Caesar, consisting of a pair of gold earrings weighing four quarters, a gold crescent weighing three quarters, a pair of silver armlets of the weight of twelve drachmas of uncoined metal, a necklace with silver ornaments worth eighty drachmas and sixty silver drachmas. Diverting the attention of his assistants and my people, he then had them conveyed to his own home by his unmarried daughter and after emptying out the aforesaid objects he threw away the box empty in my house and he even admitted finding the box, though he pretends that it was empty. Wherefore I request, if you approve, that the accused be brought before you for the due consequences. Farewell. Orsenuphis, aged fifty, scar on left forearm.

Black Magic Baby

And then there's this weird little tale of black magic, baby tossing, agricultural shenanigans:

To Heirax, also called Nemesio, strategus of the division of Heraclides of the Arsinoite nome, from Gemellus also called Horio, son of Gaius Apolinarius,

Antinoite. I appealed, my lord, by petition to the most illustrious prefect, Aemillius Saturninus, informing him of the attack on me by a certain Soras, who held me in contempt because of my weak vision and wished himself to get possession of my property with violence and arrogance, and I received his sacred subscription authorising me to appeal to his excellency the epistrategus. Then Sotas died and his brother Julius, also acting with the violence characteristic of them, entered the fields that I had sown and carried away a substantial quantity of hay; not only that, but he also cut dried olive shoots and heath plants from my olive grove near the village of Cercesucha. When I came there at the time of the harvest, I learned that he had committed these transgressions. In addition, not content, he again trespassed with his wife and a certain Zenas, having with them an infant [it is possible that this is referring to a dead foetus] intending to hem in my cultivator with black magic, so that he should abandon his labour after having harvested part of another allotment of mine,and they themselves gathered in the crops. When this happened, I went to Julius in the company of officials, in order that these matters might be witnessed. Again, in the same manner, they threw the same infant toward me, intending to hem me in also with black magic, in the presence of Petesuchus and Ptollas, elders of the village of Caranis who are exercising also the functions of the village secretary, and of Socras their assistant, and while the officials were there. Julius, after he had gathered in the remaining crops in the fields, took the infant away to his house. These acts I made matters of public record through the same officials and the collectors of grain taxes of the same village. Wherefore I may retain the right to plead against them before his excellency the epistrategus concerning the outrages perpetrated by them and the public rents due to the imperial fisc from the fields, because they wrongfully did the harvesting. Gemellus, also called Horio, about

twenty-six years of age, whose vision is impaired. Year
5 of Lucius Septimius Severus Pius Pertinax Augustus,
Pachon 27 [197AD]

Insider Trading

In the latter half of the 3rd Century the Empire experienced
a great financial crisis that saw the Senate desperately try to
control the black market by devaluing the currency several
times. This offered easy opportunity to the corrupt to make a
lot of money. Here a government official writes to his agent,
using the advance knowledge of a forthcoming devaluation
to have all his cash converted into goods.

> Dionysius to Apio, greeting. The divine fortune of our
> masters has given orders that the Italian coinage be
> reduced by half a sesterces. Make haste therefore to
> spend all the money you have and purchase for me all
> kinds of goods at whatever price you find them. But I
> tell you in advance that if you try any shenanigans, I
> won't let you get away with it. I pray you may continue
> long in health, my brother.

A Tragic Accident

The following tragic tale is from the town of Oxyrhynchusin
Upper Egypt, now known as Al-Bahnasa. It dates, precisely,
to the 3rd of November, 183AD. The interesting thing from a
legal point of view is that someone has died and the officials,
even though they know what has happened, and I'll let you
find out who it is for yourself, know there's been an accident
and someone needs to come and find out how they died and
what exactly happened. It's like CSI: Ancient Roman Egypt.
But interesting.

> Hierax, strategus of the Oxyrhynchite nome, to Claudius
> Serenus, assistant. A copy of the application which has

been presented to me by Leonides also called Serenus is herewith sent to you. Take a public physician and view the dead body referred to, and having delivered it over for burial make a report in writing. Signed by me.

The 23rd year of Marcus Aurelius COMMODUS Antoninus Caesar the lord, Athur 7 [November 3rd]. To Hierax, strategus, from Leonides also called Serenus, whose mother is stated as Tauris, of Senepta. At a late hour of yesterday the 6th, while a festival was taking place at Senepta and the castanet-players were giving their customary performance at the house of Plution my son-in-law ..., his slave Epaphroditus, aged about 8 years, wishing to lean out from the bed-chamber(?) of the said house and see the castanet-players, fell and was killed. I therefore present this application and ask you, if it please you, to appoint one of your assistants to come to Senepta in order that the body of Epaphroditus may receive proper laying out and burial. (Date and signature of Leonides.)

That the death of an 8 year old slave boy in a tragic accident would result in such official activity is interesting. You can probably be sure that at some point in all this investigating, someone is going to get the blame and that someone is going to have to reimburse Plution for the value of the boy. At the heart of all this is a poor little boy who was super excited to see the castanet-players.

Mourning

There is nothing more Roman than a bunch of laws which determine how sad you should be and for how long, especially once someone dear to you has just died. So, they invented a whole bunch of funerary laws for everyone to follow and some of them, to be fair, sound rather sensible. Like about bringing a corpse into a city, for example, which in a world full of smallpox epidemics sounds like a worthwhile precaution. Plus, there are protections against grave robbing. The following funerary laws come from Paulus' Opinions.

> It is not permitted to bring a corpse into a city, lest the sacred places of the city be polluted; and anyone who acts contrary to this is punished without delay. A corpse cannot be committed to burial or burned within the wall of a city. Anyone who strips a body committed to permanent burial or temporarily deposited in some place, and exposes it to the rays of the sun, commits sacrilege; and therefore, if he is of superior rank he is generally deported to an island, if he is of inferior rank he is sent to the mines. Persons who violate a sepulchre or remove anything from a sepulchre are, according to the rank of the person, either sent to the mines or deported to an island. Anyone who breaks open or uncovers a sepulchre belonging to another and places therein his own or another's dead is considered to have violated sepulture ... Anyone who erases an inscription on a tomb, or overturns a statue, or carries off anything therefrom, or removes a stone or a column, is considered to have violated sepulture. In a sarcophagus or vault where a body has already been deposited another body may not be placed, and he who does so can be prosecuted for violation of sepulture ...

> Parents and children over ten years of age are to be mourned for a year; minors up to the age of three years, one month for each year of their age at the time of their death; a husband, ten months; and cognates closer than the sixth remove, eight months. Anyone who acts contrary is visited with public disgrace*. Anyone who is in mourning ought to eschew banquets, ornaments, and purple and white clothing. Anything expended for

a funeral is deducted as the first claim among the debts [of the estate].

*Infamia, or public disgrace, was inflicted on Roman citizens for all manner of criminal and moral offences, from dishonourable discharge from the army to engaging in any immoral occupation like prostitution or - gasp - acting, theft, slander and that sort of thing.

Exactly what infamia entails was quite complicated, but included a loss of social standing which doesn't mean much in today's world unless you're a teenager, but in the Roman world was terrifically shameful. People who were found guilty of infamia - the infames might also lose legal protections enjoyed by citizens. Their social standing might be lowered to that of slaves and could be liable to be beaten as a punishment and couldn't run for public office.

There are also physical punishments for infames that would disgrace the person in public, something akin to the medieval pillory where they'd be stuck for a certain amount of time and have rotten tomatoes thrown at them, or they would if they had discovered tomatoes yet.

Certain professions were automatically assumed to be infames, such as prostitutes and actors, as mentioned above, but also gladiators, undertakers, dancers and anyone else who has, by their profession, put their body on public display. Citizens had the right to privacy and the right to bodily integrity and by engaging in acts in which they flaunted their bodies, they were assumed to have abandoned those rights.

Local Dispute for Local People

Local disputes, including ones between people of different cities, were usually handled by the provincial governor. If he couldn't be bothered, and who could be bothered, if you were a governor and you had money to extort from the region until you got recalled to Rome, then he would follow the old tradition of simply appointing some other shlub to do it for you. Or 'third party neutral' if you prefer. The Emperor retained the ultimate ability to rule on verdicts, in case the shlub made a stupid decision and people could appeal decisions to him. The rest of the time, the governor's ruling was final and by 'final' you can read 'Do it or I'll strangle you and throw you in whatever the drowning river is called where you live'.

> To Gaius Poppaeus Sabinus [the governor of Moesia in 11-35AD and also the governor of Achaea and Macedonia from 15AD] legate of Tiberius Caesar, from … secretary of the assembly [the league of cities of Thessaly], many greetings. You wrote to us about the dispute which Cierium and Metropolis had about boundaries, requesting the assembly to arbitrate it, as you also indicated to me in person in Aedepsus. Please be informed that as soon as I returned home I placed the arbitration on the calendar of the current assembly of the Thessalian League meeting at Larissa this month of Thyus. Both parties appeared at the arbitration and presented their cases, and the ballots were cast in secret under oath, 298 for Cierium, 31 for Metropolis, and 5 invalid. We deemed it fitting to write you this, Farewell.

Suck it, Metropolis.

> The Emperor Caesar DOMITIAN Augustus, son of the deified Vespasian, holder of the tribunician power, twice acclaimed imperator, eight times consul and designated for a ninth time, father of his country, sends greetings to the quattuorviri and decurions of Falerio in Picenum. I have ordered appended to this letter, for your information, what I have decided concerning the unsurveyed land after investigating the dispute between you and the town of Firmium. In the consulship of Publius Valerius Patruinus and Domitian, July 19 [82AD].

I, the Emperor Caesar DOMITIAN Augustus, son of the deified Vespasian, investigated the dispute between Falerio and Firmium in consultation with distinguished men of both orders and decided what is written below. I am strongly influenced both by the antiquity of the suit which has been revived after so many years by Firmium against Falerio, since even fewer years can be sufficient for the security of the possessors, and also by the letter of the deified Augustus, Emperor most attentive and beneficent toward the soldiers of his Fourth Legion in which he advised them to gather together and sell all their unsurveyed land, and I doubt not that they obeyed such salutary advice. For these reasons, I confirm the rights of the possessors. Farewell.

Suck it, Firmium.

Come Home

In 153AD there was a revolt in Egypt in which the prefect may have been killed by the rebels and which required the intervention of the Emperor, Antoninus Pius. Following the trouble, the people could not pay their taxes and hence the collectors could not deliver their tax quotas to the government for which they were personally responsible. Faced with ruin, they ran away. Several other letters give details on this panicked running from the obligations. Some of them were when people even feared being nominated to a liturgy. Even the idea of being appointed was enough to strike fear into the hearts of some. There are some examples when men scarper as soon as they see their names on the list of possible candidates.

Marcus Sempronius Liberalis, prefect of Egypt, declares: I learn that some persons have left their homes because of the recent disturbance ... and that others, who fled from certain liturgies because of the poverty about them at the time are still living away from home in fear of the proscriptions that were immediately declared. I therefore urge all to return to their own places of abode and reap the first and greatest fruit of prosperity and of the solicitude of our lord the Emperor for all men, and not to wander abroad without hearth or home. That they may comply more readily and gladly, let them know that anyone ... who is still held back for this reason will perceive the good will and kindness of our greatest Emperor in his order that there shall be no judicial enquiry against them, or even against others proscribed by the *strategi* for any cause whatsoever ...

A big section of the text is missing at this point.

... and they associate with fugitives who have chosen a life of criminals and brigands. That they may understand that I advise and do this not only for them but also for the others, let them know that their excellencies the epistrategi, the strategi, and the soldiers dispatched by me for safety and security of the country districts have been given orders to nip incipient raids in the bud by provident and timely measures, to give immediate chase when raids are committed, and to call trouble-makers caught in the act to account as fully as those engaged in actual brigandage but not to annoy others of those once proscribed who are living quietly and attending to their farming at home. Let them return, therefore, without fear, and let their period of grace be three months from the time when this edict of mine is posted in each nome. But if anyone is found wandering abroad after such great benefaction of mine, such person shall be arrested and sent to me no longer as a suspected but as a confessed malefactor. Year 18 of the lord Antoninus, Thoth 1.

So please come home and collect the taxes. They have three months grace to collect what's needed and some soldiers will protect you. But get that money. Now.

More Taxes, Jewish Edition

From Julius Caesar down to Claudius, the Emperors continued privileges handed down to the Jewish diaspora by earlier Persian and Seleucid kings, because of their religious obligations. Following the Jewish rebellion of 66-70AD, Vespasian cancelled the Jewish tax privileges throughout the Empire and established instead a special Jewish Account at the fisc. Previously, all the Jews in the diaspora had been required to pay two drachmas towards the upkeep of the Temple in Jerusalem, but considering that Vespasian's son, Titus had just burned the thing to the ground and looted all the treasure out of it, that seemed rather redundant. Instead, he ordered that the money go for the benefit of the Temple of Jupiter on the Capitoline Hill, which is rubbing the Jewish noses in it somewhat.

Josephus, in his Antiquities of the Jews, records loads of documents from Emperors and officials reaffirming and extending the rights and privileges of the Jews in the Empire. These documents, like the one below, are somewhat questionable because of the blatant inaccuracies they contain. Likely, these things aren't figments of his imagination, but he might be a bit sloppy when quoting them.

Caesar AUGUSTUS, pontifex maximus, holder of the tribunician power* declares:

Whereas the Jewish people have proved themselves grateful toward the Roman people not only at the present time but also in the past - particularly under the high priest Hyrcanus in the time of my father, the dictator Caesar - I and my council have decided ... that the Jews [are allowed to] practice their own customs according to their ancestral law, just as they used to under Hyrcanus, high priest of the highest god, that their sacred moneys be inviolable and be sent to Jerusalem and delivered to the custodians at Jerusalem and that they not [be compelled to] post bail on the Sabbath or on the day of preparation** for it from the ninth hour. If anyone is caught stealing their sacred scrolls or their sacred money whether from a synagogue or from an ark of the Law, he shall be guilty of sacrilege and his property confiscated to the public treasury of the Romans.

* This is an example of Josephus' sloppiness mentioned earlier. He fails to mention the number of years of tribunician power Augustus has held and so this letter can't be dated.
** The Greek word for 'preparation' used here, 'paraskeue' is still the Greek name for Friday.

Amazing Stories

Whilst the Greeks were analytical, rational and sober sorts of people, the Romans, both the elite and the plebs, the intellectual and the great uneducated masses alike, were fond of nothing more than a good bit of irrational tittle-tattle. A great example of this is the collection of mysteries and marvels published by Phlegon, a freedman of Hadrian, under the title 'Amazing Stories'. It reads like tabloid sensationalism, and one has to take it with a healthy pinch of salt, but in every piece of nonsense, there is a grain of truth:

There was born in Rome a hermaphrodite, in the year when Jason was Archon in Athens and Marcus Plauitius Hypsaeus and Marcus Fulvius Flaccus were consuls at Rome [125BC]. On this account the Senate bade the pontiffs consult the Sibylline Oracles, and they interpreted the oracular responses ...

The following passage describes the discovery of strange, giant bones from the ground, which, on reflection, must surely be describing fossils of some kind. If so, this might be the earliest ever mention of dinosaur bones.

Not a few cities of Sicily and the area about Regium suffered from the earthquake, and not a few of the people in Pontus were also shaken. in the fissures in the earth were revealed bodies of quite large size. The natives were astounded and shrank from moving them, but they sent a tooth of one to Rome as a sample. The tooth was not just a foot long but actually exceeded that size. The envoys showed it to Tiberius [the Emperor] and asked whether he wanted the heroic figure brought to him. The Emperor made a wise decision about this, by which he both did not deprive himself of learning its size and at the same time avoided the impiety of stealing corpses. He summoned a renowned geometer, Pulcher by name, whom he prized for his skill, and bade him reconstruct the face in scale to the size of the tooth. Pulcher calculate what the proportions of the whole body and the face would be by the size of the tooth, and quickly fashioned it and brought it to the Emperor. The latter declared that he was satisfied with this viewing of it, and sent the tooth back whence it had been brought ... One should not mistrust these stories, reflecting that in early times nature in its prime bred everything close to the gods, but that as time wasted away the size of creatures wasted with it.

There was brought to Nero a child having four heads and its other members corresponding, in the year when Thrasyllus was archon at Athens and Publius Petronius Turpilianus and Lucius Caesennius Paetus were consuls in Rome [61AD - This is the same Turplianus who was governor of Britain later that year]. And another child was born with its head growing out of its left shoulder.

There happened an incredible wonder in Rome, in the year when Demophilus was archon at Athens and Quintus Veranius and Gaius Pompeius Gallus were consuls at Rome [49AD]. One of the most esteemed serving women of the wife of Raecius Taurus, a man of praetorian rank, gave birth to an ape ...

Medicine

In Books twenty to twenty-three of Natural History, Pliny the Elder records all sorts of strange and wonderful remedies for ailments both of the body and the mind. Garlic features heavily as a cure for everything from leprosy to the plague, from animal bites to insanity. The boundaries between medicine, superstition and magic were heavily blurred, although anyone who was considered to be dabbling in the latter would soon find themselves in the Tiber. Pliny is quick to denigrate the work of such 'magicians' and condemn their 'cures' while recording them in his works on 'medicine'. He records cures that involve plants and animal matter separately, and as the ones made from plants are essentially pretty harmless, the examples below are some of the ones that include animal parts.

[Spittle]
But we have shown that the most effective protection against snakes is the spittle of a fasting person; and actual daily experience confirms other effective uses for it. We spit against illnesses like epilepsy, that is, we repel contagion; in similar manner we repel witchcraft and the danger in meeting a person lame in the right leg. We also ask pardon of the gods by spitting in the bosom for entertaining some too presumptuous hope. On the same principle it is the custom in all cases

where medicine is employed to spit three times in deprecation, so as to assist its efficacy

He doesn't explain what the danger of meeting a person lame in the right leg actually is.

[Broken Bones]
For broken bones a quick remedy is the ashes of the jawbone of a boar or swine; likewise boiled lard, tied around the broken bone, knits it with marvellous rapidity. For fractures of the ribs, goat's dung applied in old wine is especially extolled; it has aperient, extractive, and healing properties.

[For Fevers]
Deer's flesh ... is a febrifuge [reduces fever]. Recurrent fevers are cured, if we are to believe the magicians, by wearing the right eye of a wolf, salted and attached. There is a type of fever called quotidian; one can be cured of this, they say, if the patient takes three drops of blood from the vein of an ass' ear and swallows them in a pint of water. For quartan fever the magicians recommend cat's dung together with the toe of an owl to be attached to the body, and, to prevent a relapse, not to be removed until the seventh spasm ... More moderate ones recommend for quartan fever the liver of a cat killed during the waning moon, preserved in salt, to be taken in wine just before the attacks. The magicians also recommend that the toes of the patient should be smeared with the ashes of cow dung sprinkled with boy's urine, and that a hare's heart should be attached to the hands; they give hare's rennet to drink before attacks. Fresh goat's milk cheese is also given with honey, the whey being carefully extracted.

[for Melancholy, Lethargy and Phthisis]
For patients afflicted with melancholy; calf's dung boiled in wine is a remedy. Lethargic persons are aroused by applying to the nostrils the calluses from an ass' legs steeped in vinegar, or the fumes of goat's horns or hair, or wild boar's liver. This is also given to drowsy persons. The cure of phthisis [a wasting disease] is effected by a wolf's liver taken in thin wine, the lard of a sow that has been fed upon grass, or the flesh of a she-ass taken with broth - this last type is used to cure this illness especially in Achaea. They say, too, that the smoke of dried cow dung inhaled through a reed ... is good for phthisis.

Flat Earth

Strabo, in his work *Geography*, talks about how the earth is 'spheroidal'. It is a myth to think that ancient people considered the world to be flat. For most of human existence, it has been known otherwise. Stupidity is a relatively modern construct. He also commends the deduction of the Hellenistic geographer Eratosthenes, who was born in the 3rd Century BC, who deduced that "If the earth is spheroidal, just as the universe is, it is inhabited all the way round". The Polymath Posidonius (d. c 51BC) "conjectures that the length of the inhabited world, about 70,000 stades, is half of the whole circle on which it has been taken, so that, he says, by sailing straight from the west the same distance one would come to India" Posidonius calculated the circumference of the planet at 240,000 stadia which translates to 24,000 miles (39,000 km). The exact figure is 24,901 mi (40,074 km).

Most of all it seems to me, we need ... geometry astronomy for a subject like geography ... Just as these sciences prove for us in other treatises all that has to do with the measurement of the earth as a whole, and I must as in this treatise take for granted that the universe is spheroidal, and also that the earth's surface is spheroidal ... and I need only indicate, in a brief and summary way, whether a proposition comes - if it really does - within the range of sense perception or of intuitive knowledge. Take, for example, the proposition that the earth is spheroidal. Whereas the suggestion of this proposition comes to us immediately from the law that bodies tend toward the centre and that each body inclines toward its own centre of gravity, the suggestion comes immediately from the phenomena observed at sea and in the heavens; for our sense perception and also our intuition can bear testimony in the latter case. For instance, it is obviously the curvature of the sea that prevents sailors from seeing distant lights that are placed on a level with their eyes. At any rate, if the lights are elevated above the level of the eyes they become visible, even though they be at a greater distance from the eyes; and similarly if the eyes themselves are elevated, they see what was before invisible ... So also, when sailors are approaching land, the different parts of the shore become revealed progressively, more and more, and what at first appeared to be low-lying land gradually grows higher and higher.

Chapter Nine

OLD
WHITE
MEN

Biographies

Nearly all of the information you have in your hands comes from original sources. That is, it comes from the epigraphical record (inscriptions, carvings and so on), written sources, archaeological records, papyri, coins and so forth. So what you have is the information straight from the horse's mouth, so to speak. It might then be useful to know who the horses were.

The various authors referred to throughout sometimes seem like faceless names, and with good reason because although the names might be familiar, not much is actually known about some of them. What follows is a brief guide to who these people - all of them men, naturally - actually were and what, if anything, we know about them. It's not meant to be an exhaustive guide by any means, but if some of these little biographies seem surprisingly brief, that's because we don't know much about the chap.

Vergil

Publius Vergilius Maro (70–19 BC) was from the Mantua district of Cisalpine Gaul - Northern Italy, if you prefer. He was the leading poet of the Augustan age and a member of the literary circle gathered by Augustus to act as the creators of propaganda for the 'new order' Augustus was creating. He combined a Greek literary tradition with a Roman perspective and produced the *Eclogues*, ten pastoral poems, the *Georgics*, four books in praise of Italy and agriculture, both of which harked back to Rome's supposedly idyllic rural past, and his most famous work the *Aeneid*. The *Aeneid* is an artificial product, heavily in debt to Greek epic poetry, drama and philosophy, and although it is written in the style of a legendary epic, it is essentially a vehicle for the Augustan message of peace, unity, duty, morality, the revival of 'Roman virtues' and the destiny by which Augustus claims the throne. What better way for Augustus to claim that he was destined to rule Rome than to have Vergil write an epic poem in which he claims Augustus is destined to rule Rome? See? It says so in this epic poem!? It doesn't matter that he wrote it after Augustus had taken power. The *Aeneid* is fantastic, but it must be read as pure Augustan spin.

Horace

Quintus Horatius Flaccus (65-8BC) was the son of a freedman and was introduced by his friend Vergil into the same literary camp surrounding Augustus. He was originally a supporter of Brutus but made peace with the new regime and moved away from politics entirely. He then spent the rest of his career enjoying the freedom (and money) that his new patronage afforded him, writing poetry that gives a glimpse into life under Augustus. His works include *Satires, Epodes*, the *Odes* and the *Carmen Saeculare* for the Secular Games of 17BC.

Livy

Titus Livius of Patavium (Padua) in northern Italy is one of the greatest annalists of Rome. His *Ad Urbe Condita* (From the Founding of the City), all 142 books of it, supplanted all previous chronicles and still serves as the main guide to the history of the Republic. He doesn't have much of a grasp on the finer points of politics or geography, but he does have a mastery of rhetoric and drama to create what is essentially a prose epic of the glory of Rome. Critical analysis is not his aim, and instead, he focuses on the old Roman virtues of heroism, patriotism and piety. He ignores criticism of the past in favour of patriotic tubthumping. It's full of fictional speeches and verbose descriptions of battlefield glory and he recounts at great length all the traditional Roman myths. All the same, for the early Republican period, Livy is the man.

Ovid

Publius Ovidius Naso was from Sulmo in central Italy. He composed a considerable amount of erotic and mythological poetry from Rome during the Augustan age. He also composed a versified calendar, the *fasti*, which describes anniversaries and religious festivals of the first half of the year. It's full of information about legends, folklore, social customs and the like. He was exiled by Augustus for the last few years of his life to the city of Tomis, right at the very edge of the Empire on the Black Sea. Whilst he was there, he wrote *Trista* (Laments) and *Epistulae ex Ponto* (Letters from the Black Sea), poems which, as you can probably tell from the titles, are full of how miserable he is out there in the wilderness, away from the cosmopolitan fun in Rome.

People who are exiled from the hub of all that is exciting about the Empire are normally very glum. For them, this exile is a torturous punishment.

Vitruvius

Marcus Vitruvius Pollio was an architect and engineer about whom very little is known, including whether the first and last parts of his name are correct. He wrote the only surviving Roman textbook on architecture, *De Architectura*, in ten books, sometimes around 25BC. He was involved in Augustus' plans to renovate Rome, and his works deal not only with architecture but also with the water supply and machines for war.

Strabo

Strabo (64 or 63BC–c. 24AD) was a Greek scholar from Pontus who was famous as a historian and geographer. His early work, *General History*, is lost, but his *Geography*, over 17 books, is well known. It's an encyclopedic goldmine of information, not only about the geography of the known world, including some of the regions outside the reach of the Empire but also about its political and economic history.

Seneca the Elder

Lucius Annaeus Seneca (c.55BC - 37/41AD) was born in Cordoba, Spain and is the father of, you guessed it, Seneca the Younger. He wrote *Controversiae* and *Suasoriae*, which are rhetorical and philosophical exercises designed for students to discuss and mull over. They cover hypothetical situations and laws in subjects like criminal, civil and social situations.

Paterculus

Velleius Paterculus (c19BC - 30AD) was a retired army officer who wrote a history of Rome in two volumes, the exact title of which is disputed. It's full of rhetoric, very pro-aristocratic and is an exercise in worship of the imperial families, particularly Tiberius under whom he enjoyed a military career. Nonetheless, it is useful for its record of Roman colonies and provincial history and gives a full account of the reign of Augustus and Tiberius.

Philo

Philo Judeas (c20BC - 40AD) from Alexandria was the author of numerous Greek works that sought to reconcile Jewish theology with Hellenic philosophy. He wrote *Against Flaccus*, which concerns the grievances of the Jewish community against the governor of Egypt, providing invaluable information about the administration of Egypt and the place of Jews in its society, and *Embassy to Gaius* about his delegation to the court of Caligula, which gives a cool account of the madness of the Emperor.

Valerius Maximus

Valerius Maximus is another about whom very little is known, including his date of birth or death, other than he lived during the reign of Tiberius, and he wrote *Facta et Dicta Memorabilia* (Memorable Deeds and Sayings) over nine books. It contains, as you might imagine, a whole bunch of facts and anecdotes intended to act as rhetorical exercises for students, a bit like Seneca the Elder.

Seneca

Lucius Annaeus Seneca (c4BC - c65AD) was, like his father, from Cordoba in Spain. He was a prominent figure during the reign of Claudius and Nero, serving as tutor to the latter. He ended up being implicated, probably unfairly, in the conspiracy against Nero organised by Piso and was ordered to commit suicide. He's the best source for the Stoic movement in Rome. He wrote tons of stuff of which survive; *Dialogues, On Clemency, On Benefits* and 124 *Moral Epistles*. His *Natural Questions* was regarded during the medieval period as *the* reference book on cosmology and physics and gives us an idea of how the Romans saw the universe. Perhaps most famously, he is attributed as the author of *Apocolocyntosis*, the biting, bitchy satire of the deification of Claudius, who, you might have guessed, he didn't get on with particularly well. He also wrote a bunch of dramas and some philosophical musings.

Petronius

Gaius Petronius Arbiter (c27 - 66AD) was likely from Massalia, modern-day Marseilles, where the novel for which he is famous, commonly known as *Satyricon*, although the exact title isn't clear, is set. However, it might not have been him who wrote it. Confusing, hey? *Satyricon* is a, believe it or not, a satire about the wealth and excess of 'modern' Roman life and values surrounding a gaudy dinner party thrown by a rich freedman. It is snarky, cynical and overstated, yet must contain a certain level of truth; otherwise, it wouldn't have been satirical.

Columella

Little is known about Lucius Junius Moderatus Columella. He was born around 4AD in Gades, Spain and was tribune in 35AD. His *De re rustica* in twelve volumes has been completely preserved and forms an important source of Roman agriculture, whilst one about trees, *De Arborius* is about, well, trees and is usually attributed to him. The first one was only known in fragmentary form until a complete copy was discovered in the 15th Century. It's a great insight into the changes in the economy of the agricultural landscape of the Imperial period.

Pliny the Elder

Gaius Plinius Secundus (23 - 79AD) was born in Como in northern Italy and had a starry public career, particularly in the service of Vespasian. He died while serving as the head of the Roman navy at Misenum, rescuing people from the Vesuvian eruption that destroyed Pompeii. He was a great scholar, but most of his works are lost. The surviving work, *Natural History*, over thirty-seven books, is a huge and important collection of the scientific knowledge of the early Empire, although Pliny is somewhat guilty of throwing everything in there just because he can rather than taking much care about what to include and what not to include. At times, the stuff stretches the limits of credulity, and Pliny presents it all with equal value. Either way, it is rammed with information about social, religious, political, and economic aspects of Roman life, and even if some of it is absolutely bonkers, it just reflects some of the wilder beliefs of Roman society.

Quintilian

Marcus Fabius Quintilianus (c30 - c100AD) was another Spaniard who had a successful career as an educator, rhetorician and tutor to the children of the Flavian dynasty. His *Institutio Oratoria*, over twelve books, was an influential work and constitutes the most important source on Roman education. Much of his work on the education of the student from infancy to graduate deals with the technical aspects of rhetoric and oratory, but it is also a valuable source of Roman law. His greatest achievement seems to have been his ability to continue speaking his mind on a broad range of subjects without incurring the ire of Domitian, a period in which almost nobody else dared say anything at all for fear of losing their head, which shows what a skilled orator he was.

Frontinus

Sextus Julius Frontinus (c40 - 103/4AD), the former governor of Britain and the bloke in charge of the water supply in Rome under Domitian, wrote *Stratgems*, over three books, which were intended to illustrate the principles of military science via a collection of anecdotes from Greek and Roman history. His other work, *De Aquis Romae*, in two books, is a technical work on the aqueducts and pipes supplying Rome, which not only contains useful information on how it all worked but also the administrative background of running such infrastructure in the capital city.

Josephus

Flavius Josephus (c37 - c100AD) was born Joseph ben Matthias in Jerusalem. He was a prominent Pharisee, diplomat and military commander who, despite a rather pro-Roman bias, was drawn into the Jewish revolt of 66-70AD. Taken prisoner, he became an interpreter and advisor to both Vespasian and Titus and earned his freedom and subsequent citizenship, becoming very close to the Flavians. Back in Rome, he devoted the rest of his career to writing, in Greek, the *Antiquities of the Jews,* which covers the period up to 65AD, in twenty books, and *The Jewish War* over seven books. He later wrote *Against Apion,* in two books, as a defence of Judaism and *Autobiography* as a defence of himself. It's all marvellous propaganda in favour of the futility of fighting against Rome, and his later work is almost an apology for being so pro-Roman, just to prove his Jewish credentials. Despite this, they contain incredibly valuable information on Roman Imperial policy and administration and, famously, some evidence for the existence of Jesus Christ, even though some of the passages that mention him are heavily interpolated by later Christian writers. That interpolation itself is worthy of a whole chapters.

Martial

Marcus Valerius Martialis (38/41 - 102/4AD) was another Spaniard who moved in the highest circles of Roman society. His *Epigrams* over fifteen books cover the broad, cosmopolitan life of Rome and give an insight into the strata of society in the Flavian age. They are invaluable snapshots into the social and private life of Imperial Rome.

Dio Chrysostom

Dio Coccianus Chrysostomus was born in Bythina and lived between c40 and c120AD to a wealthy provincial family. His fame as a travelling speaker brought him to Rome where he became associated with the Imperial court until falling out of favour with Domitian, like everyone else, and finding himself exiled for fourteen years. He later got back into the good books with Nerva and Trajan. He wrote prodigiously, most of which is now lost. That which survives is sophistic verbosity, moral discourses and copies of political speeches. The latter has to be treated with some caution, like all political waffle, but gives information about the society and local affairs in the Greek cities of Asia Minor.

Plutarch

A rich man of letters and occasional public speaker, Plutarch (c46 - c126AD) spent most of his life in his hometown of Chaeronea in Greece but also travelled several times to Rome. The main body of his work is contained in *Moralia*, a collection of more than sixty works covering a variety of topics, mainly ethical conundrums. More important as a source is *Parallel Lives*, fifty biographies of famous Greek and Roman statesmen. His sources are secondary, and his tone is somewhat adulatory and dramatic, but nevertheless, they contain valuable material about Roman society and institutions, from the legendary foundation of Rome to the early Imperial period.

Tacitus

Publius (?) Cornelius Tacitus (c56 - c120AD) is the grand-daddy of all the Roman historians. A member of an equestrian family, surprisingly little is known about his life, including where he was born, when and even what his full name was. As a literary artist and historian, he is without a peer in the Roman historiographical world. His earliest work is probably the *Agricola*, the biography of his father-in-law and former governor of Britain, Gnaeus Julius Agricola, and *Germania*, which gives us a unique insight into a world that was otherwise never recorded or has been lost. His narrative through the latter is all about the 'noble savage' versus the morally repugnant Roman, a narrative approach he goes back to in later works. Both of these date to the years between the death of Domitian (96AD) and the turn of the first century.

This is followed by *Dialogue on Orators* and the *Histories*, written between 100 and 110. Some argue that *Dialogue* comes before, but for our needs, this isn't important. The *Annals of Imperial Rome* then come after all those. Tacitus tells us of the impressive array of sources he refers to, including the elder Pliny's history of the German wars, as well as the works of Corbulo, Cluvius Rufus and Fabius Rusticus, all of which are now lost. He consulted the records of Agrippina, Nero's mother, from which he apparently takes some facts that other historians never discover. It's fascinating to think what else of courtly intrigue he discovered and, given his proclivity to edit what goes in or not, he left out because he didn't think it important.

He also uses biographies, funeral orations, speeches, minutes of the Senate, the official imperial gazette (*acta publica*), the Emperor's personal archive (*comentarii principis*), inscriptions, pamphlets and, of course, witness testimony.

The way in which he adapts what he finds to his own ends can be seen in the differences between his version of a speech given by Claudius in *Annals* (xi.24) and the wording from an inscription found in Lyon of the same speech (ILS 212). However, we have to make it clear that his research was pretty solid, and a lot of what he says can be corroborated by other evidence, including speeches and the archaeological record.

He might pepper the history of the Boudican rebellion with his own narrative, but someone burned Colchester to the ground and razed London, and they did when he says they did it. The archaeology confirms that. If we have to treat everything Tacitus is telling us with caution, and we do, it's not because he gets the facts wrong but because of the way he is trying to spin what happened. And, naturally, one must never forget about the things Tacitus is deliberately not telling us, the wily old bugger.

Pliny the Younger

Gaius Plinius Caecilius Secundus (61 - c113AD) was the nephew and adopted son of Pliny the Elder. A rich, educated politician, lawyer and writer, he had an illustrious public career culminating in the governorship of Bythinia between 111 and 113. Of his writings that survive, there is the *Panegyricus Traiani*, a fulsome oratory delivered to the Senate in honour of Trajan on the occasion of Pliny's election as consul in 100AD and the *Letters*, some of which are his official correspondence with Trajan while he was governor. They constitute a superb source for the knowledge of Roman provincial administration and give an insight into how the Empire was run, simply not available in that depth anywhere else. The rest provide a panorama of life among the elite in Rome from a social, legal and cultural viewpoint.

Juvenal

Decimus Junius Juvenal (c60 - 140AD), about whom virtually nothing is known, was trained in rhetoric and had a military career. His *Satires*, over sixteen books, provides a quite bitter and cynical view of the depravity and immorality of upper-class Roman life in the late first and early second centuries. His sniffy indignation produces an exaggerated view of the times, but like all satires, they must contain an element of truth, or else it wouldn't work as satire. Nonetheless, they contain valuable insight into contemporary society.

Suetonius

Gaius Suetonius Tranquilis (c69 - c150AD) was born into a wealthy family but not much else is known about him. As one of the 'big four' alongside Tacitus, the younger Pliny and

Cassius Dio, he is a vital source but unlike them, he wasn't a senator. Instead, he spent a good deal of his career as a secretary to Hadrian. The courtly intrigues of Hadrian and the following Emperors are not the concern of someone like Suetonius, even though he is among them – perhaps because he is among them. The chronological accuracy of events becomes more blurred, and the analysis of events becomes less rigid. Suetonius is not concerned with events on the same political scale as the earlier Senators. Of his many works, *De Viris Illustribus*, biographies of famous men, and *The Lives of the Twelve Caesar*s, from Augustus to Domitian set new standards in historical writing that remained in place well into the modern era. *The Twelve Caesars* are methodical but anecdotal and do not have much political explanation. He is very much on the inside looking out rather than on the outside looking in.

Appian

Appian of Alexandria (c95 - c165AD) was a lawyer active in the Roman civil service. His *Roman History*, over twenty-four books, aims to write history along geographical lines. The work is fragmentary, but books xii - vxii (*Civil Wars*) are the best known. They are based on secondary and tertiary sources and are mainly concerned with military matters but are valuable sources for the end of the Republic.

Florus

Florus is an odd one. There are three names associated with the name Florus; Lucius Annaeus, Publius Annius and Julius who are all either the same person or three people. Either way, he lived at the time of Hadrian and the one extant work is *Epitome of Roman History*, over two books, covering the period from the time of Augustus. It's mostly military in nature, brief and a load of old nonsense, but it does fill in some details that are missing from other sources, so he's useful for that. Or they are.

Fronto

The Numidian, Marcus Cornelius Fronto (c100 - c166AD) was the most famous rhetorician of his time who, after a public career, became the tutor of Marcus Aurelius and Lucius Verus. His *Letters*, a collection of teachings in correspondence with his two pupils provide a valuable insight into the early life of Marcus, one of Rome's most famous Emperors, the royal court and education of the period.

Gellius

The Italian Aulus Gellius (c123 - c169AD) was a lawyer. who studied in Athens, where he began his most famous work *Attic Nights*, over twenty books, which rambles on about a lot of various topics, but is very useful because of his very obvious love of collecting facts. Someone who witters on and on about all sorts of things whilst being a total nerd about facts sounds like a nightmare, and I'm glad I don't know anyone like that in real life ... *innocent whistling* ...

Apuleius

Lucius(?) Apuleius (c125 - c171AD) was an aristocrat, orator and lawyer from Africa. He wrote in opposition to Christianity and his main area of interest lay in the mystery religions of his day, magic and philosophy. His extant works include *Apologia*, a defence of the accusation of being a wizard, Florida, excerpts from his speeches and, most famously, perhaps the first great novel in literature, *Metaporphoses* or *The Golden Ass*, a work of great beauty and enduring popularity. It's a valuable source for social history and religious weirdness in the second century.

Pausanias

Pausanias, who lived during the reign of Marcus Aurelius and about whom nothing is known, is famous for writing *Description of Greece*, over ten books, which is, maybe, the first ever tourist guidebook. It contains some historical ramblings which are of some value for the history of Greece under Roman control.

Cassius Dio

Lucius Cassius Dio (c165 - c235AD) was a historian and senator born in Bythinia. Famous as one of the 'big four' alongside Tacitus, the younger Pliny and Suetonius. He spent the last decade of his life, after having retired from public life which included the consulship, compiling and then writing his *History of Rome*. He is the de facto prime source for Augustus' reign in any detail. Cassius Dio is less expressive than Tacitus, but after him, he is the second most important source of our period. He is much more of a sober compiler of facts rather than an interpreter of events. His work dates from the early third century, going as far as his second term as consul in 229. Fragments of his histories survive from the period 68BC to 46AD and then again from his own time period. Like Tacitus, Dio sometimes reads the problems of his own time in the lessons of the past, and the long speeches he creates in the mouths of ancient people can be nothing other than anachronistic inventions. His work is defined by a bias in favour of the Imperial system. He is sometimes a little blurry with the details. Still, by the same measure, his approach is far less personal than that of Tacitus and avoids many of the pitfalls that such closeness to the subject matter entails.

Athenaeus

Athenaeus was a Greek of Egyptian origin who migrated to Rome. There hew rote *Deipnosophistae* (Savants at Dinner). This is a well of information, quotes from earlier authors and anecdotes on social and literary topics with a central focus on the dinner and food.

Herodian

Herodian (c165 - c255AD) was a Syrian in the Roman civil service. His *History*, over eight books, is an account of the Emperors from Marcus Aurelius to Gordian III. Some people are very snobbish about his work, and to be fair, it's very clouded by his own morality, and the work tends to be very biographical rather than looking at a wider picture, but he tends to write about events he has personal experience of and a lot of it consists of material for which he is the only source. And, hey! What's wrong with writing little biographies of people?

The Historia Augusta

To throw a massive spanner in the works, along comes the *Historia Augusta*, the collection of biographies of Emperors which purports to be the work of several authors, written under the reign of Diocletian and Constantine. However, they are now generally agreed to be the work of someone writing at the end of the fourth century who ascribes them to earlier authors for reasons unknown and inserts odd 'contemporary' allusions in the manner of someone writing historical fiction. The source material the author used would appear to be genuine, but they are embellished with what can only be assumed to be devilish delight. Whoever wrote them had fun writing them.

A lot of it has to be fiction, but the problem is knowing exactly what. If we consider something like Robert Graves' brilliant *I, Claudius*, which openly embellishes the known story of Claudius but does so honestly and from sources like Tacitus, and then imagine we never had any access to Tacitus himself, you can see the scale of the problem. It would be hard to know what of Graves' account to take as true or not. Generally, people tend to agree that the earlier biographies are more accurate than the latter, but that's largely because we can corroborate them more easily. The later, uncorroborated accounts must be treated with caution, but they also contain information that is not found elsewhere. We then have to apply not only common sense but also apply what we know about how writers attempted character assassination on earlier Emperors with suspicious accounts of their reign. The *Historia Augusta* is the only account that names Hadrian as the person who built the wall that carries his name, but that fact can be corroborated by archaeological evidence. It's a bizarre mix of the weird and the factually correct.

It's tempting to just say that the more lurid the story, the more likely it is to have been invented, but we have to be very careful with that approach. I reckon whoever wrote it was just playing a joke on future historians with a 1600-year-long punchline, the little shit.

The Christians

The New Testament

Vitally important as documents for social history are the books of the New Testament, which give a unique insight into aspects of Roman provincial administration and the everyday life of people at the bottom of society. Compared to the view of the Roman world as seen from the opulent villas of Senators like Pliny and Tacitus, the world of the gospels and the parables is that of the labourers and peasants of rural Judea. You don't have to believe that God is real in order to hear the voices of the people in those pages. History is, ultimately, about what the sources can tell us about the attitudes, context and beliefs of their authors, remember? If we dismissed sources simply because they contain miracles we find hard to accept as 'fact', then we'd have to throw Tacitus out with the bathwater, too, along with his accounts of the miracles performed by Vespasian.

But we don't, because 'real' or not, they are still telling us something of the attitudes of the day and the workings of the imperial mindset.

There's also additional information from the *Mishnah*, the codification of rabbinical opinions on Jewish law from the late second century, the *Talmud* and the *midrashim*. However, you'll need to be able to speak Hebrew if you don't wish to rely on translations.

Justin Martyr

Justinus Flavius (c100 - 165AD), a Palestinian and a Christian convert, is one of the very first named Christian writers. Of his works, *Dialogue* and *Apology* have survived, and the latter, especially, is valuable mostly because of its description of Christian worship and the descriptions of the criminal and moral charges brought against the early Christians.

Tertullian

Quintus Septimius Florens Tertullianus (c155 – c220AD) was born in Carthage and, after conversion, became a priest. He is arguably the founder of Western Christian theology and the first major voice in Latin Christianity. He wrote countless volumes of apologies and moral polemics, of which about thirty are extant. *Ad Nationes* (To the Pagans), over two books, and *Apology* are concerned with the defence of Christianity against charges of criminality, immorality and treason against the imperial cult.

Cyprian

Thascius Caecilius Cyprianus (c210 to 14 September 258AD) was the bishop of Carthage and a prolific writer. The most important of his many works are *Letters*, which mostly cover church administration and discipline, *De Lapsis*, which covers the persecutions of the middle of the third century, *Ad Donatum*, on the vanity of worldly goods, which describes the pagan world at that time and *De Ecclesiae Unitate*, about the unity of the church.

Lactantius

Lucius Caecilius Firmianus (c250 - c325AD) was another one from Carthage who converted to Christianity after a long career as a teacher of rhetoric and was later appointed as tutor to Crispus, the son of Constantine. Of his many works, the extant *Institutiones Divinae*, over seven books, is the most famous. It's a passionate defence of Christianity against pagan religion. His *De Mortibus Persecutorum* details the persecutions from Nero to Galerius but is valuable in the secular sense for its description of the economy under Diocletian and the Emperor's attempts at economic and social reform.

Eusebius

Eusebius (c260 - 30 May 339AD) was the bishop of Caesarea in Palestine and the 'Father of Church History'. His *Ecclesiastical History* up to 324AD, over ten books, is a goldmine of information about Christian history, the persecutions and the evolution of the church. His *Chronicon*, over two books, and *Life of Constantine,* over four books, are great sources for early Christian history.

Augustine

Aurelius Augustine, or Saint Augustine to you, (354 - 430AD) was born in Numidia and had a career as a rhetorician in Carthage and Italy, where he converted to Christianity and later became bishop of Hippo in Africa. His enormous literary output, over 118 works, consists of books, doctoral treatises, philosophical essays, philosophy, Biblical exegesis, sermons and letters. Most famous are *Confessions*, in thirteen books, and *De Civitae Dei*, over twenty-two books. The last one is a response to pagan attacks and is valuable for insights into Christian life, but also for the huge details of Roman society and pagan religion.

Orosius.

Publius Orosius (early 5th Century), a Spaniard, was a student of St. Augustine. He is the author of the first Christian history, *Historiae Adversus Paganos*, over seven books. It's based on secondary sources and is quite terrible. It's often wrong, contradictory, distorted and is essentially an apologetic dressed up as history. He carefully selected the disasters of history to support his theory that the crisis of the Roman Empire in his time had nothing to do with the spread of Christianity and the move away from paganism. He also tried to reinforce the message that divine intervention was the only way to a better world.

The Evidence

The narratives constructed around the period we're interested in were all largely composed by people at the pointy end of the Roman social pyramid, and most of the authors were Senators like Tacitus or Cassius Dio. As such, we tend to get a picture painted from close to, but not quite in, the centre of political power. As we saw in the chapter about the social ranks in Rome, the Senators were people kept dangling on the fringes of power who, in effect, didn't have much to do except pretend to be important. As such, some of these otherwise educated men filled their days with sitting around writing about history and people who sit around all day writing about history are really weird.

Watch any documentary or movie about Rome, and you'll come away with the idea that it was primarily a military-based society. Each TV adaptation is full of gruff-voiced, stern looking (white) men, mumbling about barbarians and 'hailing' each other with strange salutes whilst stomping about in full armour. This narrative is driven by the sources, of course, which are compounded by the requirement of the historiographical record to concentrate on the military efforts of the Roman state and the political actions of the ruling class. Rome appears to be a primarily military society because these are the high tide marks by which such history is recorded. In the Renaissance period or during the Age of Enlightenment, the history jumps forward in scientific or artistic leaps. In Rome, it's all about crushing enemies. Roman history tends to be the history of Emperors and what they achieve through dominance and sometimes outright terror. Roman history also includes great leaps forward in the arts, as witnessed by its influence on the grotesque styles that lit the flame of the Renaissance. Scientific discoveries abounded in Rome, too, as did geographical and astronomical ones.

Architecture and engineering achievements were some of Rome's greatest legacies, and still, to this day, people marvel in awe at the spectacular achievements of Rome's builders. But nobody makes movies about Romans who bustle about with paintbrushes or armfuls of blueprints because, unless they slapped their name across the front of them, these are not generally the achievements of the Emperors. Hadrian's name is attached to the wall he built across the middle of Britain, but this fact is only recorded in one account. Hadrian built at a ferocious pace but only put his name on one building.

Elsewhere, Emperors are depicted in statues as armour-wearing conquerors because this was the narrative they wanted to portray when generating more icons of themselves. Spreading depictions of oneself to new corners of the Empire necessarily required that one serve to remind the locals who the boss was, so the boss had to look like he would drop something heavy on you should you not learn to behave yourself. There were other statues depicting Emperors as orators and thinkers, but these are not as popular in modern eyes because they don't fit the narrative of the Emperor as a soldier.

All this, naturally, suggests that the only way the Emperors ruled was by might and fear, which was far from the case. The letters of Pliny show that Emperors like Trajan were intricately entwined in the bureaucracy of ruling. It wasn't all just smash and conquer. The genre of Emperors' biographies was effectively invented by Suetonius, who worked in the imperial household and had the advantage of being close to his subject. However, his reliance on anecdotes and his focus on the personal traits of the Emperors rather than, say, their relationship with their subjects, limits the usefulness of his work.

All of this writing has been preserved for its literary merit. Nobody ever thought, "Y'know .... I'd better preserve this in case some future historian is interested in it." So, another criterion for the preservation of literary history has to be the quality of the work. Imagine trying to piece together the history of the United Kingdom at the end of the 20th Century, but the only clue you have is a biography of Margaret Thatcher that focuses on the Falklands War, written by a Member of Parliament and only exists because someone thought it was well enough written. You begin to see how limiting the written record can be.

It would be very easy, then, to compose a history of Rome as entirely seen through the eyes of the elite. But it would be wrong to view events among this elite group as normal for the remainder of Roman society. Not much evidence survives from the western (i.e. Latin speaking) part of the Empire outside of Rome. Writers tended to gravitate towards the capital in search of patronage and an audience, with a few exceptions like Apuleius. As a result, his work *The Golden Ass* is an insight into life in the provinces as seen by someone on the fringes of the elite. Otherwise, life in the sticks is seen by the ruling class remotely in Rome.

In the Greek-speaking East, there is a mass of literary evidence that surpasses that of the West in terms of quantity but not always in quality. Some of the authors cross over from the West to the East, but many, like Pausanias, represent the East only and reflect areas such as Asia Minor or Greece. Of all of them, only Josephus composed a history of his own region in his own time. Most of the rest of Greek literature is concerned with the distant past before or around the time of Alexander the Great. There are a few exceptions, like Dio Chrysostom, but otherwise their writing is somewhat limited for constructing a narrative of their own times.

The disjointed literary record for life outside of Rome is mitigated by the extraordinary mass of physical evidence, from the archaeology to inscriptions on stone, metal and wood, the written records on papyri, and coins. The archaeology might give the impression that we know everything about Roman society, particularly given the relative lack of evidence for societies that preceded and followed that period, but the unique nature of the evidence and the biases inherent in it have to be understood in context.

One reason why there is so much Romana archaeology, besides the obvious one in that they generated so much shit to begin with, is that we can recognise it so easily. We know so much about Roman archaeology that spotting it is relatively easy, and putting it in context is an equally straightforward task. Thus, villas, towns and roads, for example, can be identified with relative ease because of the regularity of their construction. We know that Roman roads lead somewhere, and we know how far apart Roman forts tended to be, due to the limitations of the distance soldiers could march without rest. So finding new ones is sometimes just a case of looking in the right place.

Similarly, when we find Roman forts, it quickly becomes obvious what they are due to the regularity of their layout. Romans also tended to build in stone rather than in wood, like subsequent societies. There is also an abundance of pottery from the period, and the diagnostic value of such material is priceless. Pottery can also tell us a lot about the status of the people who lived on such sites, from the finest and most expensive samian ware telling us one thing about the inhabitants of a site and the total absence of any pottery at all telling us, perhaps, something else at the other scale. The recreation of settlements and lifestyles is thus possible from even the most scant of archaeological evidence, with some care.

This does raise the issue of being able to tell more about the lives of the wealthier in society simply because they tended to generate more archaeology. They built more, they consumed more, and they left more behind for us to find. A similar bias exists in the enormous epigraphical record that exists from the Roman period. Perhaps a million or more examples of Roman epigraphy exist, from the vast inscriptions of the *Res Gestae* to otherwise undecipherable scratches on shards of pottery. Most of these date to the Imperial period, and they can provide incredible detail of the careers, family, military deployments and even inter-city relations of Roman society. But this Roman habit of scratching on stuff is a strange one that wasn't particularly prevalent before them and dies out in the subsequent generations. Saxons might carry on using terrible Latin on their grave markers, but they're doing so because they wish to adopt the trappings of power that come with the use of Latin. By medieval times, the tradition of writing a whole chapter of one's life story on the outside of a building one created might be limited to a date and a family crest.

Creating this stuff requires a mason skilled in the craft, and as such, that requires someone to pay him, so again, the epigraphy tends to be the record of the relatively wealthy. It's not a custom that caught on in all corners of the Empire and didn't become popular among the classes of society who have more pressing things to spend their money on unless, of course, they do the scribbling themselves, as they did on the streets of Pompeii. If the poorer in society ever dip into their reserves to have things cut into stone, it's for funerary inscriptions where we see even ex-slaves prepared to commemorate their lives and freedom. It is, naturally, a primarily urban phenomenon. In the rural areas, it is less popular because people either didn't have the money to have their name carved in stone, and anyhow, there was nobody around to look at it. A very big part of the epigraphical tradition is that there is an audience. Outside of towns, only soldiers tend to commemorate their lives in stone and they had both an audience - other soldiers - and a certain amount of spare money to do it with. It's a tradition that we still follow to this day.

Writing on more ephemeral material has only survived the past 2,000 years due to exceptional physical circumstances or by incredible luck. Papyri survive relatively well in the dry conditions of Egypt and revealed a lot about small-town life and provincial administration. However, it must be noted that Egypt is a peculiar outlier among the provinces and such evidence can only be extrapolated to cover the rest of the Empire with great care. What happened in Egypt stayed in Egypt. Similarly, we have to be careful in remembering that, even in Egypt, we only find archaeology where the archaeology survives, and therefore, it doesn't necessarily paint a picture of the areas in which it doesn't survive. If papyri survive relatively well in the dry and desert-like conditions of Egypt, it's worth remembering that large numbers of people lived, and still live, in the areas of Egypt that are frequently inundated by flooding. In those areas, the papyri has no chance. The fluctuations in the climatic conditions of these areas may also have resulted in differing state demands of the people who lived there.

In the Near East, Judea Syria and so on, papyri exist but in fewer numbers than in Egypt. Whether this is a reflection of the bureaucratic nature of the respective provinces is a good question. More likely, the answer is down to climate. Either way, they provide a nice record of the history on their borders, in Arabia and the surrounding lands.

As we saw from Vindolanda, inscriptions on wooden slats have been discovered and are being discovered and more might appear now that archaeologists have learned huge amounts from that site, but for now, their preservation must go down to a miracle of archaeology. It might well have been that tons of this material previously existed but was overlooked by people who didn't know what they had, in similar ways that earlier antiquarians simply threw away bucket loads of pottery that they considered 'trash'.

Evidence from coins can be used to reconstruct history. The inscriptions and coin types can be used to reflect a propaganda message aimed at influencing the people who handle it. The success of this propaganda is questionable and, as such, can be seen as intended as much for a captive audience of peers rather than the population at large. The circulation of coins can also tell us much about the economy of the area and how individuals interact with the economy. The instances of coin hoards tell us about economic pressures or the threat of invasion. The spread of high value coins tells us where the money was going, and so on. Plus, coins have the advantage of being very easy to date and are incredibly valuable diagnostic items on archaeological sites. This book has deliberately steered away from using this otherwise very valuable source for the simple reasons that it is a highly specialised area of history, and I'm not sufficiently qualified to dabble in it, and it also tends to be a visual medium and thus not really suitable for this volume, unless I fancied spending six months clearing all the pictures it would have required.

It must be stressed very strongly that the only certain thing we can tell about the information we have on the ancient world is that we have but a minuscule fraction of all the information that ever existed on the ancient world. What survives of the literary record does so mainly through the preferences and prejudices of those who, in Medieval times, copied the manuscripts that we use today. And those copyists were almost exclusively Christian monks. In order to interpret what we have, we need imagination, empathy with the past and an open mind, and we have to be careful never to ignore evidence that goes against a narrative we are trying to build or that contradicts what we are trying to say.

For centuries, history has suffered from an approach in which footnotes and citations seem to be an end in themselves, and the whole thing begins to appear like an exercise in how well someone has done their homework. I hope that I have shifted away from that a little and slackened off the ropes that tie history books down in that respect. Rest assured, however, that I have done the homework. Were this such a book, these words would now be followed by another 120 pages of references and citations and that it isn't shouldn't mean that, if necessary, it couldn't be produced.

As always, the task of the historian is an ongoing one. History, even where it is literally set in stone is never ... well, set in stone. There will always be more to write, and coming to the end of a book such as this one is never a moment to regret because there will always be the opportunity to go back to the start and approach it from another angle. I haven't come to the end; I've come to the start of something else. The historian's job is never over.